Hotel Pricing
in a Social World

The Wiley & SAS Business Series presents books that help senior-level managers with their critical management decisions.

Titles in the Wiley & SAS Business Series include:

Agile by Design: An Implementation Guide to Analytic Lifecycle Management by Rachel Alt-Simmons

Analytics in a Big Data World: The Essential Guide to Data Science and Its Applications by Bart Baesens

Bank Fraud: Using Technology to Combat Losses by Revathi Subramanian

Big Data Analytics: Turning Big Data into Big Money by Frank Ohlhorst

Big Data, Big Innovation: Enabling Competitive Differentiation through Business Analytics by Evan Stubbs

Business Analytics for Customer Intelligence by Gert Laursen

Business Intelligence Applied: Implementing an Effective Information and Communications Technology Infrastructure by Michael S. Gendron

Business Intelligence and the Cloud: Strategic Implementation Guide by Michael S. Gendron

Business Transformation: A Roadmap for Maximizing Organizational Insights by Aiman Zeid

Connecting Organizational Silos: Taking Knowledge Flow Management to the Next Level with Social Media by Frank Leistner

Data-Driven Healthcare: How Analytics and BI Are Transforming the Industry by Laura Madsen

Delivering Business Analytics: Practical Guidelines for Best Practice by Evan Stubbs

Demand-Driven Forecasting: A Structured Approach to Forecasting, Second Edition by Charles Chase

Demand-Driven Inventory Optimization and Replenishment: Creating a More Efficient Supply Chain by Robert A. Davis

Developing Human Capital: Using Analytics to Plan and Optimize Your Learning and Development Investments by Gene Pease, Barbara Beresford, and Lew Walker

Economic and Business Forecasting: Analyzing and Interpreting Econometric Results by John Silvia, Azhar Iqbal, Kaylyn Swankoski, Sarah Watt, and Sam Bullard

The Executive's Guide to Enterprise Social Media Strategy: How Social Networks Are Radically Transforming Your Business by David Thomas and Mike Barlow

Financial Institution Advantage & the Optimization of Information Processing by Sean C. Keenan

Financial Risk Management: Applications in Market, Credit, Asset and Liability Management and Firmwide Risk by Jimmy Skoglund and Wei Chen

Foreign Currency Financial Reporting from Euros to Yen to Yuan: A Guide to Fundamental Concepts and Practical Applications by Robert Rowan

Fraud Analytics Using Descriptive, Predictive, and Social Network Techniques: A Guide to Data Science for Fraud Detection by Bart Baesens, Veronique Van Vlasselaer, and Wouter Verbeke

Harness Oil and Gas Big Data with Analytics: Optimize Exploration and Production with Data Driven Models by Keith Holdaway

Health Analytics: Gaining the Insights to Transform Health Care by Jason Burke

Heuristics in Analytics: A Practical Perspective of What Influences Our Analytical World by Carlos Andre Reis Pinheiro and Fiona McNeill

Hotel Pricing in a Social World: Driving Value in the Digital Economy by Kelly McGuire

Human Capital Analytics: How to Harness the Potential of Your Organization's Greatest Asset by Gene Pease, Boyce Byerly, and Jac Fitz-enz

Implement, Improve and Expand Your Statewide Longitudinal Data System: Creating a Culture of Data in Education by Jamie McQuiggan and Armistead Sapp

Killer Analytics: Top 20 Metrics Missing from Your Balance Sheet by Mark Brown

Mobile Learning: A Handbook for Developers, Educators, and Learners by Scott McQuiggan, Lucy Kosturko, Jamie McQuiggan, and Jennifer Sabourin

Predictive Analytics for Human Resources by Jac Fitz-enz and John Mattox II

For more information on any of the above titles, please visit www.wiley.com.

Hotel Pricing in a Social World

Driving Value in the Digital Economy

Kelly A. McGuire, PhD

WILEY

Published by John Wiley & Sons, Inc., Hoboken, New Jersey.
Published simultaneously in Canada.

For general information on our other products and services or for technical support, please contact our Customer Care Department within the United States at (800) 762-2974, outside the United States at (317) 572-3993 or fax (317) 572-4002.

Wiley publishes in a variety of print and electronic formats and by print-on-demand. Some material included with standard print versions of this book may not be included in e-books or in print-on-demand. If this book refers to media such as a CD or DVD that is not included in the version you purchased, you may download this material at http://booksupport.wiley.com. For more information about Wiley products, visit www.wiley.com.

Library of Congress Cataloging-in-Publication Data:

McGuire, Kelly Ann.
  Hotel pricing in a social world : driving value in the digital economy / Kelly A. McGuire, PhD.
      pages cm — (The Wiley & SAS business series)
  Includes bibliographical references and index.
    ISBN 978-1-119-12996-7 (cloth); ISBN 978-1-119-19241-1 (epdf);
ISBN 978-1-119-19240-4 (epub); ISBN 978-1-119-16228-5 (obook)
  1. Hotels—Rates.   2. Online social networks—Economic aspects.
  3. Electronic commerce.   4. Revenue management.   I. Title.
  TX911.3.R3M35 2016
  910.46068—dc23
                                                        2015033007

Printed in the United States of America

10 9 8 7 6 5 4 3 2 1

*To the Girl Geek Gang, for the support,
the inspiration, and the memories!*

Contents

Foreword

"Reset your thinking and see the future of revenue management." In today's competitive marketplace, revenue management is an incredibly hot topic because well-conceived revenue strategies and tactics can grow a hotel's market share and profits significantly . . . making you the hero of the day.

As an early pioneer in airline and hotel revenue management in Asia Pacific, I have experienced tremendous and unrelenting changes in the global travel marketplace. The rapid growth of worldwide wealth has fueled global travel, the explosion of ecommerce and social media has brought a new generation of digitally savvy travelers and with them, the era of big data and analytics. Never has there been a more exciting time in hospitality and its fast evolving discipline of revenue management and pricing, and never has your role as a revenue manager been more strategic yet more complex.

How do you understand these changes in marketplace, technology, and consumers, and the impact that they will have on your business? How will you evolve your pricing strategy to exploit these revenue opportunities to gain competitive share and transform your role from a revenue manager into chief revenue strategist?

Read this book, and take your revenue management game to a new level. In *Hotel Pricing in a Social World*, Kelly McGuire helps you to understand and navigate these new forces that have swept the travel landscape and changed the strategic nature of revenue management forever. She helps you to develop the knowledge and skills required to stay current and be successful.

I have profound admiration for Kelly, and how she has over the years, with passion and commitment, challenged the old conventions of revenue management and pricing and helped to transform industry thought and practice. Kelly is a revenue management and analytics evangelist to the hospitality and travel industries. Through her research work and leading role in hospitality at SAS, Kelly has been a persuasive advocate for integrating consumer psychology into the discipline of revenue management and pricing, through the application of big data and advanced analytics.

Pricing strategies need to evolve with the changing mind-set of the consumer. Travelers are now self-reliant and resourceful—they research more than 12 websites to plan a trip, trust user-generated content over hotel marketing, compare prices using metasearch, expect instant gratification with 24/7 connectivity and book last minute on mobile devices. Less than 30 percent of travelers have a preferred hotel brand, half of what it was eight years ago, and decreasing still. Consumers are loyal to their needs, not to a hotel brand. Hotel supply has increased exponentially over the past 10 years and players in the sharing economy, like Airbnb, have brought even more private rooms into the market. Choice is abundant, competition is fierce, and consumers have full transparency on the web.

The distribution landscape has also become more crowded, with proliferation of online travel agencies like Expedia, Booking.com, and CTrip, and search players like Kayak, Qunar, and Google Hotel Finder. Revenue managers not only have to craft pricing strategies to account for different consumer needs and price sensitivity, but they also find themselves having to comprehend and manage among direct consumer channels, the online intermediaries, and traditional agreements with wholesale, group, and corporate accounts—each incurring different transaction costs and having different impacts on profitability.

Hotel Pricing in a Social World is timely and relevant. You will learn from Kelly how revenue management systems today should take advantage of innovations in analytics and data visualization to drive more profitable business decisions. It will help you identify opportunities for revenue management to play a larger and more strategic commercial role within your organization. And it will provide you with a compelling vision for the future, where revenue management professionals are encouraged to step out of the box, embrace innovations, and develop a holistic understanding of consumer behavior. I believe that this book will give you the road map to transform your revenue management capabilities and build a sustainable long-term competitive advantage for your company. You will feel energized and empowered to develop critical thinking around key topics influencing our industry:

- How do we take advantage of the explosion of big data in revenue management? Kelly provides some definitions, frameworks, and cautions about how to approach new data sources and new technology options to improve revenue performance.

- Does your hotel's online reputation impact pricing? Kelly shares her research findings on how consumers combine user-generated content with price to make a purchase decision, and she helps you understand how the impact differs for various purposes of travel.

- What did Peter Drucker mean when he coined the phrase "Culture eats strategy for breakfast"? We all intuitively understand the importance of instilling an integrated revenue culture across revenue management, sales, marketing, and operations in order to achieve truly superior performance results. Here, Kelly helps you to achieve the vision of "intelligent demand management" and provides tips on how to start your organization moving in this direction.

- How do you forecast and manage demand when the prevalence of the mobile culture encourages instant and last-minute bookings? In the book, Kelly shows how changes in consumer behavior are influencing the way revenue management needs to think about pricing. She also provides a framework for applying revenue management to other revenue-generating assets and explores the role of the guest in total hotel revenue management.

- What is the role of revenue management in building loyalty and increasing marketing returns as the marketplace becomes increasingly crowded? Learn the crucial part that revenue management plays in the creation and execution of consumer personalization initiatives.

- How do you develop the right revenue management talent for success in this new future? The book describes the skills and competencies that will be required for the revenue manager of the future, and it helps hotels understand how to attract and retain top talent into the discipline.

Hotel Pricing in a Social World has masterfully combined the art and science of pricing and taken it to higher ground. Kelly has succinctly and powerfully described the winds of change in our industry and provided frameworks, tips and critical thinking to take us into the future. If you are serious about creating and sustaining superior revenue management performance for your organization, this is a must read and must practice. Change favors the prepared, and with the knowledge and skills acquired from this book, you will be ready to succeed and win.

Jeannette Ho
Vice President—Revenue Management,
Consumer Insights and Analytics
FRHI Hotels and Resorts Worldwide

Acknowledgments

I have been privileged in my role at SAS to be able to travel around the world speaking at events and meeting with individual hotel companies. I have appreciated the opportunity to listen and to advise. Questions, comments, and discussion points from hundreds of conversations are represented in this book. I have endeavored at all times, and particularly for this book, to be respectful of the need to keep specific company business strategy and internal processes private, while providing advice that will raise the discipline as a whole to the benefit of all. Thank you to those who were willing to be quoted, and especially also to those who helped to inform my thinking but needed to remain anonymous.

There are many people who deserve my deepest gratitude for their support and contributions to this book. I must particularly express my thanks to my dear friend and research partner Dr. Breffni Noone. The genesis of the title of this book was a chance meeting with her at the HSMAI ROC conference in Orlando in 2010. Although we became colleagues and friends during the PhD program at Cornell, I hadn't seen her in a few years. We snuck out of a session to have a chat about how we could maybe do some research together, and that meeting turned into the research I describe in Chapter 4, and eventually the title of this book. The opportunity to work with her on the research has been a great source of inspiration and joy for me. She also took on the role of technical editor for this book during a very busy time, for which I am very grateful. She provided feedback that was critical to the quality of the final version. I also remain thankful to her and her incredibly supportive husband, James, for convincing me to go back to Cornell for my PhD to begin with. If I had not done that when I did . . . well . . . things would have turned out very different!

I am grateful to Jeannette Ho for writing the foreword to this book, but even more so for her inspiration throughout my career (and the careers of many other revenue managers). Jeannette sponsored the function space revenue management (RM) internship in Singapore at the Westin Stamford that led to my honors monograph and first published article with Sherri Kimes. This was a crucial factor in my having the opportunity to work with Sherri during my PhD. It is an honor to continue to have Jeannette's support today. She is a role model for revenue managers in general, and women in revenue management in particular.

I am also very grateful to Chris Crenshaw, Nicole Young, Tim Wiersma, and Neal Fegan, who also took time out of their busy schedules to review the outline and content of the book for me. Their feedback helped me immensely and the book is much better because of our conversations, and their quotes and case studies.

I have been privileged to work with an incredibly talented and dedicated team at SAS, particularly Natalie Osborn and Alex Dietz, who have been instrumental in shaping much of the thinking that went into this book. I am grateful for your dedication to your work and to the industry—and very appreciative that you have the patience to let me burst into your office to talk over my latest crazy idea or work through my writer's block. I am also incredibly grateful to Natalie for creating the beautiful visualizations in Chapter 4. She is so very talented in many ways, but her ability to graphically express complicated concepts is particularly impressive. Thank you, Natalie, for making me look good! Analise Polsky, another SAS colleague, assisted me with a lot of the visualization content, including pointing me to the fantastic pie chart in the big data chapter. Suneel Grover worked with me on the digital intelligence content in Chapter 8, helping me to describe the data collection and analytics available to digital marketers today.

Speaking of SAS, I would like to thank SAS Publishing for the opportunity to write this book, and for their support during the publication process. In particular, I appreciate the advice that Shelley Sessions provided during the proposal process, and the support and editing skills of Brenna Leath (and also her therapy sessions over the phone during the last few weeks before completion). I would also like to thank my manager, Tom Roehm, who pushed me to write this book (mostly by appealing to my highly competitive nature by pointing to other SAS authors in our group). Without the opportunity, support, and encouragement from SAS, this book would not have happened.

Big thanks as well to all of the talented revenue leaders who allowed me to share their insights in this book. I know how busy everyone is, so your willingness to take time for a phone call or to respond to a lengthy list of questions in an e-mail is much appreciated. Thanks in particular to those who provided the longer case studies, including Joerg Happle, Ivan Oliveira, Tarandeep Singh, Rich Hughes, Tugrul Sanli, Mark Molinari, Chinmai Sharma, Hari Nair, Monica Xeureb, Lennert de Jong, Maarten Oosten, Stefan Wolf, Rhett Hirko, Brian Payea, and Kathleen Cullen. Thank you also to IDeaS product marketing, particularly Ezra Kucukciftca and Bonnie Hollenhorst, for providing screen shots of the product to use as examples.

I also appreciate the connections and insights my work with HSMAI has facilitated. I have been privileged to serve on the Americas Revenue Management Advisory Board, which has allowed me to spend time with talented and dedicated revenue leaders (many of whom are featured in this book). I have also had the great opportunity to speak at all of HSMAI's global Revenue Optimization Conferences (ROC) in 2015 in the United States, Europe, and Asia. Thanks to Bob Gilbert, Juli Jones, Ingunn Hofseth, and Jackie Douglas for including me in your conferences and roundtables, and for giving me access to your resources and your content for this book. It's a great organization and I feel fortunate to be able to be involved! Every revenue manager should join and get involved with HSMAI. It provides great access to knowledge and to networking opportunities around the globe.

I am grateful to my advisor and friend, Sherri Kimes, for inspiring me to get involved in this discipline and for guiding me through the PhD. Your tireless dedication to your students, current and former, and to this discipline, is an inspiration, and I feel fortunate to be a small part of your legacy.

Thanks to Brad Weiss for supporting me, taking my panicked phone calls, and for making me dinner when I was deep in the writing process.

Finally, my deep appreciation to my family, particularly my parents, who have always supported my endeavors.

About the Author

Kelly A. McGuire, PhD, leads SAS's Services practice, which is comprised of a team of domain experts in hospitality, gaming, travel, transportation, communications, media, entertainment, and the midmarket. She is an analytics evangelist, helping particularly SAS's hospitality and gaming clients realize the value from big data and advanced analytics initiatives, to build a culture of fact-based decision making. Internally at SAS, she is responsible for setting the strategic direction for the practice and defining the industry portfolio and messaging for her industries. She works with sales, alliances, product management, services, field marketing, and R&D to ensure that SAS solutions meet the needs of the market. Before taking on this role, she was the industry marketing manager for Hospitality and Gaming at SAS. She was responsible for the outbound messaging regarding SAS's Hospitality and Gaming capabilities, particularly in the areas of revenue management and price optimization. She also worked with the joint IDeaS and SAS product management team, where she was responsible for gathering requirements for ancillary revenue management solutions such as function space, spa and food and beverage. Kelly was also responsible for defining requirements and creating the market strategy for SAS Revenue Management and Price Optimization Analytics, which is also the analytics engine for IDeaS G3 RMS.

Before joining SAS, Kelly consulted with Harrah's Entertainment to develop restaurant revenue management strategies for the casinos in their major markets. Kelly was a senior consultant at Radiant Systems, working with contract food service clients on web-based administrative solutions to manage cash handling, inventory management, supply chain, and labor. She also worked for RMS (Restaurant Revenue Management Solutions) on menu-item pricing strategies for chain restaurants, and designed a prototype function space revenue management system for the Westin in Singapore. She managed an upscale Creole restaurant in New Orleans, and was the general manager of a franchised Ben and Jerry's Ice Cream Shop in the French Quarter.

Kelly has a BS from Georgetown University and a MMH and PhD in Revenue Management from the Cornell School of Hotel Administration, where she studied with renowned revenue management researcher Dr. Sherri Kimes. Her dissertation was on the impact of occupied wait time on customer perceptions of the waiting experience. Her research has been published in the *Cornell Hospitality Quarterly, Journal of Pricing and Revenue Management, Journal of Hospitality and Tourism Research,* and the *Journal of Service Management.* She is also a frequent contributor to industry publications, speaker at industry conferences, and is coauthor of the SAS/CHR blog "The Analytic Hospitality Executive." Her latest stream of research, with coauthor Breffni Noone, Associate Professor, The Pennsylvania State University, deals with the influence of user-generated content (social media) on consumer reaction to price in the hotel room purchase process.

New Analytics for a New Environment: The Evolution of Hotel Revenue Management Analytics, Technology, and Data

CHAPTER 1

The Social World Has Changed Revenue Management Forever

Revenue management has a lot less control today
than we like to think we do. It used to be that we could
influence guest behavior by putting a particular pricing
strategy in the market. With price transparency, rate
parity, user generated content, mobile and all of the
other myriad of influences on guest behavior, we can't
change behavior with just a price. Our guests are in
control, and we need to understand them better to be
effective. Price alone won't do the trick anymore.

—Nicole Young, Vice President, Revenue Management and Sales, SBE Hotels

The chapter opening quote perfectly illustrates the challenges revenue management faces today. In today's interconnected social world, getting it right is harder than it used to be. Pricing and competitive positioning are becoming more complicated by the day, as service triumphs and mistakes are laid out for the world to see. Revenue managers are asked to build profitable pricing strategies in the face of price transparency, distribution complexity, increased competition, changing market conditions, hyperconnected consumers, and evolving technology. The market has changed, the technology has changed, and the revenue manager has changed as well. Hoteliers are left wondering how to evolve to manage through these changes.

Any statistics I provide about the evolution of the social web and its impact on the search and booking process will likely be outdated before the book is out of copyediting, but the trend will be directionally correct. It is clear that social media has gone mainstream, and it has changed the way consumers engage with one another and the vendors they do business with. Pew Research Center, in a 2014 study, estimated that 52 percent of American online adults use two or more social media sites, with Facebook being the most popular at 71 percent. Seventy percent of Facebook users engage with the site daily and 45 percent interact several times per day (Duggan et al. 2015: www.pewinternet.org/files/2015/01/PI_Social-MediaUpdate20144.pdf). To illustrate how this has changed behavior, the 2014 Pew study reports that nearly half of web-using adults get their news about politics and government from Facebook. A Harris poll found that half of Americans get recommendations about something good to try from social media (www.mediapost.com/publications/article/241179/half-of-americans-get-product-recommendations-from.html). My own research has shown that 55 percent of leisure travelers (Noone and McGuire 2013b) and 80 percent of business travelers (Noone and McGuire forthcoming) read reviews some or all of the time when researching a hotel purchase.

This evolution of the social web came close on the heels of the revolution of ecommerce, which completely transformed the way that consumers research and buy products. Online travel agencies (OTAs), like Expedia (founded in 1996) and Orbitz (founded in 2001), took advantage of the Internet as a buying platform to build online storefronts that display multiple hotel options in a market, so that consumers have easy access to price, location, and feature comparisons across the market. TripAdvisor (founded in 2000) provides a platform for user-generated content describing the travel experience. Today, TripAdvisor has more than 225 million reviews and opinions about more than 4.9 million accommodations, restaurants, and attractions worldwide (www.tripadvisor.com). Review sites are now integrated with Facebook so that consumers can identify reviews generated by friends, or friends of friends. Metasearch sites like Trivago and Kayak aggregate prices and information from booking sites across the web, helping consumers identify the "best" deals (even though with rate parity, they should be finding the same rates for the same hotel offered everywhere).

Facilitated by this robust and complex digital ecosystem, consumers today look at dozens of websites during the search process, making it challenging for hotels to understand where demand is sourced, and which partners are generating bookings. A 2013 report from Expedia Media Solutions and Millward Brown Digital found that leisure travelers visited up to 38 sites before booking a vacation package, an average of 15.5 of them in the week before booking (http://info.advertising.expedia.com/path-to-purchase). The OTAs had a 47.2 percent share of site visits in this study. Let's not forget that all of this digital activity is rapidly shifting from computers to smart phones, tablets and other mobile devices.

Before I describe how this book will help hotel revenue management survive and thrive in the new social world, it is important to briefly describe where hotel revenue management started, and why the changing marketplace I discussed earlier has put pressure on traditional revenue management systems and practices.

THE CHANGING MARKETPLACE

Based on the success of revenue management in the airlines after deregulation (Smith, Leimkuhler, and Darrow 1992), major hotel companies saw an opportunity to adapt this model to their business, which shares similar characteristics. Yield management, or revenue management as it came to be known, is a pricing methodology that is well suited for industries that have a limited capacity (only 300 rooms in the hotel), perishable inventory (if the room goes empty one night, you lose the opportunity to sell it for that night), segmentable demand (business travelers and leisure travelers value the product differently), time-variable demand (at a business hotel, weekdays are busy, weekends are slow), and a low cost of sale (compared to the cost of operating the hotel, the variable cost associated with booking one more room is relatively low) (Kimes 1989).

Hotels followed the airline model of forecasting demand and preserving inventory for higher paying guests. Overbooking policies protected against no-shows and length of stay controls helped to fill the days around busy periods ("shoulder days") (Vinod 2004). These measures were very successful, even when implemented in a relatively manual environment. However, this methodology originated at a time before the Internet existed, so it was difficult for consumers to "price shop" in the market. Demand was relatively stable, and assumptions about the independence of rates held for the most part. After realizing substantial value from manually applied overbooking and length of stay controls, rudimentary forecasting techniques, and pricing strategies like threshold models to shut off lower rates as demand started to build, hotels were only just starting to implement automated revenue management systems based on airline models in the late 1990s.

Suddenly, the Internet went mainstream, ecommerce became widespread, and consumer behavior started to change dramatically.

Distribution opportunities expanded, and third parties started to sell hotel rooms online on behalf of their hotel customers. Just a few years later, the social web connected consumers to one another and to their preferred vendors across distances and networks. Consumers were suddenly empowered to take control over how they researched, how they made a decision of where to book, and what channels they used.

Today, online travel agents (OTAs), price transparency, social media, mobile, search, review sites, last-minute booking apps, and flash sales have created a market that is more dynamic and generates more data than ever before. Consumers have easy access to price and value information about all the hotels in a market, which means more pressure on hotels to understand and account for competitive dynamics. Disruptive events like economic downturns, political disruptions, and catastrophic weather events have shaken consumer confidence. Booking windows are shortening, driven by the shift to mobile devices and new last-minute booking apps that promise the very best deal on hotel stays. All of this activity means the past is no longer the best predictor of the future.

Traditional revenue management systems have been unable to cope with these changing market conditions primarily because the airline model they were based on assumes that prices are relatively stable, so availability for different prices could be controlled without impacting demand. The models assume that predetermined rates could be open and closed based on independent demand levels. With rate parity agreements, price transparency and the disintegration of traditional rate fences, simply opening and closing rates according to demand forecasts no longer provides optimal price recommendations. Pricing for the mass market must account for price sensitivity of demand and also be balanced against the traditional agreements with groups, wholesalers, and corporate accounts.

THE EVOLUTION OF THE REVENUE MANAGEMENT FUNCTION

Cross, Higbie, and Cross (2009) provide an overview of the evolution of revenue management in the lodging industry, from the inventory-focused role it played in the late 1980s and 1990s, to the post-9/11 shift toward a more expansive role within the organization. Historically, as described previously, revenue managers were tasked with opening and closing predefined room rates based on predicted demand such that the best combination of occupancy and rate was achieved for any given night. More recently, with the emergence of the digital economy as described earlier, revenue management has begun to evolve from this tactical orientation to a more strategic role that encompasses marketing, sales and channel strategy. With this evolution has come a broader set of responsibilities across a number of domains including pricing, management of the entire revenue stream (total hotel revenue management), and a customer-centric approach to developing demand (Figure 1.1). Consequently, the background and skill set of an "ideal" revenue manager have evolved. I will address all of these topics, and their implications on the practice of revenue management, in this book.

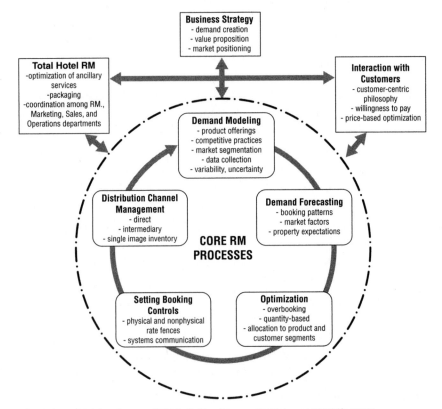

Figure 1.1 Evolving Scope of RM Activities (Noone, McGuire, and Rohlfs 2011)

Cross and his coauthors conducted the research for this article before the social web became mainstream, before the economic crisis of 2008, before everyone had a smartphone and therefore, before the guest experience went digital. These impacts have only exacerbated the effects that Cross and his coauthors discuss in their article, and revenue management has become further complicated by emerging opportunities in digital marketing, such as personalization.

The success of revenue management programs in general has raised the visibility of the discipline, and increased the scope of revenue management activities. Revenue managers are now asked to take on additional responsibilities including ecommerce, business strategy development, analysis of competitive dynamics, application of revenue management to nontraditional areas of the hotel or to new categories of hotels, and more recently understanding and accounting for the impacts of digital marketing, social media, review sentiment and mobile in a pricing strategy. These expanding responsibilities require revenue management to develop new relationships across the organization, working cross-functionally with counterparts in sales and marketing as well as in the restaurants, spas, function space, and even retail outlets.

Technology has also evolved since the advent of revenue management systems, providing the opportunity to incorporate more data, use more complex mathematical algorithms, and get better answers faster. Data volume, variety, and velocity are increasing exponentially, as the influences on hotel pricing expand. Systems can handle this data deluge, but the practical question arises about what data should be incorporated into revenue management algorithms, which data has a place more in strategic decision making, and what data will only be a distraction for revenue managers.

Technology evolutions are also impacting the way that data can be visualized and consumed. New data visualization software puts the power to consolidate disparate data into a single source, and visualize that data through a flexible, dynamic interface. Reporting is moving away from static charts and graphs and into highly visual displays available wherever and whenever needed. As revenue managers are increasingly called on to explain their strategy to broader audiences and in the face of a complex marketplace, there is a huge opportunity to leverage these new visualization tools and techniques to create compelling stories that inspire action.

With the widespread adoption of automated revenue management systems, revenue managers are no longer required to go through the manual process of acquiring data and building models in Excel. There is now more time to spend on developing and implementing a pricing strategy around system recommendations. With this evolution, the role and skill sets required of a revenue manager are evolving as well. The traditional hard-core data- and analytics-focused revenue manager is evolving into a more business-oriented leader.

WHAT TO EXPECT FROM THIS BOOK

As I have traveled around the world in the past few years, speaking with revenue managers about the value of data and analytics to move their business forward, I hear several common themes:

- Revenue management analytics are evolving, driven by price transparency, and now the social web. The way that revenue management problems are solved needs to change, both because of changing consumer behavior, and also because new technology enablers are available that can provide better, more detailed answers faster. Revenue managers are eager to understand the opportunities that come with evolving pricing and revenue management analytics.

- Revenue leaders are also anxious to take advantage of new data sources to improve their day-to-day pricing decisions and their overall pricing strategy; for example, reputation data or web-shopping data. Before they can even consider new "big data" sources, they struggle to get access to and information from their more traditional data sources. Technology moves fast. It is challenging to keep up.

- Effective pricing to the connected consumer requires working cross-functionally in the organization and better synchronizing activities with counterparts in marketing, sales, and operations.

Technology can be the glue that binds these departments together, but developing a framework for interaction is also crucial, and challenging.

- As revenue management has demonstrated success in generating revenue for full-service hotels, there is a strong desire to apply these techniques more broadly, both to other revenue-generating assets in the hotel and also to different types of hotels, like economy or limited service. Yet, there are technology and business process limitations to making this happen.

- There is a talent shortage across all analytical functions, and revenue management is no exception to this. Revenue managers are highly concerned about where they will find the talent to take their organizations into the next decade and beyond. As the practice of revenue management is evolving, so are the talent, skill set, and organizational structure of the revenue management function.

- Hotel executives, owners, and asset managers are beginning to understand the value of revenue management, but in many cases, they still have limited understanding of its application and value. Revenue managers are struggling to communicate their value to stakeholders outside of the revenue management function.

Through my blogs and articles, I have tried to make sense of the impact of changing market and technology dynamics. From the reaction to that work, I realized that there was a real need to lay out in more depth the realities of the current environment, describe how that has impacted the modern practice of revenue management, and provide strategies for revenue management, and hotels in general, to meet the challenges and take advantage of the opportunities.

This book is not a "how to" for the property level revenue manager. If you are looking for that, I would suggest that you sign up for HSMAI's Certified Revenue Management Executive program and take advantage of the *Evolving Dynamics* book that accompanies it. Nor will this book describe in detail the math behind pricing and revenue management systems. There are two great resources for that information,

Pricing and Revenue Optimization by Robert Phillips and *The Theory and Practice of Revenue Management* by Kalyan Talluri and Garrett van Ryzin.

One of the revenue leaders I spoke to about the content of the book remarked to me that the book seemed to be less about the practice of revenue management itself and more about the implications of changes in consumer behavior on revenue management. She is right. The changes in consumer behavior driven by the market factors I described earlier have fundamentally changed how hotels need to think about the revenue management function. Using research from leading experts, my own experience, and the experiences of revenue leaders from around the world, the book will help hotel revenue managers make the right decisions about data, technology, and business processes to move their business forward in the face of this changing consumer behavior. In fact, I hope that this book will be useful to a broad range of hoteliers even beyond revenue management who want to understand revenue management better, and that revenue managers can pass this along to their colleagues in marketing, asset management, or operations to help them better understand the crucial role of revenue management and the pressures that are facing it.

In today's social world, the job of the revenue manager is both more complex and more strategic. In the book, I describe the modern practice of revenue management to help revenue managers develop the knowledge and skills required to stay current and be successful. Starting with the core of revenue management, the pricing systems, I describe innovations in analytics and technology that are improving the accuracy and reach of pricing decisions, both tactical and strategic. Then, I discuss the expanding role of revenue management, and address some of the current pressures that the discipline is facing, including understanding the role of reputation in pricing, working more closely with marketing, and embracing total hotel revenue management. Finally, I describe some broader strategic opportunities that revenue management should be prepared to get involved with, such as personalization initiatives. As new opportunities present themselves in the future, revenue management must be prepared to address them. The final chapter describes how to identify the right skill sets and organization to facilitate the ongoing success of revenue management programs, as well as provides some predictions from revenue leaders about where the discipline will evolve. The following section describes in more detail what you can expect to learn from the book.

WHAT'S IN THIS BOOK

Data, technology, and analytics have always played a crucial role in the revenue management discipline. As the social world has evolved, rapid innovation in technology has followed. The first part of the book, **New Analytics for a New Environment**, outlines how today's revenue management systems should take advantage of innovations in analytics, processing power, data management, and data visualization. I take a broad approach to this discussion so that revenue managers can be prepared to participate in conversations not just about the revenue management system, but about the hotel's broader data and technology strategy.

Chapter 2: Demystifying Price Optimization covers the analytic implications of price transparency, by describing the differences between price optimization and traditional inventory optimization. It identifies when applying price optimization is appropriate, and when traditional inventory optimization is still needed. By understanding these concepts, revenue managers will be better equipped to effectively apply them, or to evaluate a vendor that claims to do so.

Now that the variety, velocity, and volume of data available to hotels are expanding, it is important to understand how to capture, store, and access this data, and how to identify opportunities to leverage it to improve decision making in revenue management, but also, across the organization. Revenue management has always been a "big data" problem, so much so that traditional revenue management systems had to make sacrifices to overcome technology constraints that limited the amount of data that could be processed in time to deliver a price recommendation. In **Chapter 3: Big Data, Big Analytics, and Revenue Management**, I describe the innovations in data management and analytics that are enabling revenue management algorithms to handle more data faster, providing more profitable pricing recommendations and new opportunities for understanding demand. Evolving consumer behavior creates new data and new influences on pricing. I also talk about how to evaluate new data sources to understand their place in the revenue management decision.

The second part of the book, **The Expanding Role of Revenue Management**, describes how revenue management's role in the organization has expanded over the past few years to meet the needs of an evolving marketplace. Revenue management is incorporating new impacts into pricing tactics and pricing strategies to help others understand how to take a revenue management approach to their areas of responsibility. This part identifies opportunities for revenue management to work across functional areas to generate additional value for the organization. It focuses on expanding the pricing strategy to include new data and new functions.

The biggest change in the hotel environment recently is the emergence of the social web. With the growing popularity of review and rating sites, consumers have a new source of information to rely on when making a hotel purchase. The question for revenue managers is: How are consumers using all of this information, with price, to make a purchase decision? **Chapter 4: Hotel Pricing in a Social World** describes the results of some research I conducted with Dr. Breffni Noone to answer this question. This chapter teaches revenue managers how to use user-generated content in a pricing strategy.

Chapter 5: Integrated Revenue Management and Marketing presents the opportunities that come from revenue management and marketing working closely together. Revenue management is responsible for demand control, and marketing is responsible for demand generation. These functions are really two sides of the same coin. Working closely together, revenue management and marketing can achieve the vision of "intelligent demand management," with marketing only generating demand during need periods, and revenue management ensuring that promotional demand is accounted for in pricing and allocation decisions. This improves the effectiveness of pricing strategies.

Discussions about "intelligent demand management" and synchronizing decision making across departments lead naturally into the concept of total hotel revenue management. With the success of hotel room revenue management, hoteliers naturally see an opportunity to extend the practice beyond rooms. **Chapter 6: Total Hotel Revenue Management** provides a framework for applying revenue management to other revenue-generating assets, and explores the role of the guest in total hotel revenue management. I talk about the importance of an integrated revenue culture across all departments in the hotel and provide tips about how to start your organization moving in this direction. This chapter expands pricing strategy to new revenue-generating areas.

The final part, **The Future of Revenue Management: Pricing as a Business Strategy**, provides advice to revenue management to elevate the discipline to the level of an overall business strategy. Price can be an important strategic lever and an important component to support the success of an overarching business strategy. This part describes how revenue management can align itself to the organization's overarching strategy, both overall and at the level of an all-encompassing initiative like personalization.

Chapter 7: Pricing as a Strategic Tool describes the opportunities to elevate the pricing discipline to the strategic level and outlines how revenue managers should position themselves to take on a more strategic role in the organization.

Consumers today expect that the companies they do business with will treat them as individuals instead of a member of a large market segment. As distribution costs rise and alternatives flood the market, hotels must create an experience that differentiates the brand to stay competitive, and one that can only be accessed by booking directly with the hotel. Many hotel companies are beginning personalization initiatives to engage with their guests at a more individual level. In **Chapter 8: The Path to Personalization**, I present a vision for personalization in the hospitality industry and describe revenue management's crucial role in the creation and execution of personalization initiatives. I emphasize throughout the importance of finding the balance between providing that excellent guest experience and "crossing the line to creepy."

The final chapter in the book, **Chapter 9: The Future of Revenue Management**, describes the skills and competencies that will be required for the revenue manager of the future. At the same time, as hotel companies struggle to redefine the function to meet the needs of the changing marketplace, it is important to also understand how that impacts the skills required to be a successful revenue manager. This chapter helps hotels define the new role of a revenue manager, understand how to attract and retain top talent into the discipline, and organize revenue management departments to take best advantage of the talent that is available.

Throughout the book, I provide examples, quotes, and testimonials from revenue leaders who are helping their organizations to meet some of these challenges.

I hope that this book inspires revenue managers to continue to evolve the discipline with the changing marketplace and changing consumer. It is an exciting time to be in revenue management, but it's also a critical one. Unless revenue leaders are equipped to manage pricing in a social world, they and their companies will fall behind.

CHAPTER **2**

Demystifying Price Optimization*

At the core of a hotel revenue manager's job are the data and analytics in the revenue management system that form the foundation for day-to-day pricing decisions. The better the data and the more accurate and robust the analytics, the better the pricing decisions will be. Better pricing decisions lead to a more effective revenue management strategy, and, of course, to more revenue. This is why the industry must be concerned about the latest and greatest analytic techniques to support effective pricing in a changing marketplace. In the next two chapters, I discuss the innovations in systems and processes that support the execution of more accurate pricing for the day-to-day, tactical task of determining the right price to charge for each product for sale over the booking horizon.

Price transparency has brought about what is probably the largest and most widely discussed change to revenue management analytics. When consumers were given access to every price in the market, hotels had to compete on price more directly, which meant revenue managers had to start paying more attention to competitors' prices, and revenue management systems needed to consider how consumers react to price (Figure 2.1). Rather than simply opening and closing rates based on demand patterns or occupancy forecasts (traditionally referred to as "yielding"), the analytics must now consider consumers' reaction to price changes, the hotel's and the competition's. This pricing methodology, based on demand sensitivity to price, is called *price optimization*, and it is the focus of this chapter.

Price optimization has been talked about in industry for a decade or so, but it has not been widely implemented. This has been partially due to the fact that in order to provide price optimization, the commercially available revenue management systems would have to completely redo their data integrations and analytic engines—an expensive and technologically difficult task. It is also partially due to the fact that the move to price optimization requires revenue managers to think about their

* Portions of this chapter were taken from www.hotelexecutive.com/author/348. HotelExecutive.com retains the copyright to the articles published in the *Hotel Business Review*. Articles cannot be republished without prior written consent by HotelExecutive.com.

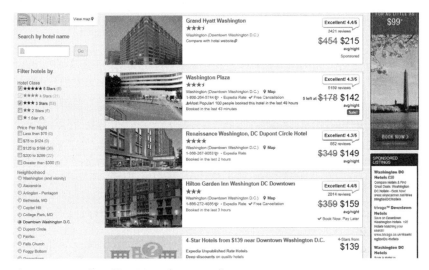

Figure 2.1 Hotel Booking Screen from Expedia
As you can see from this screen, the prices are in by far the largest size font, focusing the consumer's attention directly on prices in the market.

demand differently, resulting in a good deal of change management. However, market conditions today are such that any hotel that is not considering price sensitivity of demand will miss out on a huge revenue opportunity. The good news, as I describe in this chapter and the rest of this part, is that technology is rapidly evolving such that it is becoming possible for hotels to access this capability, even through commercially available revenue management systems, if they know what to look for.

With all the hype, price optimization has become one of the most frequently misused and misunderstood terms in revenue management. Clearly, it is crucial that revenue managers understand what price optimization is, how it relates to traditional revenue management, and what advantages will be gained from this approach. In this chapter, I describe how and why pricing in hospitality has evolved, define price optimization, and then discuss how it should be applied.

After reading this chapter, you will understand exactly what price optimization is (and isn't), and be able to define its advantages as part of hotel pricing in a social world. You will be better prepared to evaluate its impact on your analytic platform and your business processes.

A HISTORY LESSON: YIELD MANAGEMENT IN THE AIRLINES

To put price optimization in context, it is important to understand how pricing has evolved. Here is a brief history lesson.

Yield management started after deregulation in the airline industry, as a method for airlines to control the number of discounted fares they sold. The idea was to move away from first-come, first-served selling and start preserving the right number of full-fare seats for higher-paying demand (Figure 2.2a). Airlines started by forecasting demand by fare class and protecting a certain number of seats for higher paying fares. *Fences*, which are rules to qualify for purchase, were created around the discounted fares, such as advance purchase or a Saturday night stay. This was designed to discourage those who would pay a higher fare from booking the lower fares.

As this business process evolved, airlines saw the opportunity to add more discount levels to drive even more incremental revenue (Figure 2.2b). As the number of fares increased, the problem started to get more complicated, so mathematicians began to model the problem to find the mathematically optimal protection levels that would maximize revenue. The output was the number of full-fare seats to protect, and the number of each of the many discounted products to sell in order to maximize revenue. The early systems developed for this purpose were known as yield management systems (Smith et al. 1992).

After the carriers began to move toward a *hub-and-spoke* model, where a significant percentage of passenger itineraries involved a stop at the carrier's hub, yield management systems needed to account for the large numbers of connecting passengers produced by this approach. This involved managing demand for a specific segment, known as a *leg*, of an itinerary when many different kinds of itineraries, all with different values to the airline, also flowed over it, and optimizing the availability of different fares on these connecting itineraries.

For a simple example, think about a flight from Ithaca, New York, to Philadelphia, Pennsylvania, a hub for US Airways. This is considered a *leg*. There are passengers on that flight who are going to Philadelphia, but there are also passengers connecting to flights around the world. If

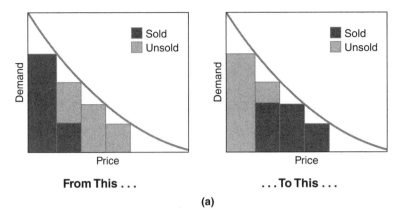

(a)

Figure 2.2a Evolution of Airline Yielding

The area under the curve represents all demand for a flight by price. There is more demand for the flight than available seats. For flights, leisure travelers tend to book further in advance and they are more price sensitive. If the airline uses first-come, first-served selling, as on the left, the plane will fill with lower rated demand. If the airline saves seats for higher-paying customers who book later, as on the right, more revenue is generated through higher prices charged for the same limited number of seats. This is the basis for the first yield management systems, preserving inventory for higher rated demand.

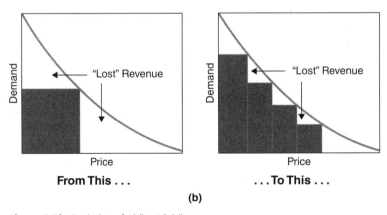

(b)

Figure 2.2b Evolution of Airline Yielding

The white area under the curve represents lost revenue opportunity. If you only offer one price, you lose revenue opportunity from consumers who would have paid more. Increasing the number of prices offered means you can capture more of the revenue opportunity, while still preserving seats for those who would pay higher prices.

the airline does not balance passengers who will stop in Philadelphia with those continuing on, it may end up with many empty seats on connecting flights. It might be better for the revenue over the entire system to make it more expensive to stop in Philadelphia than it is to continue to say, Tampa or San Francisco.

This is called the *network effect*.[1]

Yield management was highly successful for the airlines, which naturally generated interest from businesses with similar operating conditions. Revenue management, as it came to be known, was specifically designed for industries that met certain necessary conditions (Kimes 1989; Kimes and Chase 1998):

- Fixed capacity (only 75 seats on the plane or 300 rooms in the hotel).
- Perishable product (once the plane takes off, you can't sell the empty seat).
- Advance reservations (requiring inventory to be "protected" for more valuable business).
- Time-variable demand (peak and off-peak periods).
- Segment-able demand (demand segments place a different value on access to the inventory).
- Low cost of sale (compared to the cost of running the hotel, the cost of selling one more room is minimal).

Modeling after the success of airlines, hotel companies began to adapt the airline methodologies to their business problem, first manually through better length of stay and overbooking controls, and then analytically, using optimal pricing recommendations derived from an automated revenue management system.

THEN THINGS CHANGED . . .

The original revenue management algorithms were based on the use of fences to ensure that consumers who would be willing to pay a higher price could not access lower priced inventory. In other words, demand could be perfectly segmented according to the value consumers placed on access to the inventory. Another key modeling assumption for these algorithms was that the fare amounts were relatively stable over time. In addition, these models assumed that even though different fare products used the same inventory unit (an airline seat), each different fare type could be treated as a separate product, servicing a distinct and separate market of customers. This last assumption meant that demand for these different products could be treated as independent—a key assumption that underpins traditional revenue management forecasting and optimization.

Three important trends, driven by evolving market conditions, have emerged since the original revenue management algorithms were developed:

1. Low-cost airlines introduced simplified fare structures with fewer fares and significantly reduced fencing, meaning everyone "qualifies" for all of the fares. Today, these simplified fare structures dominate most air travel markets—effectively invalidating the assumption of demand independence made in revenue management models. Figure 2.3 represents a typical online airline purchase. In this case, a consumer could purchase any of the available fares, instead of being fenced into one bucket according to her travel pattern.

2. Revenue management has been introduced into markets where strict fences on rates or fares don't really exist. Hotels, rental cars, and cruise lines have rate or fare structures that do not contain strict fences. Prices are tiered based on product characteristics (room type, number of connections) as opposed to consumer characteristics (business traveler who won't stay over the weekend)—thus, demand independence cannot be assumed, because the same consumer can qualify for multiple rates or fares.

3. In addition to price transparency, the advent of ecommerce and OTAs also introduced rate parity. Hotels are forced to offer only one generally available price in the market for *unqualified transient demand,* guests who are not part of a group and do not have an arrangement for a special rate. Now consumers can freely shop all available rates for all hotels in the market.

All fares are rounded up to the nearest dollar.

Depart	Arrive	Flight #	Routing	Travel Time	Business Select $629 - $641	Anytime $601 - $613	Wanna Get Away $278 - $388
6:00 AM	10:50 AM	414 1604	1 stop Change Planes MDW	7h 50m	⊙ $637	⊙ $609	⊙ $326
6:50 AM	9:10 AM	4480	Nonstop	5h 20m	⊙ $629	⊙ $601	⊙ $278
8:20 AM	12:15 PM	491 1027	1 stop Change Planes STL	6h 55m	⊙ $637	⊙ $609	⊙ $326
8:20 AM	1:00 PM	491 3226	2 stops Change Planes STL	7h 40m	⊙ $641	⊙ $613	Unavailable
9:10 AM	1:50 PM	752 4026	1 stop Change Planes DEN	7h 40m	⊙ $637	⊙ $609	⊙ $388
10:40 AM	3:25 PM	490 611	1 stop Change Planes MDW	7h 45m	⊙ $637	⊙ $609	⊙ $326
12:10 PM	4:20 PM	482 747	1 stop Change Planes PHX	7h 10m	⊙ $637	⊙ $609	⊙ $326
3:00 PM	8:15 PM	4089 3673	1 stop Change Planes TPA	8h 15m	⊙ $637	⊙ $609	⊙ $326
5:15 PM	9:20 PM	315 134	1 stop Change Planes MDW	7h 05m	⊙ $637	⊙ $609	⊙ $286
7:10 PM	10:50 PM	2774 1282	1 stop Change Planes DEN	6h 40m	⊙ $637	⊙ $609	⊙ $326

Select Returning Flight:

Figure 2.3 Airline Booking Screen
Note that there are three fare options, but they are available to any customer who is booking. They are differentiated by product-related options like no cancellation policy or higher priority for picking seats, but every shopper "qualifies" for any option.

These recent trends have taken hospitality revenue management away from the assumptions made by the original hotel revenue management scientists, who modeled according to the airline revenue management problem. No demand independence, no rate fences, simplified rate structures, rate parity, and easy access to competitors' rates have made "traditional" revenue management algorithms relatively ineffective. It is these factors that have created an environment better suited to *price optimization*.

PRICE OPTIMIZATION

As airlines evolved their revenue management practices, other industries that did not meet all of the necessary conditions for revenue management were also attempting to maximize revenue and profits through analytic pricing. In industries like retail, products are made available at a single price to a broad market. Each customer has a different ability or willingness to pay, and the retailer can change the price of the product over time (typically through discounting). As in economic theory, if the price of the product is increased, the price will exceed the willingness-to-pay level of some customers and demand decreases. If the price is decreased, the product price drops below the willingness-to-pay level of more customers, and demand increases.

This theory is the basis for *price optimization.* In price optimization, demand for a product is estimated as a function of price, and the price becomes the decision variable that is used in maximizing revenues or margin. So, as opposed to protecting rooms for higher-paying guests, like classic revenue management models would, price optimization determines the optimal single price to change the broader market (*unqualified demand*), considering that demand changes as the price changes (Phillips 2005).

Let's think about why this approach is well suited to hotels. Think about a roadside hotel. It may meet many of the necessary conditions of revenue management, such as fixed capacity, perishable product, and advance reservations. However, it very likely does not have clearly fenced segments, so there is no need to protect inventory for higher valued segments. Generally, the hotelier chooses one of several possible rates to charge on any given date for any customer who wants a room. Once again, there is no independence of demand between these rates. They all have the same set of characteristics. Therefore, the prospective consumer will always select the least expensive one. This is an extreme example of *price-able demand*—demand that can be offered an optimized price, based on the price sensitivity of demand.

The unqualified guest in limited or full-service hotels also could be considered to be price-able. Based on distribution agreements, hotels need to offer one publicly available price for a room type in the market through all channels, like OTAs and brand.com, creating a price-sensitive demand environment.[2]

Table 2.1 provides a very basic example of the importance of accounting for price sensitivity. The hotel in this example has 50 rooms but is not forecasted to sell out on this particular day. A revenue management

Table 2.1 Price Sensitivity of Demand Example

Price Point	Demand	Revenue
200	10	2,000
180	12	2,160
160	**15**	**2,400**
140	17	2,380
120	19	2,280
100	21	2,100
80	23	1,840

system that used strictly yield-based controls (set by a threshold rate or hurdle rate, for example), would recommend the lowest price point, in this case, $80. This is because, without a sellout, inventory-based optimization models calculate the hurdle rate at zero, and the selling system offers the lowest rate.

However, if the pricing system has access to the information in Table 2.1, according to the price sensitivity of demand illustrated in this table, pricing at $160 actually results in higher revenue. While the $80 price results in the highest occupancy, if the hotel had chased the occupancy strategy, they would have missed out on a significant amount of revenue. This is a very simplified example, clearly, but it does illustrate a case where accounting for price sensitivity of demand can result in higher revenue.

Price-able hotel products represent a significant portion of demand in today's market. In fact, in highly competitive markets, there is a significant advantage to using price sensitivity of demand, or price elasticity, in revenue management modeling. The analytics can account for the price sensitivity of demand for your hotel, and also account for the impact of your competitor's pricing moves on your own demand.

Many consultants and vendors claim that they provide price optimization capabilities. In fact, optimization itself is a pervasively misused term across all facets of hospitality, as well as in business in general. To understand whether a specific solution will meet your price optimization needs, it is important to be able to identify not only what true optimization is but also the specific nuances of the price optimization problem and how it is best solved. This is the goal of the next few sections.

WHAT IS OPTIMIZATION?

To understand price optimization, it is important to understand the general mathematical technique behind it. *Optimization* is a specific mathematical technique that solves for the best possible answer to a specific objective, accounting for all of the operating constraints unique to the problem.

All optimization problems involve the following elements:

- **Objective.** The equation that describes the desired outcome of the problem, always written as a goal. For example, in price optimization modeling, the goal is to maximize revenue. The objective equation is expressed in terms of *decision variables*.
- **Decision variables.** These are the outputs of the optimization problem. They represent the decisions you must make to achieve the best possible outcome. Price optimization algorithm output is the price to charge (by date, length of stay, and room type), that maximizes revenue across the booking horizon.
- **Constraints.** The constraints are how you express the operating conditions under which the problem should be solved. For example, you can't sell more rooms than the hotel has, so the capacity of the hotel is a constraint. Also, you will not sell more rooms than there is demand for, so the amount of expected demand by segment, or by willingness to pay, is also a constraint.

Optimization problems are solved by testing different values for the outcome variables over and over until the objective is achieved. The process of solving the problem through these iterations is managed by an optimization *algorithm*, which is basically a set of rules that are followed in calculating the answer to a problem. At each iteration, the algorithm must verify that no constraints are violated and compare the answer to the previous iteration to see if it is better. The algorithm stops when the best possible answer is found.

Revenue management and price optimization problems are further complicated by the presence of the network effect I mentioned earlier. In the case of hotels, as I described in the notes, this is the length of stay. This network effect is important because the remaining rooms to sell are a crucial constraint in the optimization. If there are a lot of rooms left to sell, and demand is sensitive to price, you could lower the price to sell more. If you have only a few, you could raise the price to get more value from them. The number of two- or three-night stays sold on a Friday could change the price decision you would make for a Saturday or Sunday, because it changes the number of rooms available to sell for those nights. In order to account for this in the hotel revenue management problem, the optimization has to solve for every possible forecasted length-of-stay combination for every day in the booking horizon, and its impact on the preceding and following days. Obviously, that's a lot of iterations!

Optimization problems are among the hardest problems in mathematics. The complexity of the problem, and the number of iterations it takes to solve, requires highly specialized algorithms and intensive processing power. Some mathematicians spend their entire careers just figuring out how to solve these problems faster and more efficiently. Even so, in some cases, using traditional technology infrastructure, solving the full problem can take days or weeks. I talk more about this issue and how advances in technology have helped to overcome it in the next chapter, "Big Data, Big Analytics, and Revenue Management."

If the solution you are considering is not based on an optimization problem, and solved using an optimization algorithm, as described earlier, it will not provide an "optimal" or "optimized" answer. If you are only looking at a graph of historical data, or a forecast of expected demand, you are not getting an optimal solution. If your revenue manager is expected to derive the answer by looking at reports or forecasts, you are not optimizing. You get the idea. Revenue management problems are simply too complex to solve without the aid of technology, including optimization algorithms that can automate the process of testing every possible alternative.

INDUSTRY DEFINITIONS

Since I have seen several terms used interchangeably in industry publications relative to price optimization, it is worth defining them so the distinctions are clear.

Price Optimization: As described in this chapter, this is a mathematical calculation of an optimal price derived from the price sensitivity of demand. Price sensitivity of demand can be calculated at room type and market segment level, to provide a very detailed set of optimal prices, depending on how price can be deployed in the selling systems.

Continuous Price Optimization: This refers to the specific output of a price optimization calculation. There are two ways to derive the optimal price in an optimization algorithm. In continuous price optimization, the algorithm can freely select a price according to price sensitivity of demand, meaning the output could be $176.32. Alternatively, price can be calculated against the best available rate (BAR) spectrum (which can be set at a very granular level, if desired). The optimization algorithm is restricted to selecting a price from that spectrum according to the price sensitivity of demand. For the first option, every possible penny of revenue potential is captured. The second method is useful when there are concerns about consumer reactions to such granular pricing, or if there are restrictions in the selling system that require a predetermined rate spectrum to be preloaded.

Dynamic Pricing: In contrast to the previous two mathematical techniques, *dynamic pricing* is a blanket term referring to a pricing strategy where price is allowed to fluctuate with some frequency according to demand. Dynamic pricing is basically an execution methodology for price. The dynamic price could be calculated through price optimization, inventory optimization, threshold modeling, or any number of methods, including gut feel.

Price Optimization for Hotels

In price optimization, the goal is to maximize revenue over the booking horizon by setting optimal prices for each product available for sale; in other words, a price for each combination of room type, arrival date, and length of stay. The optimal price is subject to demand and capacity constraints, and considers the price elasticity of demand. There are several specific nuances to this problem that make the solution tricky, including calculating price elasticity, determining the impact of competitor pricing and accounting for "yieldable" demand.

Calculating Price Elasticity

Price elasticity, or the price sensitivity of demand, is an economics term that refers to how demand for a product or service changes with changes in price. This measure is generally negative; as price increases, demand decreases. Products with elasticities less than one (absolute value) are generally considered to be inelastic, whereas products with elasticities greater than one are relatively elastic and sensitive to price changes. Price elasticity is required to model demand as a function of price, the metric at the core of true price optimization. However, there are some factors in the hotel problem that make calculating price elasticity particularly challenging.

For instance, demand does not just vary according to price. Demand can vary dramatically according to a number of factors including:

- Time of the year
- Day of the week
- Special event periods
- Time remaining until arrival
- Competitive effects

Hoteliers have long recognized the impact of the above factors on demand and even without technology solutions, have actively managed price according to expected demand patterns. For example, many hotels have a low price available during the off-season and offer higher rates during peak periods. This means that for most hotels, even those without a formal revenue management function, when demand is high, prices tend to be high.

Because to some extent hotel room prices are already managed according to demand, simply graphing the relationship between price and demand in hotels provides a misleading picture of price elasticity (Figure 2.4). It would appear that price elasticity is positive, that is, as the price goes up, demand goes up. We know this is not the case. This

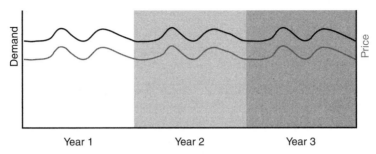

Figure 2.4 Example of price and demand relationship in hotels

effect is known as *price endogeneity*. It must be broken in order for hotel revenue management analytics to effectively calculate price elasticity and derive an optimal price (Dietz et al. 2012).

In order to account for price endogeneity, you have to look at demand and price within each period, as opposed to across periods, watching how it responds to your pricing and your competitors' pricing. There are fairly complex analytical techniques that address this issue. The important thing to understand is that if the elasticity model is not accounting for this effect, the output will be incorrect.

My advice for the businessperson is to just ask the consultant or vendor who is pitching price optimization whether their model accounts for price endogeneity. You don't need to understand the answer much beyond yes or no. If they look confused, or try to tell you it isn't a big deal, find another partner to work with. If they have a technical answer, find a scientist you trust to verify if it will work in your environment. Of course, once this book is published, I imagine (or hope, because that means they all will have read this book), that every vendor will understand and talk about this concept, so you will definitely need to find that scientist!

Competitive Price Effects

As I allude to earlier, competitor price effects are also an important component in the price optimization decision. Consumers consider your price relative to the competition when making a purchase decision, so this impact must be accounted for when setting the optimal price. Typically, this has been accounted for by adjusting the system recommended price according to certain automated business rules describing how the hotel would like to be positioned relative to the market. If the hotel is not using a revenue management system, the process would be similar but just implemented manually. The revenue manager reviews the competitor pricing, which is typically provided by a third-party data provider. Then she applies a predetermined competitive pricing strategy like "My hotel must always be top of the market" or "I want to be $20 less than the Sheraton."

There are many problems with this approach. First of all, a business rule approach does not fully account for consumer decision-making processes. Do you understand the consumer's value proposition for each of the hotels in the competitive set? If not, then $20 is a pretty arbitrary number. Business rules also do not account for the market conditions that might be impacting your competitors' pricing decisions. Does the Sheraton have a large group in-house, and only a few rooms left to sell—or maybe you do and they don't? Finally, it assumes that you have selected the right set of competitors, so that you are benchmarking against the same hotels that your customers are looking at.

Competitive set selection is a well-known and persistent problem in the hotel industry, driven by management contracts, aspirations of ownership groups, and incomplete market knowledge. I could write a whole chapter on the right way to select a competitive set, and all of the reasons why that will never happen, but suffice it to say I think we all realize that if you aren't comparing yourself against the right competitors, you'll always be missing an important piece of the equation.

Hotels feel the impact of poor competitive pricing decisions where overreacting to competitor pricing starts a price war that drives the market down, and underreaction causes the hotel's demand to spiral down as the rest of the market captures more than their fair share with lower prices. It is crucial to make the right decision. Leaving it to business rules is not enough.

My favorite example of the problem with business rule–driven competitive pricing comes from Amazon.com, and the $23,698,655.93 book about flies (www.michaeleisen.org/blog/?p=358). Two sellers on Amazon Marketplace had the book *The Making of a Fly* for sale,

	profnath	bordeebook	profnath over previous bordeebook	bordeebook over profnath
8-Apr	$1,730,045.91	$2,198,177.95		1.27059
9-Apr	$2,194,443.04	$2,788,233.00	0.99830	1.27059
10-Apr	$2,783,493.00	$3,536,675.57	0.99830	1.27059
11-Apr	$3,530,663.65	$4,486,021.69	0.99830	1.27059
12-Apr	$4,478,395.76	$5,690,199.43	0.99830	1.27059
13-Apr	$5,680,526.66	$7,217,612.38	0.99830	1.27059

Figure 2.5 Business Rules for Competitive Pricing

profnath and bordeebook. They were each using a business rule to price against the other competitors. Profnath had a new copy for sale and wanted to be the lowest in the marketplace, but only slightly. They set their algorithm to price at 0.998 below the cheapest new book in the market. Bordeebook, probably relying on an inflated perception of themselves, decided that their consumers would pay slightly more for the new copy if it were bought from them, so they set the algorithm to price at 1.27059 above the lowest in the market. Figure 2.5 demonstrates what happened when they set their business rules and let the system make decisions unchecked by "reality."

The price increase over the market set by bordeebook was enough to offset the paired decrease by profnath that the book price eventually rose to *$23,698,653.93 plus $3.99 shipping and handling* (Figure 2.6).

Figure 2.6 The Danger of Business Rule–Driven Competitive Pricing

Now, biologists will tell you that this book is an important reference in their work, but I'm pretty sure not even the author would claim it was worth $23 million. (My book, on the other hand, will help you make decisions that will directly impact the bottom line. . . . I'll leave it to you to decide how much that's worth to you!)

Clearly, proper competitive pricing requires more thought than setting unmonitored business rules and walking away. An algorithmic approach to competitive pricing effects helps to estimate and calibrate price elasticity, as well as to refine future demand forecasts to account for market conditions. There is a good discussion of an approach to this in the white paper I reference at the end of this chapter. The technique works by tracking the movement of competitor prices relative to your prices and detecting any demand effects that are not accounted for by other factors like seasonal patterns or special events. This not only identifies the impact of specific competitor movements on your demand, but it also eliminates any identified competitors that may not have an impact on your demand at all. (Like the one the owner made you include, even though it's in a completely different class of service.) Unlike business rules, the algorithms incorporate the hotel's current demand patterns and remaining capacity left to sell in pricing recommendations, ensuring you do not under- or overvalue your inventory as rooms are sold just because a competitor needs to move inventory, or happens to have a large group in-house.

Not All Demand Is Price-able

Price-able demand represents a large portion of demand, particularly for economy and limited service hotels, but a good portion of hotel demand is still *yieldable*, meaning the price is prearranged, but the hotel can determine how many rooms they want to sell at that price. This is particularly true for full-service hotels that have a high percentage of group business, agreements with wholesalers, or any channel agreement that does not include last room availability, meaning you have the option to shut it off.

The decisions that are made about yieldable demand have an impact on capacity, and therefore change the decisions that would be made about an optimal price. Strictly relying on price optimization, therefore, leaves out what could be a large portion of hotel revenue, which, when mismanaged, has a big impact. For many hotels, optimizing price and availability together will balance the crucial components of revenue maximizing decisions.

This is how this works. For price-able demand, price changes change expected demand levels. The amount of expected demand impacts the optimal availability decision. The amount of yieldable demand you accept changes the number of rooms left to sell, and therefore would impact the optimal pricing decision. For example, if there is a sufficient amount of high-rated yieldable business (a valuable group or a wholesaler agreement), the hotel would accept that demand, and then could generate incremental revenue from raising the transient rates for the remaining rooms because there are fewer left to sell. The optimization algorithm tests all of these impacts against one another and provides a price and an availability control that jointly maximize revenue.

Hotel pricing is also complicated by contractual agreements that include *linked rates*. More and more, contracts include rates that are derived from, or linked to, the BAR. For example, a corporate contract is offered a 10 percent discount off of BAR for any given night. This demand is not technically price-able on its own, but also not technically yieldable either, as these rates are typically offered with last room availability and therefore cannot be turned off.

The challenge with these linked segments is that their price sensitivity can be vastly different than the unqualified demand they are linked to. Not accounting for these sensitivities can result in a huge missed revenue opportunity. For example, when demand from corporate travelers with linked rate agreements is high, the system might recommend setting the best-available rate higher than the price sensitivity of the transient segment might indicate. This will ensure that the less price sensitive corporate travelers pay more, making up for any transient demand you may have turned away.

If this capability had been available during the recent recession, hotels might not have gotten into as much trouble. The leisure segment all but dried up but some business travelers were still booking. Given a less sensitive segment linked to the leisure rate, hotels might

Table 2.2 Difference between Revenue Management and Price Optimization

	Revenue Management	Price Optimization
Assumption	Demand independent—Each consumer only qualifies for one product or rate	Demand dependent—Each consumer could qualify for multiple products or rates
Inputs	Demand by product or rate	Price elasticity, demand, competitor rates
Output	Protection levels or controls, set the number of each rate or product to sell	The optimal price to charge for a single product considering demand sensitivity to price
Business Problem	Qualified customers with an agreed-upon rate, highly fenced rates	Unqualified customers, no fences exist
Best Fit Segments	Groups, wholesaler agreements, channels with no last room availability agreements, highly discounted rates with clear restrictions	Transient, OTA, leisure, corporate agreements with last room availability agreements, brand.com prices, linked rates

have kept rates a bit higher and generated some incremental revenue from the demand that was there, instead of dropping rates to try to stimulate demand that didn't exist.

Table 2.2 summarizes the difference between revenue management and price optimization.

As you can see, the hotel industry is now in a position where different techniques are required to continue to maximize revenue, applied according to market conditions and business mix. Applying price optimization to the appropriate demand segments will result in significant revenue gains in the right context, but yieldable demand must also be considered.

AND THE MONEY CAME ROLLING IN . . .

This is an aspirational subhead for sure, but, in summary, in today's social world, price optimization will generate more revenue than traditional revenue management techniques because:

- Demand from unqualified segments is well suited to be priced using price optimization. Traditional revenue management techniques apply the wrong behavioral assumptions to the problem, resulting in a less-than-optimal price recommendation.

▪ During periods of low demand, price optimization will drive more revenue for hotels. If the hotel is not expected to sell out, a traditional revenue management approach would probably recommend opening the lowest available rate—because there is no reason to protect inventory. Because it considers the price sensitivity of demand, price optimization might recommend a slightly higher price based on demand forecasts by segment and the price sensitivity of those segments. You'll be able to capture additional incremental revenue even if the hotel doesn't sell out.

▪ Price optimization techniques help in competitive pricing situations. You can calculate demand sensitivity of price to your own demand and the impact of competitors' price movements on your demand. This means rather than overriding pricing decisions based on business rules about competitive positioning, you can get an analytically derived pricing recommendation that is based only on those competitors that actually impact your demand.

However, keep in mind the following cautions:

▪ For hotels, if you simply graph out the price-demand relationship, it would look like demand increases as price increases. Price endogeneity must be accounted for when calculating price sensitivity of demand, or the price sensitivity metric will simply be wrong.

▪ Price sensitivity can vary widely by market segment, so one overall price sensitivity at the hotel level is not useful for optimizing price. There is an advantage in considering price sensitivity by segment, particularly if the hotel uses linked rates.

▪ As I mentioned earlier, while a significant portion of demand is price-able in hospitality, there is also a good amount of demand that is only yieldable (groups, promotions). Decisions you make for your price-able demand will impact availability for yieldable demand and vice versa. It is crucial that your revenue management modeling accounts for the impact of decisions made for each type of demand on the other. There are very few problems that are purely price-able (or purely yieldable), so be sure to think about whether a combined approach of yieldable and price-able is best for you.

As I have described in this chapter, price optimization, when applied properly, has significant revenue advantages for hotels. Not only are the data and analytics required to solve this problem different from traditional revenue management approaches, but the outputs (i.e., recommendations) will also change. This means there will also be business process change associated with applying price optimization. As the industry moves in this direction, well-informed revenue managers and hospitality executives will need to understand the benefits and limitations of this approach to appropriately apply price optimization to their hotels.

Adopting price elasticity into the revenue management system definitely impacts the way the revenue manager works with the system. Everything is connected in a way it never was before. For example, price changes for unqualified demand impact availability restrictions for qualified rates, and demand forecasts have to be thought of relative to price position. This level of interconnectivity in decisions can make revenue managers feel like when they first started thinking about length of stay effects, and they suddenly realized just how important shoulder days are to revenue maximization. It can take a while to get used to this, even if the reasoning behind the changes is quite intuitive.

I asked Joerg Happel, Product Manager for IDeaS G3 RMS, a new revenue management system that has introduced price optimization and simultaneously optimizes price and inventory allocations, how the revenue manager's interactions with the system change when price optimizations is part of the pricing algorithms. Here is his response:

"In the past, if revenue managers were unhappy with the prices the system recommended, they would just override the price. After a while, when the increased price slowed down demand, the system forecast would begin to adjust, and the impact on that day and surrounding days would begin to be noticed—possibly too late to respond to market opportunities.

"If they override a price in a price optimization–based system, demand forecast will instantly change, corresponding to the price/ demand relationship. Forecasts and decisions on those days, as well as surrounding periods, adjust, and ADR and RevPAR are impacted. Everything is now interrelated. These complex relationships can be difficult to comprehend. To help revenue managers understand these impacts, we provide a what-if analysis that allows revenue managers to test the impact of any adjustments, but it is no longer as simple as an override in one place to force the system to provide a price or a forecast that the revenue manager might want.

"In the past, solutions did not have the capability to deal with all the dynamics of market, price, volume, and value of demand and network effects. Although it has become more complex to operate a revenue management system, a skilled user gets a chance to push the right levers to get the desired outcome, and a less advanced revenue manager is prevented from making costly mistakes that would harm their business."

A CASE STUDY IN PRICE OPTIMIZATION: IHG[3]

CASE STUDY

About IHG: Intercontinental Hotels Group (IHG) owns, manages, leases, or franchises more than 4,500 hotels with more than 650,000 guest rooms in nearly 100 countries and territories worldwide. It owns the hotel brands InterContinental Hotels, Hotel Indigo, Crowne Plaza Hotels and Resorts, Holiday Inn Hotels and Resorts, Holiday Inn Express, Staybridge Suites, and Candlewood Suites. About 85 percent of IHG hotels are franchised, 14 percent are managed, and 1 percent are company owned

Why Price Optimization: Between the advent of the OTAs ushering in a new era of price transparency, the impact of the economic downturn in 2001, and the breakdown of traditional revenue management fences, IHG realized that traditional revenue management processes were not as effective as they had been in the past. Revenue managers were having to

(Continued)

(Continued)

do a lot of work manually, outside of the revenue management system, to account for price transparency and competitive pricing effects.

Goal: To manually manage pricing in this new environment, DORMs (directors of revenue management) were spending 30 percent of their time gathering price intelligence, 30 percent forecasting, 20 percent strategy and business planning, and 10 percent managing inventory controls. IHG's desired state for the DORMs was 40 percent forecasting, 40 percent strategy, 10 percent pricing, and 10 percent managing inventory controls.

Solution: IHG worked with revenue analytics to build automated, analytical price optimization capabilities, which integrated into its existing environment to minimize change management. These capabilities optimized prices for the retail segment, considering competitor rates, by generating a price-adjusted forecast based on price sensitivity and optimizing across that forecast.

Benefits: Because of the rigorous process required to justify investment for this project, IHG conducted a multiphase project, calculating benefits after each phase. First, they deployed a simulation model, which estimated that benefits from deploying a price optimization solution would be between 2.75 and 6 percent revenue uplift on the retail segment. Then they deployed the process with a test group, which noticed a 3.2 percent improvement in RevPAR, and provided some critical feedback for the beta phase. The beta group achieved 2.7 percent improvement in RevPAR ($145M translating to $400M system-wide). IHG began the full rollout in 2010.

ADDITIONAL READING

Alex Dietz, "Demystifying Price Optimization: A Revenue Manager's Guide," white paper, www.sas.com/en_us/whitepapers/demystifying-price-optimization-revenue-managers-guide-106156.html.

Alex Dietz, Natalie Osborn, and Tugrul Sanli, "Are You Awash in a Sea of Competitive Price Intelligence? Let Analytics Be Your Life Raft," white paper, www.sas.com/ro_ro/whitepapers/are-you-awash-in-the-sea-of-competitive-price-intelligence-1990558.html.

Dev Koushik, Jon Higbie and Craig Eister, "Retail Price Optimization at InterContinental Hotels Group," *Interfaces*, 41, no. 1 (2012): 45–57.

Robert L. Phillips, *Pricing and Revenue Optimization*, Stanford University Press, 2005.

REVENUE MANAGEMENT PERSPECTIVES

Revenue management is a relatively new discipline in hotels and is evolving quickly. As the evolution progresses, issues emerge that create discussion or debate within the industry. While I, and others, may have opinions on these issues, the evidence is not yet there for the industry to make a final decision. For the rest of the book, at the end of each chapter I include a revenue management perspective. This section presents information that will help you think through a current issue or get exposed to a new concept so that you can help us work through the issue toward the right solution. I will typically interview experts who have taken a position or are experimenting with answers. At times, I will offer my own opinion. In all cases, it is up to you to decide what you think!

Rethinking the Revenue Management Process: Are We Too Obsessed with Forecasts?

As revenue managers, we typically get obsessed with the forecast and its accuracy. This is for good reason, as it makes sense that a more accurate forecast leads to better pricing decisions. The problem is that in many cases we can become so obsessed with the forecast that we are unable to move past it to actually make decisions. I spoke with one of my colleagues at SAS about this issue, and he provided the following perspective.

Ivan Oliveira, Director, Advanced Analytics and Optimization Services, SAS

SAS is the leader in business analytics software and services, and the largest independent vendor in the business intelligence market.

You know how sometimes you have a conversation with someone that turns everything you thought you knew completely upside down? I had a chance to have a chat with Ivan Oliveira of SAS. His

Figure 2.7 Revenue Management Process

team is composed of a group of experts in really hard analytic techniques, like optimization.

Ivan introduced a concept to me that seemed totally counterintuitive, but, once explained, started to make perfect sense. Ivan and his team tend to work on custom analytical projects. These are implementations where the client desires to gain competitive advantage from building a pricing or inventory optimization system that is configured to its unique operating conditions and business process.

Traditionally, revenue management analytic implementations follow a very defined process (Figure 2.7).

Outputs from each step become inputs to the next, so this order has always seemed logical. Good data leads to accurate demand modeling, which improves forecasting, and we all know accurate forecasting leads to much better pricing recommendations. Most off-the-shelf revenue management systems follow this process, but they enforce that the user adhere to a well-defined and strictly laid out format for data and a specific demand modeling and forecasting method to feed into optimization.

Ivan made two key observations about what happens when you apply this methodology during a custom revenue management and price optimization system development process, where the data and demand modeling steps are more flexible.

1. Optimization provides the biggest "bang for the buck" in a pricing solution. However, because this phase is last, the majority of the value only comes in the last phase of the project. Given the complicated, interconnected nature of these problems, when optimization is last, a good amount of time can go by before the organization is able to get to the point of where it can realize the full value of the implementation.

2. Many analytics departments can get bogged down in the forecasting phase, becoming obsessive about fine-tuning the forecast to the point that they add time and drain resources from the

project—testing multiple methodologies, disagreeing about how to determine what is the metric to assess the "accuracy" of the forecast, determining which set of parameters is optimal, and so on. All of this effort eventually results in diminishing returns on forecast accuracy, and the constant iteration results in the forecast becoming the end itself, rather than a step in the process.

Ivan offered the suggestion that instead of waiting until the end to build the optimization, the projects should start with the optimization and pull from there (Figure 2.8).

Ivan pointed out that optimization is the only part of the pricing cycle that actually provides a recommendation. Every other step may provide insight, but does not give users a specific action that they should take (or not). Any optimization output that is based on some reasonable approximation of business expectations and constraints should provide a pricing recommendation that is better than a manual or "gut-feel" price. Additionally, the optimization output should also provide guidance toward the most impactful way to configure the inputs to improve the recommendations.

(This was the point at which he started to make a startling amount of sense to me, by the way.)

Optimization experts, like Ivan, always advocate that the simplest possible optimization problem that solves the problem at the right level of detail will always be the one that provides the best answers. In fact, this holds true for any statistical or mathematical modeling problem. Ivan suggests that you can start by defining a simple set of outputs, or

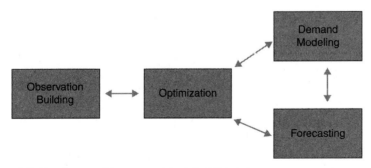

Figure 2.8 New Revenue Management Analytical Process

recommendations, that could add value to the company, and then formulate the optimization problem based on that. These scenarios may be such that demand forecasting isn't even required as an input. For example, many companies that price multiple products have to occasionally rationalize those prices to eliminate conflicts. In freight, customers might not be willing to accept price lists that produce a higher price for transportation legs that are shorter versus the longer legs. The optimization would provide recommendations of how to best rationalize issues like this, without requiring a demand forecast.

For problems that do require a demand forecast input, Ivan says it makes perfect sense to agree on a reasonable estimate of demand, possibly derived from some simple time series or booking curve forecasting methods. You could use broad stroke estimates of other demand modeling outputs like cancellation rates, no shows, price sensitivity by segment, and so on, as the baseline inputs.

The optimization can then become the barometer of what analysis and development the organization should take on next. Remember that one output of the optimization is to identify the binding constraints—which inputs, or constraints, are preventing a "better" answer, and by how much. This information, combined, of course, with the users' knowledge of the problem, can inform the road map for future development, including which inputs should be refined next. Meanwhile, the optimization continues to provide recommendations that drive value for the firm.

Ivan also pointed out that the optimization can also be the arbitrator in forecasting discussions. If a forecasting "improvement" does not make a difference in the optimization output, then there is no point in spending time working on it. "What-if-ing" using the optimization can serve to test the impact of refining any element of the process, saving time and resources to dedicate to those data and analytic projects that actually improve recommendations, or even influence the recommendations at all.

Ivan stressed to me that he feels this methodology is probably going to be most valuable for nontraditional problems—pricing problems that have not yet reached mainstream. For problems that have been solved many times before (hotel rooms and airline seats, for example), there is enough institutional knowledge that following the standard process can be faster and more reliable.

Given the cautions that Ivan outlines, this approach may not be necessary in hotel revenue management, but I thought it would give our more analytical hotel executives something interesting to think about, particularly when they are considering applying revenue management to other revenue-generating assets in the hotel. It is important to also keep in mind that the hotel room revenue management forecast can be used for other applications like labor scheduling or budgeting in addition to driving the revenue management process, so accuracy and detail are important for other applications besides pricing.

NOTES

1. For hotels, length of stay creates a similar issue. Think about a hotel that is popular on weekends. The decision of what demand you accept on a Saturday night has an impact on the surrounding nights. If you sell too many one-night stays on a Saturday night, you block out demand that would have stayed Friday and Saturday or Friday, Saturday, and Sunday. This can have a significant revenue impact for hotels, particularly if the majority of demand for Friday night is for two-night length of stay. You would fill the hotel on Saturday, but leave rooms empty on Friday. It is important to consider the peak night along with the surrounding nights, or shoulder periods, to truly optimize revenue.

2. This section is referring to the BAR (best available rate) or base price by room type. That price is offered to the OTAs or used as the base for packages and promotional rates (i.e., breakfast included).

3. This case study was adapted from D. Koushik, J. Higbie, and C. Eister, "Retail Price Optimization at IHG," *Interfaces*, 41, no. 1 (2012): 45–57.

CHAPTER 3

Big Data, Big Analytics, and Revenue Management*

Big data is what happened when the cost of storing information became less than the cost of making the decision to throw it away.

—George Dyson, The Long Now, *March 19, 2013*

Ecommerce and price transparency haven't just impacted pricing algorithms. The data resulting from the evolution of ecommerce and the social web, along with rapid innovation in data gathering and processing technology, is generating a phenomenon that has become known as *big data*. Given the important role of data and technology in the revenue management function, revenue management has been placed front and center in the big data discussion in hotels.

Gartner says organizations have a big data challenge "when the volume, variety, and velocity of data exceed an organization's storage or compute capacity for accurate and timely decision making" (Laney 2001). While big data has certainly become a big buzzword, the concept is driven by some very real evolutions in technology that have made it possible to access and unlock insights from larger and more complex data sets than ever before. This big data phenomenon is not just caused by the data itself, but more so now that we finally have the technological capacity to capture, analyze, and derive insights from it.

To a certain extent, revenue management, among the most data-intensive applications in hospitality, has always been a big data problem. Revenue management systems require several years of historical demand data to develop detailed forecasts at the rate, length of stay, and arrival day levels across the booking horizon, which can be up to a year.

A typical hotel has the following input data:

- Detailed customer or market type segments (optimal for revenue management analytics): 60

- Room types: 12
- Historical dates (2 years of history): 730
- Future dates (1 year): 365
- Length of stay types: 8
- Snapshots stored for each occupancy date: 40

The combination of all of this input data for just one property amounts to 252 million observations. If you generate and store decisions based on this data, you will need to store 10 to 20 gigabytes per property. For a hotel chain with 2,000 to 4,000 properties, that would equal 20 to 80 terabytes of data. This may be only a fraction of the data generated by a large credit card company or a major online retailer, but if the internal infrastructure is not set up to manage this amount of data, you have a big data challenge.

Compounding data size issues, the complex forecasting and optimization algorithms in the revenue management system require a lot of processing power to execute. However, prices need to be updated at least once a day to account for demand changes. Traditional revenue management systems had to make sacrifices in the amount and detail of the data they used and the type and sophistication of analytics in order to solve the problem in time to provide price recommendations daily. Recent advances in the technological underpinnings of analytical solutions no longer require systems to make these kinds of compromises.

As the technology has evolved to support more detailed data and more advanced and complex analytics, market changes have produced new influences on revenue management pricing decisions, like competitor pricing, forward-looking market demand information or reputation scores. These new data sources add to the volume, variety, and velocity of data that goes into the execution of a pricing decision, as well as the pricing strategy as a whole. Some data may be extremely useful in pricing algorithms, while others may just add noise and overhead to the analysis. On top of this, revenue managers are also challenged by disparate systems, antiquated technology, and a lack of technology infrastructure (even outside and around whatever revenue management solution they might be using).

In this chapter, I provide a high-level description of the innovations in technology that have facilitated the ability for hotels to take advantage of big data. I describe innovations in analytics specifically for revenue management that have been made possible by innovations in technology. I define at a high level the data storage and processing innovations that are enabling a big data approach to revenue management strategy and tactics, and describe the delivery methodologies system providers are using to help hotels take advantage of these opportunities. Finally, I provide a practical framework for identifying and evaluating the right uses for new data sources, big or not so big (after all, no one would want to admit their data is small, right?).

It is important to keep in mind that the characteristics of the business problem you are trying to solve impact the kind of data and technology you will utilize. For example, revenue management systems are operational in nature, providing daily (or even within day) recommendations. The data and technology they must leverage need to be suited for this condition. In contrast, the ad hoc analyses that you may conduct to support a revenue management strategy may require access to a broader range of data and different types of analytics, requiring a different infrastructure. This chapter helps you understand these distinctions, without requiring you to become a database architect.

WHAT IS BIG DATA?

The Gartner definition of big data in the chapter introduction is worth exploring a bit more here. Two key components of the definition are particularly relevant for hospitality. First consider the "three Vs": volume, variety, and velocity. The important point here is that it isn't just the amount of data that challenges organizations. The social world is creating a variety of new data sources, many in nontraditional formats like text, video, audio, location data, or click stream from websites. Organizations are not used to storing or analyzing this unstructured data. Experts, including analysts like Gartner and IDC, estimate that 70 to 90 percent of data generated today is unstructured. This puts tremendous pressure on a traditional IT infrastructure that was not set up to handle this kind of data. Data is coming at us fast, too. A tweet is stale almost at the moment it is created, and if you can't identify a guest's location fast enough to act on it, there's not much point in tracking it.

This brings me to the second important point in the definition: "exceeds an organization's storage or compute capacity for accurate and timely decision making." If the data is such that you can't derive value from it at the speed of business, you have big data. Most legacy technology infrastructures have been set up to manage structured, transactional data (and not very much of it). It is difficult to "fit" some of these new unstructured data sources into these legacy environments. Additionally, these environments were optimized for quickly and efficiently extracting, transforming, and loading transactional data, not for performing complex analytics across a massive data set.

Recent technology innovations have made it possible to capture, comprehend, and act on all this big data. These technology innovations are evolving quickly, and there is plenty of very detailed information available through a variety of sources, some of which I've listed at the end of this chapter. I am certainly not suggesting that revenue managers need to become information technology strategists or big data experts, but I suspect you will hear more and more about big data technology solutions in the years to come. It is important that you have a high-level understanding of what is happening in this space, so you can participate in discussions with your counterparts and help to identify opportunities to leverage this within your organization.

Revenue management is directly impacted by these technology innovations, but they, of course, have benefits to the entire organization as well. It is important to think about big data and big analytics both in the context of individual functions, like revenue management, and also broadly at the hotel level. In this chapter, I use examples that apply directly to revenue management, but also to the hotel business in general. First, I address the technology innovations that facilitate storing unstructured data (the "variety" and "velocity" big data problem), then I talk about the technology innovations that allow for processing the "volume" of data.

Storing Unstructured Data

As the variety and velocity of data increase (adding to volume), data storage needs to be cheaper (because you need a lot of it), more flexible (to handle nontraditional data formats), faster (at the speed of data creation), and scalable (because you will continue to collect more and more data). Technology innovation happening today is addressing these four key needs. To put the issue of big data databases in context, let's first look at why some of these unstructured data sources caused technology problems by contrasting them with more traditional structured data.

Structured data is any data that has relationships such that it can be sorted into rows and columns. Think about sales data, which can be associated with a store, a date, or an item. Or think about customer profile information, which can be associated with a customer or customer ID (see Figure 3.1).

Contrast this with *unstructured data*, which does not have any predefined relationships within or among similar data (Figure 3.2). This could be reviews, emails, call logs, surveillance clips, or web data. Imposing structure on this data requires some effort, and depends greatly on what you plan to do with it. For example, reviews could be used to identify important conversation topics, understand consumer sentiment, profile guests for targeted marketing, or identify value drivers. Depending on who wants to access the data and what they will do with it, the imposed structure could be very different. Unstructured data can get large very fast (think about the size of a daily security video file compared to the size of an outlet's daily sales files).

The challenge with these two different data types is the storage and access methodologies required to take full advantage of the insights contained in the data. Structured data is typically stored in a *relational database*, which sorts the data points according to their relationships with other data points in the database. Relational databases are set up with a predefined data schema that the data is then sorted into as it is loaded into the database. New data is added according to its relationship to the data already contained in the data set. Most of today's technology infrastructures are set up to handle this kind of data, which is then generally made available through static reports.

125	94	62	32	116	41	-25	0	0	0	0	12,012.00	12,012.00
125	81	27	54	118	10	-58	0	0	0	0	3,094.00	3,094.00
125	54	27	27	87	20	-20	0	0	0	0	2,995.40	2,995.40
125	71	31	40	87	16	-7	0	0	0	0	5,444.40	5,444.40
125	101	28	73	87	10	-13	0	0	0	0	7,981.00	7,981.00
125	84	20	64	72	22	-21	0	0	0	0	6,287.00	6,287.00
125	111	26	85	93	39	-20	0	0	0	0	9,508.75	9,508.75
125	96	30	66	87	30	-8	0	0	0	0	8,255.35	8,255.35
125	40	14	26	81	6	-62	0	0	0	0	3,192.00	3,192.00
125	46	17	29	42	18	-18	0	0	0	0	2,900.00	2,900.00
125	51	18	33	42	24	-7	0	0	0	0	4,372.50	4,372.50
125	61	36	25	42	25	-15	0	0	0	0	5,228.50	5,228.50
125	25	10	15	42	4	-40	0	0	0	0	1,687.00	1,687.50
125	68	40	28	42	32	-8	0	0	0	0	6,272.50	6,272.50
125	92	48	44	42	11	-11	0	0	0	0	8,022.50	8,022.50
125	52	29	23	42	19	-50	0	0	0	0	3,279.00	3,279.00
125	60	29	31	42	15	-15	0	0	0	0	3,478.00	3,478.00
125	62	36	26	42	16	-12	0	0	0	0	4,125.00	4,125.00
125	39	23	16	42	3	-16	0	0	0	0	2,474.00	2,474.00
125	36	20	16	42	10	-13	0	0	0	0	2,541.00	2,541.00
125	65	32	33	42	30	-5	0	0	0	0	5,146.00	5,146.00
125	80	35	45	42	23	-17	0	0	0	0	8,496.40	8,496.40

Figure 3.1 Structured Data

Figure 3.2 Text Reviews—How Do You Structure These?

I like to think about relational databases as a silverware drawer you may have in your kitchen. The silverware drawer sorts your place settings: forks, knives, and spoons, in separate, but related, slots. A row across the drawer makes a place setting. Before you put the silverware in the drawer, you probably had to buy an insert. This insert is the predefined schema for the drawer. Now, every time you empty the dishwasher, you sort forks, knives, and spoons into the appropriate slots. If you buy new place settings, you add them to the predefined slots.

But what happens if you decide you need iced tea spoons or a new set of serving utensils? If you didn't plan for these utensils ahead of time, they won't fit neatly into your silverware schema. What if you got rid of that predefined schema (insert), and just put all the silverware together in one drawer? When you needed to add new utensils, any utensils, you would not need to know ahead of time what their relationship was to the rest of the silverware in the drawer, you could just place them in there. Further, if the drawer filled up, you could start using another drawer, or put the silverware in a shoebox or plastic storage bin. It is easy to add more storage space without needing to buy any specialized equipment (more inserts).

New databases are moving toward this more flexible structure, which does not require a predefined schema. This is why some have been talking about Hadoop as an emerging platform for storing and accessing big data. Hadoop is a database that is designed to handle large volumes of unstructured data, by deploying a methodology similar to my no-insert drawer above. Hadoop works because it is cheap and scalable, flexible, and fast.

- **Cheap and scalable.** Hadoop is built on commodity hardware, which is exactly what it sounds like—really cheap, "generic" hardware. It is designed as a "cluster," tying together groups of inexpensive servers. This means it's relatively inexpensive to get started, and easy to add more storage space as your data inevitably expands. It also has built-in redundancy—data stored in multiple places, so if any of the servers happen to go down, you don't lose all the data (there are forks in every drawer, so you always have access to forks, even if one drawer jams).

- **Flexible.** The Hadoop data storage platform does not require a predefined data structure, or data schema (like the silverware drawer insert). You can just "throw the data in there" and figure out the relationships later.

- **Fast.** Hadoop is fast in two ways. First, it uses massive parallel processing to comb through the databases to extract the information. Data is stored in a series of smaller containers, and there are many "helpers" available to reach in and pull out what you are looking for (extending the drawer metaphor: picture four drawers of silverware with a family member retrieving one place setting from each at the same time). The work is split up, as opposed to being done in sequence. The second way that Hadoop is fast is that because the database is not constrained by a predefined schema, the process of loading the data into the database is much faster (picture the time it takes to sort the silverware from the dishwasher rack into the insert, as opposed to dumping the rack contents straight into the drawer).

Many companies have put a lot of effort into organizing structured data over the years, and there are some data sets that make sense to be stored according to traditional methods (like the silverware you use every day, which has a specific, defined, and routine purpose). Databases are not only optimized for efficient extraction, transformation, and loading, but they also make it really easy to render and build standard reports, because the schema has been optimized specifically for this purpose. Because of this, most companies see Hadoop as an addition to their existing technology infrastructure rather than a replacement for their relational, structured, database. At the risk of overextending the metaphor, you have silverware drawers with inserts in your kitchen, as well as free-form drawers for serving utensils and kitchen gadgets.

Because of the flexibility of the data stored in Hadoop, it is not best suited for operational analyses or production models. It is really designed to facilitate reporting, exploratory analysis, or model development. For this reason, Hadoop will likely not be the basis for a revenue management system, but rather, will support revenue management's ad hoc analyses for innovation and strategy development.

Keep in mind that revenue management systems are operational systems. They connect directly to selling systems with two-way interfaces. As I described earlier, many of the big data databases are not designed to support operational systems like revenue management. They are great at being repositories for large volumes of information that will be analyzed on an ad hoc or experimental basis. They are not as good at any real-time, or near real-time, applications as relational databases are. It is likely that the data for your day-to-day operational revenue management system will not be stored in one of these unstructured database formats.

Further, the interconnected analytic processes in revenue management systems do require a predefined data structure, so even if the system is incorporating some data that originated as unstructured (i.e., reputation data), it will need to be "structured" before it is incorporated into the revenue management system. Again, it may be faster and more efficient to store this information in a relational database than to pull it out of a Hadoop environment.

Revenue management systems suffer more from the "volume" data problem. In order to provide the most accurate recommendations, detailed transactional information is required, which can add up quickly and bog down analytical processes. In the following section, I describe the technology innovations that allow analytical systems to process more data faster.

Innovations in Executing Analytics

Big data is of no use unless you can turn it into information and insight. For that you need big analytics. Every piece of the analytics cycle from reporting to advanced analytics has been impacted by big data. In reporting, billions of rows of data need to be quickly rendered into a report form, and users want the flexibility to slice and dice and drill down into the data according to their specific needs. Advanced analytics like forecasting and optimization require complex math executed by multiple passes through massive data sets.

Without changes to the technology infrastructure, analytic processes on big data sets will start to take longer and longer to execute—even if you can capture and store that big data. Businesses today can't be run by pushing a button and then waiting hours or days for an answer. Today's advanced analytics need to be fast and they need to be accessible. This means more changes to the technology infrastructure.

Analytics companies like SAS have been developing new methods for executing analytics on large data sets more quickly. Below is a high-level description of some of these new methodologies, including why they provide an advantage. Once again, the intention is to provide enough detail to start conversations with IT counterparts (or understand what they are talking about), certainly not to become an expert. There is a ton of information out there if you want more detail. See the end of the chapter for some references.

1. **Grid computing and parallel processing.** Calculations are split across multiple CPUs (central processing units) to solve a bunch of smaller problems in parallel, as opposed to one big problem in sequence. Think about the difference between adding a series of eight numbers in a row versus splitting the problem into four sets of two, and handing them out to four of your friends. To accomplish this, multiple CPUs are tied together, so the algorithms can access the resources of the entire bank of CPUs.

2. **In-database processing.** Most analytic programs lift data sets out of the database, execute the "math," and then dump the data sets back in the database. The larger the data sets, the more time-consuming it is to move them around. In-database analytics bring the math to the data. The analytics run in the database with the data, reducing the amount of time-consuming data movement.

3. **In-memory processing.** This capability is a bit harder to understand for nontechnical people, but it provides a crucial advantage for both reporting and analytics. Large sets of data are typically stored on the hard drive of a computer, which is the physical disc inside the computer (or server). It takes time to read the data off the physical disc space, and every pass through the data adds additional time. It is much faster to conduct analysis and build reports from the computer's memory

instead of the physical disc. Memory is becoming cheaper every day, so it is now possible to add enough memory to hold big data sets for significantly faster reporting and analytics.

To give you an idea of the scale of the impact, here at SAS we have applied these methodologies to render a summary report (with drill-down capability) from a billion rows of data in seconds (in-memory). Large-scale optimizations, like risk calculations for major banks or price optimization for thousands of retail products across hundreds of stores, have gone from hours or days to minutes and seconds to calculate (grid computing and parallel processing). As you can tell, the advantages are tremendous. Organizations can now run analytics on their entire data set, rather than a sample. It is possible to run more analyses more frequently, testing scenarios and refining results.

Innovations in Solution Delivery

Solution providers are innovating in the way that technology is delivered as well, and this has an impact on revenue management solution decisions. While we are talking about technology innovations, it is worth defining available solution delivery options in order to understand the advantages and disadvantages of each.

Hoteliers are likely hearing a lot about solutions delivered via *the cloud* versus requiring the technology to be managed on-site or *on premise*. Cloud-based solutions are accessed via the Internet, and the applications are *hosted* at a remote site. On-premise solutions require the company to invest in the hardware and IT resources to manage the solution. At a high level, there are two different types of cloud solutions:

1. **Software-as-a-Service (SaaS).** These cloud-based solutions are complete end-to-end software packages that are standardized for the entire user base. While they can be configured, generally, the software is the same for all companies that access it. The application sits on a layer above the individual users' databases. Security is maintained between the users' databases, but all databases access the same application layer.

2. **Hosted.** A hosted, or managed, solution is a proprietary solution for each client that is effectively the same as the client having an on-premise solution, except it is located at a remote data center and managed by the vendor. This enables a more proprietary, client-by-client application delivery, but without the client's organization having to own the technology infrastructure or invest in resources to maintain it.

Four advantages of a cloud solution over an on-premise solution are:

1. **Reduced burden on IT.** The vendor assumes all responsibility for maintaining the environment, including regular maintenance, upgrades, data transfers, or managing memory and storage capacity.

2. **Guaranteed service levels.** Cloud providers guarantee a minimum up-time for the solution, and build in the mechanisms required to achieve this. You have the security of knowing the system will be available when you need it.

3. **Implementation speed.** Particularly for SaaS applications, the time to implementation is dramatically reduced for cloud solutions.

4. **Security.** Most cloud providers have extensive data encryption and cybersecurity measures in place. In fact, some financial services companies use hosted solutions to manage credit card fraud activity, and are able to meet all their internal and regulatory security measures to ensure that credit card numbers are not stolen and that the privacy of the credit card owner is respected.

Three advantages of an on-premise solution over a cloud solution are:

1. **Control.** An on-premise solution is 100 percent in the control of the company that installs it. The data flow in and out is controlled by the company, as is the system configuration. Many companies see their data as a strategic asset, and do not want it to be managed by a third party.

2. **Regulatory issues.** Some industries' data is highly regulated (casinos, for example), and these regulations prohibit some data from ever leaving the facility where it is created. While

the data centers for cloud solutions may have every protection mechanism in place, these companies are simply not allowed to leverage them. This is particularly an issue for customer data.

3. **Cost.** While the up-front cost of many on-premise solutions may be higher, the long-term costs can be significantly less. For hosted solutions, you pay all of the up-front hardware and software costs plus an ongoing maintenance fee for the solution. SaaS solutions are frequently subscription-based, which means a regular fee while the software is being used. Over the life of the solution, these can be significantly more than up-front software costs for an on-premise solution.

Here are some of the differences between pure SaaS and a hosted solution:

- The time-to-value of SaaS solutions, or any out-of-the-box solution, can be significantly shorter than any proprietary option, even including custom-built hosted solutions. The implementation process is standardized, so the solution can be up and running much faster. There generally are standardized training materials available, as well as extensive support mechanisms for users at every stage of the lifecycle.

- SaaS solutions are multitenant, meaning that all users share a common application layer (although each company's data is kept separate). This means that upgrades happen simultaneously and automatically for all users. They are included in the monthly subscription fee, so do not require additional service fees. This means you are always using the latest version of the software package.

- SaaS applications are standardized to an industry or an application, so they do not offer room to customize to meet specific customer requirements. Some companies have unique requirements that would make a proprietary solution highly valuable (for example, a unique operating constraint like the capacity of a kids' club or a minimum occupancy requirement driven by other on-site services). Depending on how complex or specific they are, unique requirements can be difficult to accommodate in a SaaS application, and if they are incorporated, they become generally available to any user of the application. A proprietary hosted (or on-premise) solution incorporates any unique business processes or operating constraints and maintains them as a competitive advantage for the company.

■ SaaS applications include specific user interfaces and workflows. There is some flexibility, but in general, users must be trained on and conform to the methodology as laid out by the application. When a company decides to move to one of these applications, the change management can be extensive, and the opportunity for company-specific business processes is either reduced or must be developed within the context of the application. For a company brand new to revenue management and revenue management systems, this can be an advantage, as business processes are baked into the solution implementation, so there is no need to invent new ones. For a more mature company that desires to upgrade, this can be burdensome and restrictive.

WHERE BIG DATA MEETS BIG ANALYTICS FOR REVENUE MANAGEMENT

So, what does all this mean for revenue management? You might be thinking, "But I have been using an automated revenue management system for years, and it is working fine, or, you know, working okay anyway. Why do I need to start worrying about data and technology now?" The game has changed for hotels over the past few years, and technology is becoming more accessible. Now is the time to take advantage of advances in data availability and technology innovations to drive revenue and profits. There are more, and more varied, influences on pricing today than when analytic pricing using revenue management technology first became available. As I described in the preface, we are now in a world of price transparency, reviews and ratings, shortening booking windows, and the proliferation of third-party distribution channels. In Chapter 2, I described the implication specifically on price optimization, but the effects are also broadly felt. All of this activity means that more data, different data, and a new mathematical approach are required to drive revenue, profits, and share.

Revenue management systems that were originally built years ago had to make sacrifices because of the limitations of the technology platforms. Data storage was expensive, and systems got bogged down executing analytics and reporting as data volumes increased. Data limitations like duration of storage, reporting access, or level of detail were imposed to ensure that performance was not negatively impacted.

> Without question, the biggest challenge faced by today's revenue manager is a lack of access to the appropriate technology. The result has left most revenue professionals filling their time troubleshooting technology errors, rebuilding the wheel in Excel and reacting to market trends far too slowly.
>
> —*Calvin Anderson, Director of Revenue, New York Hilton Midtown*

System providers also had to balance the time it took to run complex analytics against the need to update prices as conditions changed. Forecasting and optimization calculations have to be completed, at minimum, overnight to keep up with changing market conditions. Processing limitations meant revenue management systems had to take analytic shortcuts to meet this time frame—for example, relying on only one forecasting method and employing heuristics (i.e., rules-based optimization) instead of true mathematical optimization.

At the time, these systems represented the latest thinking in revenue management and generated a great deal of benefit for the companies that implemented them; most are still generating some benefit today. The advances in data management and processing power I described earlier mean systems can store and analyze more data and more detailed data faster. Reports can be more flexible, configurable, and contain more data. System providers have leveraged the processing gains to innovate in forecasting and optimization science, like the price optimization algorithms I described in the previous chapter. It is now possible for the system to test multiple forecasting methods to find the most accurate method for each forecast and run true optimization algorithms, resulting in more accurate pricing recommendations that reflect current market conditions.

With increases in processing speed, revenue management systems can not only employ more accurate forecasting and optimization algorithms, but they can also perform more complex calculations, like calculating price sensitivity of demand at a market segment or room type level. Systems can also account for more data sources, like the influence of competitive rates or reputation scores on demand patterns or price sensitivity. As I described in the previous chapter, these new algorithms and new influencers will provide huge competitive advantages in pricing for companies that can take advantage of them properly.

The bottom line is that companies that are already good at revenue management can become even better by modernizing systems and processes to account for these changing market conditions. As of the publication of this book, most of the major hotel companies globally have made investments in modernizing their revenue management systems to meet the challenges of the changing marketplace.

DATA VISUALIZATION AND BIG DATA

The same advances in technology that facilitated storage and access to big data and the execution of big analytics are changing what is possible in terms of data visualization. This is particularly important to revenue management. The development and execution of pricing strategies relies on the ability to visualize disparate data sources together in a unified whole. This has traditionally been managed in manual, Excel-based environments, which is clumsy, error prone, and time consuming. In addition, revenue managers are constantly being called on to present past performance and future projections to decision makers across the hotel enterprise, increasingly to executives, asset managers, or owners, who are not familiar with revenue management data or decisions. The ability to easily access information, use that to build simple and compelling visualizations, and tell the right story that inspires action will continue to be a critical component of a revenue manager's role.

There are many strategic and tactical components that go into a price. We congratulate ourselves when we get the price right and when we deploy the price correctly. However, sometimes I worry whether our strategy and decision making in making this happen is either accidental or reactive. Like most hotels, we have many data variables in our decision making of the price. It is difficult to pull all this data together, and statistically interpret which factors contribute to success. We want to become more forward looking, and make this process more intentional and proactive by using tools that can help us visualize the data quickly and streamline the data access and analysis.

—*Malcolm Leong, Head, Revenue Management and Distribution, Far East Hospitality Management*

They say a picture is worth a thousand words. For data-obsessed revenue managers, it is easy to forget this simple statement. Revenue managers love a good data set, and are extremely comfortable determining relationships and deriving insight from rows and columns of performance data. For most intelligent but "a-numeric" people, it's difficult to see the forest for the trees in a complex chart full of numbers. If you really want to inspire others to take your recommended action, you need to tell a highly visual, simple, and compelling story with that data.

Figure 3.3 is one of my favorite examples of a compelling visualization. It tells exactly the story, no more and no less, that the viewer needs to interpret what the chart represents.

Building a visualization from complex and varied data sources today is nearly as simple as the "pie chart." As data volume, velocity, and variety has increased, the tools to visualize that data have evolved as well. Reporting tools have become faster, more flexible, and more accessible to a wide variety of users. Tools like Tableau, MicroStrategy, and SAS® Visual Analytics provide users the flexibility of self-service reporting, putting the power into the hands of the end user and removing reliance on IT to create reports. Big data reporting tools can render

Figure 3.3 Simple, But Compelling, Visualization
Source: Mike Hlas, "The Most Accurate Pie Chart You'll Ever See," Gazette, March 31, 2014, http://thegazette.com/2011/05/25/the-most-accurate-pie-chart-youll-ever-see.

reports from billions of rows of data in seconds, and users no longer have to predetermine what type of chart or graph they want to create. The reporting tools will render the report in the format that makes sense for the data, and let the users tweak it as they'd like. Some visualization tools no longer require building complicated OLAP cubes or imposing any kind of restrictive data structure. This provides a good deal more flexibility for end users to create their own ad hoc views, with drill-down capabilities on the fly.

Furthermore, visualizations are now available on a variety of devices, so the information can be where the viewers are, instead of the viewers having to wait until they are in front of a computer. It's becoming easier for anyone to build mobile apps, deploy information via email, or create a visualization on the fly during a meeting. This easy access to information is helping organizations make decisions proactively, rather than waiting for the report to show up on their desk hours or even days after the information is created.

> One of the analysts on my team happens to be really good at creating reports in our visualization tool. The tool makes it really fast and efficient, has a mobile integration, and most importantly, doesn't require us to call IT any time we need something new. One morning, just before lunch, she and I were discussing the challenges we had with this daily email report that

was automatically sent to everyone in the organization right up to the CEO. The report at times came in blank or with data problems. Before we could follow up and correct it, our CEO would always notice, and we would end up in a fire drill to get the right information. We decided it made more sense to turn this daily report into an app, so the C-level would always have the "latest" info and not have to follow up on a blank or incorrect email. I asked my analyst to build the app, and by the time I was back from my lunch meeting, the app was done. If I had to go to IT to build the app, it would have taken three months!

—*Executive from a global hotel company discussing the advantages of self-service reporting*

These technological advances are of great benefit to revenue management, because now revenue managers no longer have to be dependent on IT or the revenue management vendor to create the reports and visualizations they rely on to get the job done, whether it's a routine analysis or a new report. Every revenue management vendor and every technology vendor will tell you (if you can get them to admit it) that reports are the most requested enhancement, and that they can never create enough reports in the right formats to satisfy the user base. Every company wants to see its data in a slightly different way, and every company wants to see more than just the data that is in the revenue management system. Now, with these flexible reporting tools, users can create their own visualizations exactly how they want them, easily and automatically accessing data from multiple sources across the organization.

The self-service capabilities as I have described them are a benefit, but one that comes with responsibility. I have provided a practical application section in the appendix to help you create powerful visualizations and the story around them that will compel your organization to action. As this book illustrates, as the job of the revenue manager becomes broader and more complex, it will be even more crucial to be able to reduce that complexity to a clear and actionable story. Please refer to that section for some important practical tips for leveraging visualizations to tell a story with your data.

RESPONSIBLE USE OF BIG DATA

So, now that I've gotten you excited about big data opportunities, you are probably ready to run out and grab every piece of data you can get your hands on. That is certainly the message coming from third-party data resellers, big data vendors, and technology experts. It sounds so easy, it's tempting to think that you can just shove all of that new data into a database and you're good to go.

> Before we can get big data, we need small data, and before small data, we need clean data.
>
> —*Tarnadeep Singh, Director, Revenue Analytics, Asia, Middle East, and Africa, IHG*

Regardless of how inexpensive storage space is getting and how fast processing is becoming, capturing, storing, and analyzing data still takes resources, both in technology and human capital. Administrative overhead is required to ensure that the data is updated regularly and integrated properly into the data infrastructure. If the data will be used in the analytics, it will need to be stored differently than if it is used for reporting or ad hoc analysis. You may have to pay for some data sources, so they need to have a return associated with them. Some data sources may not be captured in a format that fits well with your data infrastructure—it might be summarized too much or collected with a different frequency.

"In revenue management, the first thought when approaching a new data source is often 'How can I get this data in the system?' Really, our first thought should be 'What different decisions can I enable with this data?' We should be more creative and thoughtful about how we approach new data sources. We make many types of decisions, and such data may well have significant value outside tactical day-to-day pricing decisions, where the data may or may not add value," says Alex Dietz, Advisory Industry Consultant, SAS Revenue Management and Price Optimization Practice.

Perhaps more important, sometimes adding more data to an analysis simply does not result in a better answer. In this case, I am talking about additional data sources, as opposed to more of the same kind of data. More of the same kind of data can add confidence and statistical rigor to an analysis.

Additional data might not result in a better answer if:

- The data does not have a significant causal relationship with demand patterns or price sensitivity (it simply does not influence these factors, so it won't make a difference in the answer).

- The data does not change significantly over time, so adding it to an algorithm would not change the day-to-day forecast or price recommendations enough to result in a different answer. Think about weather data, for example. Weather data might do a good job of explaining what happened to demand in the past (identifying a storm in the past as a special event so the forecast would treat those dates differently in the future), but how do you incorporate weather into a forecast for future dates? If it's March now, and I'm setting prices for November, I only have the "average" forecast for that time period (temperature). Is this really useful?

- The data is extremely volatile or "dirty," so it is too unreliable for the algorithms. In other words, it would just add to the uncertainty of the forecast or the pricing recommendation. Regrets and denial data fall into this category for revenue management. Theoretically this information could help in demand unconstraining, but this type of data is very unstable. Collected by a call center agent, it is subject to user error. Collected via a website, it is subject to noise from shopping, inability to identify unique visitors, or inability to identify exactly what the user was focused on in a page with multiple products. Not collected across all demand sources would bias the response toward one channel's characteristics, when others may have very different demand patterns.

These are all important considerations when it comes to what data belongs in a revenue management algorithm versus what data a revenue manager would use for strategic analysis outside of the revenue management system. Regrets and denials, for example, could help in a marketing analysis or website performance analysis, even if they add too much noise to an unconstraining algorithm.

There are myriads of detailed technical and analytical methodologies for assessing and transforming data to make it useful for reporting and analysis, which I won't go into here. I provide some business-oriented suggestions for how to think about a new data source, and discuss potential problems that could arise from throwing too much data at a problem. Regardless of whether you are collecting this data for yourself or evaluating a revenue management vendor's data requirements, you should think through the benefits and drawbacks, as I describe next.

Identifying the Data Source

I always advocate starting with the business problem you are trying to solve (increase forecast accuracy, understand price sensitivity, track market activity, etc.), and then determining what data is necessary to solve that problem. In reality, you are likely to be offered or come across data sources that seem like they might be useful, but it's not clear how. Having the goals of your function or organization in mind will help you understand how to place that data. Will it meet a tactical (day-to-day pricing) need or fit into a more strategic analysis (market position, future opportunity)? Are there ongoing projects that might benefit from this new data? You could match the data source to the revenue management cycle I presented in Chapter 1 and have reproduced here (Figure 3.4), or a similar process map to determine where the data might fit.

For example, one recently available data source is forward-looking demand data from Travel Click (www.travelclick.com/en/product-services/business-intelligence-solutions/demand360). This data source provides future demand for a hotel and its competitive set across channels and segments. Once revenue management determines some basic information about the data set, like how often it is updated, what level of detail is provided, and what fields are included, revenue management could look at the cycle described in Figure 3.4. There is

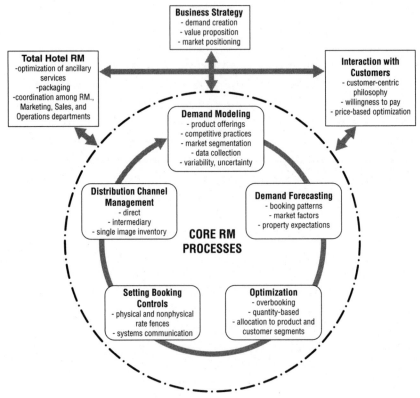

Figure 3.4 Revenue Management Framework
Taken from Noone, McGuire, and Rolhfs 2011.

the possibility that the forward-looking demand data could improve forecast accuracy by providing a directional input about market performance. However, the level of detail and included fields needs to match with the forecasting and optimization algorithms, and the data needs to add some explanatory power that is not already picked up by the booking pace or demand patterns.

Moving to the outside of the circle, the forward-looking demand data can help revenue management assess their competitive value in the market. The hotel's pace by segment over time as compared to the competitive set will provide some intelligence about how the hotel books relative to the competition, and can help reinforce who the primary competitors are and which market segments are most attracted to the hotel's offering. As the team tests out distribution strategies, they can validate the success against the benchmark for the market. All of this activity can be done proactively, so that adjustments can be made in advance of the stay date, instead of reactively, after the stay is done.

Revenue management can find a lot of potential uses for the data set, but the final step in the analysis is to think through whether other departments might make use of the data. For example, marketing could evaluate the success of targeted promotions to certain segments, time periods, or channels by benchmarking against the competitive set. Again, this can be done proactively, so adjustments can be made in advance of the stay date. Sales might have a similar use for the data, ensuring they are getting their fair share of group or other high-valued business.

Evaluating the Data

The first important step in evaluating a potential new data source is to determine what business value you will gain from accessing that data. You should clearly and specifically define not just the insight you expect to be able to gain from that data source, but also who will benefit from that insight and what actions will be taken as a result. Knowing the "fit" at the level of business value will help you justify the investment in acquisition.

I spoke with a head of analytics for a major hotel company who said he constantly pushes this philosophy with his team, whether they come to him with a new data source or a new analysis result. He says, "I always ask them 'so what,' what would I do differently now that I know this? If I find out that my gender split for one brand is 55 percent women whereas another is only 45 percent, what does that change? What could I realistically do with that information, and so, do I really care?" Thinking of the "so what" is a crucial first step to ensure that your analysis stays focused and you aren't wasting time on data with no real value.

Once you understand the potential business value, you need to be sure the data can actually deliver. The second step is to understand the characteristics of the data source. Ask the following five questions:

1. What is this data? Where does it come from, how is it collected, and what does it look like? You should start by understanding who is collecting the data, how it will be collected, and what the data looks like. Does it come from a reliable source that will provide the data at regular intervals? How does it get transmitted to you? How big is it? What fields are included? Are there many missing values? How are the fields calculated? Is it closely related to any data you are already collecting? Understanding where the data comes from will give you a sense of how reliable it is. If it is heavily driven by user entry, then you need to assess the business process around the data collection. User-entered data is notoriously unreliable unless it has a tight business process for collection around it. The more familiar you become with the data itself, the better you will be able to answer the rest of these questions.

2. How will the data fit within your database structure? Next evaluate how the data will fit within your existing structure. Will you need to integrate it with other data? If so, you need to ensure that the data is at similar levels of detail, and has common fields to match. Will you need to link it to other data tables somehow? Will it need special permissions to access? For example, a property level manager should only be able to see his property's data, but the regional rep must see multiple levels of data. Do you need to do any summary or drill down on the fields?

3. How often is the data updated and how? Your systems will need to be set up to receive and store the data in a timely fashion. If the data comes too fast, and the extraction, transformation, and loading (ETL) process takes too long, it might be useless by the time you are able to access it. For example, tweets or geolocation data are stale almost as they are created, so if you aren't able to process them in time to use them, it's not worth

the trouble. Further, if the data delivery process is unreliable (as in, it frequently doesn't show up, or shows up with missing values, etc.), and you are counting on it for a critical piece of insight, you may want to look elsewhere.

4. What tools/algorithms will you need to analyze the data? Report on the data? Determine whether you will need to bring on any specialized technology to analyze the data at the level that you can unlock the insights. For example, unstructured text data requires different analysis tools than forward-looking demand data. Reporting on the data may require a different type of technology, which depends also on who needs to have access and at what level of detail. If the data source will require new technology investment, you need to be able to justify the investment with the value that you will unlock from the data.

5. Who will want access and what will they need to do with the data? This is a crucial final question once you understand the data structure. If, after careful evaluation, no one will want access to the data (or analytical results), it is not worth spending the time and resources to collect, store, and manage that data. On the other hand, if multiple groups want access, and would take different actions on that data, all of the stakeholders' needs must be considered so that you do not make any decisions in the collection, storage, or access process that restricts usage.

These questions are very high level, and can quickly become very complex. You should have a partner in your IT organization who can take this to a more technical level. If you have already gotten started by assessing the questions I listed here, however, you will save everyone time and energy—and probably make some new friends in IT while you are at it!

If you are collecting this data yourself, I would suggest forming a cross-functional team within the organization that can help you to assess data needs and brainstorm opportunities in this area. You will likely find that other departments could benefit from access to a new data source, but they might require expanded information or additional parameters. Knowing this up-front helps save work later. This group could also help provide data governance—establishing a set of agreed-upon rules for defining, accessing, and storing all the data across the organization.

If your revenue management system provider is collecting this data on your behalf, challenge it in the same way you would challenge yourself internally. Make sure you understand all of the data inputs and their influence on the outputs. After all, you need to be able to trust the pricing recommendations and explain where they come from!

The Problem with Big Data in Analytics

If you are just interested in using a new data source for reporting, or for descriptive statistics, the previously outlined steps will keep you out of trouble. Incorporating more data into a predictive model or forecasting analysis is trickier. I am going to introduce some statistical concepts that you should be aware of as you plan to add data to an advanced analytic application, or evaluate a vendor that is talking about new or additional data sources.

The principle known as *Occam's razor* comes into play in analytical applications. It is a principle of mathematics developed in the fourteenth century, which basically states that "simpler explanations are, other things being equal, generally better than more complex ones." Occam's razor cautions us that simply throwing more data at a statistical problem might not necessarily generate a better answer. Many statisticians follow this guidance, believing that you should always select the simplest hypothesis, or simplest formulation of the problem, until simplicity can be traded for predictive power.

In fact, practical statistical analysis generally supports this theory. Note that when I talk about "more data" in the next few paragraphs, I am talking about more "predictor variables"(columns), not more observations (rows) within the same data set. Generally speaking, more observations will help to increase the reliability of results, because they will help to detect patterns in the data with greater confidence.

Two different statistical phenomena can occur in predictive analysis with the addition of predictor variables to a model: multicollinearity

(Ott and Longnecker 2001) and overfitting (Burnham and Anderson 2002). In both cases, the addition of variables decreases the reliability or predictability of the model (I'm only going to define them at a very high level here, so that you can verify with your analysts whether there's a concern).

1. **Multicollinearity** happens in a multiple regression analysis when two or more predictor variables are highly correlated, and thus do not provide any unique or independent information to the model. Examples of things that tend to be highly correlated could be height and weight, years of education and income, or time spent at work and time spent with family. The real danger in multicollinearity is that it makes the estimates of the individual predictor variables less reliable. So, if all you care about is the model as a whole, it's not that big of a deal. However, if you care about things like what variable has the biggest impact on overall guest value, or on likelihood to respond, then you do have to watch out for multicollinearity.

2. **Overfitting** happens when there are too many parameters relative to the number of observations. When this happens, the model ends up describing random error, not the real underlying relationships. Every data sample has some noise, so if you try to drive out too much error, you become very good at modeling the past, but bad at predicting the future. This is the biggest danger of overfitting a model. This is particularly problematic in machine learning algorithms, any models that learn over time, like revenue management forecasting.

Talluri and van Rysin (2005), well-known revenue management researchers, say, "It is natural to suppose that a model that fits historical data well. . . [and] has low estimation errors, will also generalize well and give low forecast errors. This, however, is NOT the case." In the forecasting world, this is known as the *bias-variance trade-off*. For revenue management forecasts, there are two kinds of errors that can be reduced. Variance error can be improved by adding more data that fits the model. The second kind—bias—is adversely affected by more data. So there is a trade-off between minimizing variance and minimizing bias. Adding more data to historical data may reduce the variance, but it creates the "overfitting" problem as described earlier, which increases the bias.

Again, it is most important to know that these problems exist and to use this information to determine whether a vendor you might be evaluating knows and has dealt with them, than it is for you to really understand the statistical underpinnings and the methods for accounting for them. There is plenty of very technical information in statistics and forecasting research if you want more details. The one thing I want you to take from this discussion is that more is not necessarily better. Make sure that your vendors or analysts have shown that adding more predictor variables to the forecast (or any analysis) has actually improved accuracy or predictive power before you accept that it is a good idea to burden the system by including it.

CONCLUSION

The technology advancements that provide for the capture, analysis, and storage of larger and increasingly complex sources of data will provide a huge opportunity for hospitality in the coming years. Now is the time to ensure that your organization is prepared to responsibly take advantage of these opportunities. Although no revenue manager needs to become a big data expert, it is important to understand how big data impacts technology infrastructure, analytics, and the business process. In this chapter I explained why complex data, particularly unstructured data, is challenging organizations today, and provided a framework for you to evaluate the usefulness of new data sources. I explained some key concepts about databases, data processing, solution delivery options, and potential analytical pitfalls from the improper use of big data. This is all designed to help you have better conversations with your counterparts in IT and across the organization.

So, what is the bottom line here? Don't assume that more is better—prove it! Big data represents a big opportunity for revenue management—and the hotel industry in general. Taking on any new data source, big or not, requires strategic planning and careful thought. Just because you *can* collect big data does not mean you *should*.

In the next chapter, I talk about the most important new source of big data that organizations *should* be utilizing, reputation data. Reputation data is classic big data because it has variety, being comprised of unstructured text data from reviews, quantitative scores from ratings, and derived metrics like TripAdvisor rank. It has velocity—tweets are stale nearly as soon as they are created, but they can have a huge reputation impact in the moment. And it has volume, growing every day as social media and review sites continue to gain popularity and traction. Most organizations have recognized the importance of monitoring reputation from the branding and marketing perspectives, but there are broader impacts that I describe in the next chapter, particularly on demand and pricing, putting reputation squarely in the purview of revenue management.

ADDITIONAL READING

Alex Dietz, "Can Big Data Help Revenue Management?" *Analytic Hospitality Executive Blog*, www.sas.com/en_us/offers/15q1/non-geeks-big-data-playbook-106947.html.

Tamara Dull, "Hadoop in a Data Environment: A Non-Geek's Big Data Playbook," SAS white paper, www.sas.com/en_us/offers/15q1/non-geeks-big-data-playbook-106947.html.

Big Data, Data Mining, and Machine Learning: Jared Dean, *Value Creation for Business Leaders and Practitioners* (Hoboken, NJ: John Wiley & Sons, 2014), www.sas.com/store/books/categories/business-leadership/big-data-data-mining-and-machine-learning-value-creation-for-business-leaders-and-practitioners/prod-BK_66081_en.html.

Multicollinearity: T. Krishna Kumar, "Multicollinearity in Regression Analysis," *Review of Economics and Statistics*, 57, no. 3 (1975): 365–366. JSTOR 1923925.

Overfitting: I. V. Tetko, D. J. Livingstone, and A. Luik, "Neural Network Studies. 1. Comparison of Overfitting and Overtraining," *Journal of Chemical Information and Computer Sciences*, 35, no. 5 (1995): 826–833. doi:10.1021/ci00027a006.

REVENUE MANAGEMENT PERSPECTIVES: THE ROLE OF BIG DATA IN REVENUE MANAGEMENT SCIENCE

I have seen two schools of thought emerging on the future of revenue management analytics. With the advent of big data analytics, some are advocating for a more exploratory, data-oriented approach to solving the revenue management forecasting problem, throwing more and more varied data sources at the problem. Others are leveraging improvements in processing power to innovate around the existing revenue management forecasting and optimization algorithms, employing more complex and accurate analytics to solve the problem. Here, I present two perspectives on the advantages and disadvantages of a big data approach to revenue management.

In order to get a perspective on the impact of big data on pricing and revenue management science, I interviewed two people who are at the forefront of their fields, one who is working in the new frontier of big data science for pricing and revenue management and one who is innovating within established pricing and revenue management techniques.

Rich Hughes, SVP and Chief Data Scientist, RealPage, Inc.

RealPage is the biggest SaaS provider in the largest vertical in the U.S. economy, with software deployed on more than a trillion dollars of assets.

Rich has a background in revenue management, statistics, and technology. He has been in the apartment revenue management industry for the past 15 years, first on the supplier side and then on the vendor side. Apartment revenue management has some similar characteristics to the hotel problem (capacity constrained inventory, time variable demand, high fixed costs with low cost of sale); however, there are some significant differences as well. Transaction density in the apartment context is relatively sparse, with the average inventory cycle close to a year rather than a handful of days. Think about how often an apartment—even in short-term corporate housing—is rented, versus a hotel room. There are also many attributes associated with apartments, like number of bedrooms, floor, view, or layout that could impact demand and price.

Rich has had to innovate in his approach to data and analytics to account for some of the unique challenges in apartment revenue management, giving him an interesting perspective on the evolution of big data analytics in revenue management. I asked him about this.

"We all know that pricing and revenue management is a data and information technology-reliant industry. While we may intuitively understand what is meant by *information technology*, many don't take the time to really unpack that statement. Technology is, of course, the platform, a practical application of science. Information is defined by Claude Shannon as a reduction in uncertainty, basically telling you things about something you don't already know or making you more confident about things you might. In the pricing and revenue management context, supply is generally well understood, but demand is what we need information about. I approach the problem of demand from the perspective of *consilience*, which is the principle that when multiple sources of evidence are in agreement, the conclusion can be very strong, even when none of the individual sources of evidence are very strong on their own. This is where big data sources can provide an advantage. If my social media, web traffic and historical demand patterns are converging toward expected demand, for example, I can be more certain in the demand forecast.

"The Internet lets us know much more about people much sooner in the sales cycle. We need to understand not just the data itself, but also the *metadata*, data about the data. For example, I could potentially learn from the time stamp on an e-mail inquiry, the domain name, or the length of the e-mail just as I can from understanding the content of that e-mail. Any of these factors help to model demand more accurately, which, of course, is the goal. Also, having an indication sooner gives a strategic advantage. As we move backward in time away from (in front of) the purchase event we have more candidates, less certainty and less information. Rather than pick an arbitrary event to measure demand, we need to understand the whole funnel and be able to credit each activity appropriately.

"What is equally important to understanding demand is to not be a victim of it. Marketing is considered a cost center in most organizations, and is, at times, not well measured or well managed. Revenue management should provide targeted direction in terms of what is needed to fill the sales funnel that will eventually materialize into the right demand at the right price. Marketing can determine how to generate that demand at the lowest cost to the organization. This represents a huge opportunity that has not yet been exploited in most organizations."

Tugrul Sanli, Senior Director, Revenue Management and Price Optimization, SAS

SAS is the leader in business analytics software and services, and the largest independent vendor in the business intelligence market.

Tugrul leads the development team at SAS that builds revenue management and price optimization analytics for hospitality and travel. He has a PhD in operations research, specializing in stochastic optimization. Prior to running this team, he worked in the group that built SAS's Markdown Optimization product. Tugrul's team is comprised of master's and PhD level scientists who are experts in demand modeling, forecasting, and optimization. When SAS acquired IDeaS in 2008, Tugrul and his team were able to sit down with the hotel revenue management experts at IDeaS and a blank sheet of paper to rethink the revenue management problem in the context of the changing marketplace. I asked him about how he approaches the idea of big data in revenue management for hotels and casinos.

"First of all, in the context of business today, I don't think that revenue management data is that big. When you compare hotel transactions to, say, a credit card company or a big retailer, or the volume of data created by sensors and GPS, it really isn't that big at all. We take advantage of increased processing power and efficiencies in coding to make sure the analytics run at the speed of business, but for SAS, hotel transaction data is really no problem size-wise."

I asked Tugrul about how he thinks about incorporating new data sources into the revenue management process. He said for him, the most important thing is to understand whether and how the data adds value to the process (for example, the forecast).

"For example, one of the sources could be weather forecast. Weather data can really only add value if its effects aren't already captured in historical demand patterns in the transactional data. We do a lot of testing to make sure that the data source will improve the forecast accuracy, decrease variability, or improve pricing recommendations.

"Even if the data does have value, if it isn't clean, it causes problems. Dirty or unreliable data causes problems in modeling, including adding noise (variability). We also test whether the data is clean and accurate, whether it reflects the behavior of the customers or the market. Bottom line, if the data source does not add any significant benefit to the process or it is not reliable, then including it will make things worse." Clearly, within an established discipline with a rich primary data source, Tugrul thinks it's really important for revenue managers to be cautious in their evaluation of new data sources.

I also talked to him about his analytics approach. Tugrul said that when it comes to analytics, one of the biggest challenges in hospitality is working within the constraints of the selling system. "It doesn't matter how accurate the forecast is, or how advanced the optimization, if the selling system can't take the controls, it doesn't matter. In my opinion, the next big opportunity in revenue management will come when hotels replace their selling systems with options that can be more flexible in data collection and utilize decision controls generated by advanced optimization systems. Until that happens, hotels will always be limited."

Something to Think About . . .

Big data scientists are employing new techniques to gain insight from large data sets. From a revenue management perspective, data scientists are exploring alternate forecasting methods involving big data techniques that detect patterns within large data sets. Their contention is that in this complex social world, these big data methods can incorporate more data, deriving better patterns and a more accurate forecast. A forecasting or operations research scientist would argue that big data should only be added if it adds unique value to the process. Unstable data or dirty data can create too much noise in revenue management algorithms. So, at the cusp of what we might call the *big data revolution*, is revenue management going to be out with the old and in with the new, or are data scientists just reinventing a solution to a problem that is already being solved properly?

NOTE

1. Note that not every problem can be easily divided and aggregated. Revenue management forecasting is done at a very detailed level (property, market segment, day), which already results in many small problems instead of one big one. Forecasting is an input to optimization, so forecasting needs to be finished before optimization can begin. There are other ways to speed up forecasting algorithms to handle greater levels of detail or to evaluate multiple forecasting methods to improve accuracy. This parallel processing is, however, very useful in optimization algorithms.

PART TWO

The Expanding Role of Revenue Management

CHAPTER 4

Hotel Pricing in a Social World: Price, UGC, and Buying Behavior

With Dr. Breffni Noone, Associate Professor, The Pennsylvania State University

As soon as our revenue managers began paying attention to our hotels' reputation as compared to the competitive set, in addition to monitoring our price position, they became more confident in taking a more aggressive price position. This made a big difference in our performance.

—Monica Xuereb, Chief Revenue Officer, Loews Hotels

In the previous chapters, I talked about how the data, technology, and analytics at the core of revenue management pricing recommendations are evolving to meet the needs of the changing market, taking advantage of innovations in technology driven by the big data era. Now that these technology innovations are available to revenue managers, it is important to understand how they impact both tactical and strategic decision making as the role of revenue management expands to encompass new data and new departmental relationships. In the next three chapters, I discuss emerging areas of opportunity for revenue management to improve both the calculation of optimal pricing recommendations, and also the process of building an integrated pricing strategy that accounts for all of the new influences on price. This chapter talks about the role of reputation in pricing, the next chapter talks about the opportunities associated with integrating revenue management and marketing data, analytics and decision making, and the final chapter in this part discusses total hotel revenue management and how to apply revenue management thinking to the entire hotel enterprise. These chapters describe new data that is becoming available to improve the tactical generation of a price, and the opportunity to leverage technology and business process to support the development of a more profitable pricing strategy.

After price transparency, the emergence of the social web has probably had the largest impact on consumer buying behavior, and because of that has quickly become front of mind for revenue management. As user-generated content (UGC) proliferates on social media sites, review sites, and other social sharing mechanisms, there is a wealth of new information about a hotel experience in just about every place consumers look, and it is changing how consumers purchase hotels. Consumers can now evaluate hotels based on the opinions of their peers, information that some consider more genuine—and therefore more credible—than traditional, firm-generated content. With this, the hotel industry finds itself in a new buying environment that has not only price transparency, but also *value transparency*. The question is, how are consumers using this information to assess value, and ultimately, to make a purchase decision?

In order to continue to build profitable pricing and positioning strategies, revenue managers must understand the relationship among reputation, pricing, and consumer decision making. In other words, it is crucial for revenue managers to understand how a hotel's reputation should be factored into revenue management's pricing strategy.

In this chapter, I first describe the results of original research I conducted with a colleague from Penn State, which investigates how consumers use user-generated content with price to make hotel purchase decisions. This research identifies which types of UGC consumers rely on, how they trade off this UGC with price and brand, and how this influences buying behavior. I then provide answers to common questions that arise from revenue managers attempting to understand the impact of UGC broadly on consumer perceptions and lodging performance. Finally, I talk about how revenue managers should incorporate reputation into their tactical and strategic pricing activities.

PRICE, RATINGS, AND REVIEWS: HOW CONSUMERS CHOOSE

Revenue managers today pay close attention to their price as well as competitors' pricing, and use this information to better understand demand for their hotels. Consumers are also looking at your price and the competitors' prices, but they are using this information to assess value, and that is what ultimately drives them to make a decision. If revenue managers do not account for value, they are missing an important piece of the pricing equation.

Value is defined as a trade-off between what you give (price) for what you get (the hotel room night). When consumers only had access to price and some firm-generated content, the decision was a bit simpler. Now that there is more information than ever before available at the point of purchase, the question of how consumers assess value has become more complicated. Breffni Noone, associate professor at The Pennsylvania State University, and I have been conducting a series of studies to understand how consumers use UGC with price to evaluate value and ultimately make a purchase decision. Our goal is to help revenue managers (and marketers) develop more profitable pricing and positioning strategies.

Study 1: UGC, Price, and Quality and Value Perceptions

Academic research tells us that quality is a driver of value perceptions and both quality and value drive purchase decisions. Our first project was designed to evaluate how the interplay between price, consumer reviews and aggregate consumer ratings influences consumer quality and value perceptions. This would help us to establish a baseline of which of the key UGC metrics were influencing value perceptions and to what degree.

We designed a study that replicated the experience of purchasing a hotel room online (Noone and McGuire 2013a). For the study, we recruited a representative sample of the U.S. population to participate in an online survey. Participants were presented with one of eight scenarios based on a typical online purchase of a four-star hotel room for a three-night leisure trip. In each scenario, we varied the following:

- Price (low and high relative to an established reference price).
- Aggregate rating (low or high out of five).
- Review sentiment (mostly positive or mostly negative).

We asked participants to evaluate the quality and value of the hotel in the scenario they were presented with. The definitions of the eight scenarios are shown in Figure 4.1.

Code	Price	Rating	Review
LHP	Low	High	Positive
HHP	High	High	Positive
LLP	Low	Low	Positive
HLP	High	Low	Positive
LHN	Low	High	Negative
HLN	High	Low	Negative
LLN	Low	Low	Negative
HHN	High	High	Negative

Figure 4.1 Eight Study Scenarios

Perceived Quality

In Figure 4.2, you can see the mean perceived quality by scenario (on a scale of 1 to 7). The light gray bars represent high price, and the dark gray bars represent low price. You'll notice that there does not

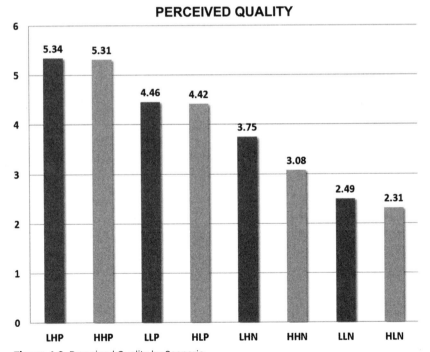

Figure 4.2 Perceived Quality by Scenario

appear to be much difference between low- (dark gray) and high-price (light gray) scenarios at the same levels of ratings and reviews. You'll also notice that the scenarios with positive reviews (P) had the four highest-quality perceptions.

Our statistical analysis showed that, in fact, price had no significant relationship with quality. Positive reviews were associated with higher perceptions of quality. Aggregate ratings also had a positive relationship with quality perceptions, but it was much weaker than the review relationship.

Perceived Value

Because value is defined as what you give for what you get, economic considerations (price) should come into play when consumers are asked about value. So, not surprisingly, looking at the low-price (dark gray) and high-price (light gray) bars in Figure 4.3, the low-price

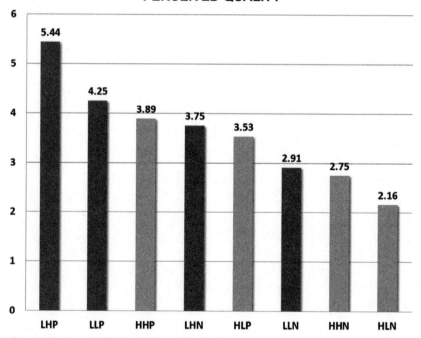

Figure 4.3 Perceived Value by Scenario

scenarios tended to have higher value perceptions (on a scale of 1 to 7). But there are still some high-priced scenarios (light gray) mixed in with the low-priced scenarios—so not all low-priced scenarios received higher value perceptions. Ratings and reviews also seemed to have some impact on value perceptions, altering the straightforward relationship that as price increases, value decreases.

Statistically, there was a three-way interaction among price, aggregate ratings, and reviews. This means that UGC altered the magnitude of the negative relationship between price and value perceptions. To investigate these effects, we split out the high- and low-priced scenarios and looked at the value perceptions by rating and review levels.

In Figure 4.4, the high-priced scenarios are on the top. The dark gray bars represent high ratings, and the light gray bars represent low ratings. So the first dark gray bar on the high-priced chart (a) represents the average value perception for the high-priced, positive-rating, positive-reviews scenario. The dark gray bar in the same location on the low-price chart (b) represents the average value perceptions for the low-priced, positive-review, high-ratings scenario. For both high and low prices, positive reviews increase value perceptions (see the first two bars on each chart compared to the second two bars). Ratings have no statistical impact in the high-priced scenario.

The interaction came into play when price was low, aggregate ratings were high, and reviews were positive. In this scenario, the aggregate ratings gave a bump to the value perceptions—as if the consumers were using the high aggregate rating as a signal that they were getting a really good deal. You can see this effect when you look at the difference between the first two bars in the high-priced scenario compared to the first two in the low-priced scenario (the bold font shows the impact of the interaction).

Finally, notice the "worst-case scenario" bars, the low ratings and negative reviews, high price (top chart) versus low price (bottom chart). There isn't a statistical or practical difference in the two value perceptions. This means that consumers saw no additional value in the low-rated, negatively reviewed hotel with a lower price.

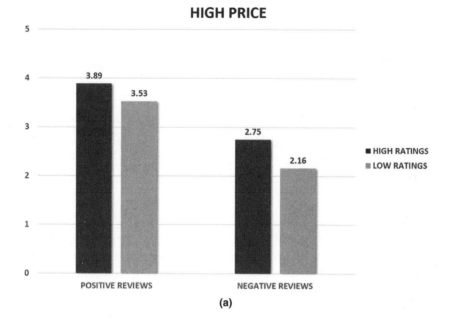

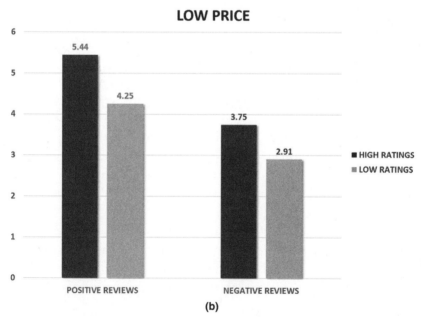

Figure 4.4 Perceived Value, High Price versus Low Price

What Is the Impact on Revenue Management?

There are five key takeaways for revenue managers from the results of this study:

1. **Price and quality.** Consumers do not use price as an indication of quality if ratings and reviews are available. This is good news for revenue managers, because it means that they can adjust price (within reasonable bounds) to generate short-term demand without affecting long-term quality perceptions.

2. **The important role of UGC.** Competing on price alone is not a winning strategy. Consumers will look closely at your UGC, and that of your competitors, when making a purchase decision. This means you should *not* just adjust your price simply based on the price movements of your competitors. You must understand how your reputation compares to understand consumers' value perception of your hotel versus the competition.

3. **Power of reviews.** Reviews are more important to consumers than ratings. Our research showed that consumers look to reviews over aggregate ratings to form quality and value perceptions. This runs counter to some theoretical arguments that suggest consumers are "information misers," preferring a metric that's easier to consume (like an aggregate rating), as opposed to an information-rich review. We hypothesize that the uncertainty associated with a hotel experience leads consumers to want to gather as much information as possible to mitigate risk.

4. **Reputation and price.** Good reviews are not a license to charge more. Consumers still prefer to pay the lowest price. This means that if all other things are equal, you'll drive demand to your property if your price is lower. If you are clearly better than the competition, you'll be able to push the price. If you aren't, it's not that simple.

5. **Poor reputation.** It's hard to overcome bad UGC. Our results indicated that lowering the price of a badly rated and negatively reviewed property provides no additional value in the

minds of consumers. If you happen to be in that unfortunate position, you should keep the price up, and take what you can get—which, according to our results, won't be much. Use your energy to fix the problems with your property instead of worrying about how it is priced.

Study 2: The Power of the Negative Review

In the first study, we asked consumers to evaluate their perceptions of one hotel property so we could evaluate how the presence of UGC and price influenced quality and value perceptions. Knowing this, and understanding the power of the reviews in particular, we wanted to explore how consumers make trade-offs among price and nonprice information when forced to choose among alternative hotel properties. Analyzing these trade-offs will help us to understand how consumers use these different attributes to assess value. Using the same context as the study described above (an online purchase of a four-star hotel for a weekend leisure break in a major city center), we designed a choice modeling experiment.

In the experiment, we asked consumers to select the hotel they would buy from a choice of three, with varying levels of key attributes (Noone and McGuire 2013b). Participants were told that all three hotels were equally convenient in terms of location, and they were all four-star hotels with equivalent amenities. By tracking their pattern of choices, it is possible to statistically assess the importance of each attribute in decision making, and the value that they place on the attribute and its levels. We again used a representative sample of the U.S. population through an online survey. Table 4.1 shows the attributes and the attribute levels we tested in the study.

Because our first study clearly demonstrated the power of reviews in consumers' assessment of the quality and value of a hotel purchase, we wanted to learn more about how consumers react to reviews. In this study, we also tested if what the reviewers talked about (content) and the way they talked about it (language) had an influence on choice behavior. We also added TripAdvisor rank, based on a survey

Table 4.1 Choice Attributes and Levels Tested

Attribute	Level 1	Level 2	Level 3
Hotel name	Known brand	Unknown brand	
Price	$195	$235	$295
Aggregate rating	2.8	3.5	4.8
TripAdvisor rank (out of 217 Hotels)	Low	Mid	High
Review valence	Negative	Positive	
Review content	Physical property	Service	
Review language	Descriptive (e.g., the bed was comfortable)	Emotional (e.g., I loved the bed)	

of the popular press and some interviews of hoteliers that anecdotally reported an impact on performance as they moved up in TripAdvisor rank.

Demographics

Figure 4.5 describes the demographic characteristics of the leisure travelers in our study. We specifically recruited participants who had traveled at least once for leisure in the past 12 months, and who booked the trip

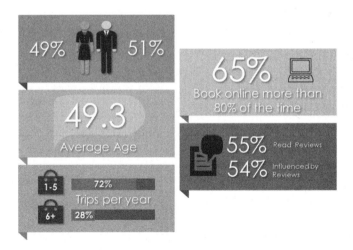

Figure 4.5 Leisure Traveler Demographics

themselves online. You can see here that our participants were evenly split in terms of gender, and the majority traveled one to five times per year. When asked how often they book their travel online, 65 percent reported booking travel online more than 80 percent of the time. We also asked them how often they read, and were influenced by, reviews on a scale of 1 (never) to 7 (always). Fifty-five percent reported that they read reviews most or all of the time (6 or 7), and 54 percent reported being influenced by reviews most of the time (6 or 7).

Choice Modeling Overall Results

The first output of a choice modeling experiment identifies the list of attributes that had a significant impact on choice behavior and the order of impact. For the leisure traveler, the following attributes, in order of importance, influenced their choices:

1. Review sentiment (positive or negative)
2. Price
3. Ratings
4. TripAdvisor rank
5. Brand

Review sentiment was the most influential, followed by price. This supports the results of our first study, but for a segment that is considered to be very price-sensitive, the fact that price was second to reviews is very interesting. Ratings, TripAdvisor rank, and brand were significant influencers, but statistically, their impact was much less than sentiment and price. Notice that neither review content nor review language were significant.

After understanding which attributes are significant, the next step in choice modeling is to understand how these attributes, and the levels of these attributes, influence value perceptions. This more detailed analysis helps to explain why the attributes are significant influencers of choice behavior.

Attribute Levels and Value Assessments

Figure 4.6 shows the impact of changes in attribute level on value perceptions. In this type of analysis, the number associated with the changes in attribute levels is less important to interpret than the magnitude and direction of that number relative to the other attribute levels. Attribute levels with a star (*) in the chart were significant predictors of choice. The line down the middle is zero, so the dark gray bars that go to the left represent a negative impact; the lighter gray bars that go to the right represent a positive impact. The following list details the impact of all levels of attributes on value perceptions:

- The top dark gray bar represents the significant negative impact on value of a negative review (over a positive review). It is larger than any of the other bars on the chart—explaining why it was the most significant attribute.

- The next two bars represent the negative impact of a midrange price over a low price, and then a high price over a midrange price. As the price goes up, the value goes down, with the high over mid having a larger impact on value than mid over low. For a price-sensitive segment, this is not surprising.

- The next set of bars (fourth and fifth) are the impact of ratings levels on value perceptions. The first bar, okay ratings over terrible ratings, is not significant. Consumers only notice, and

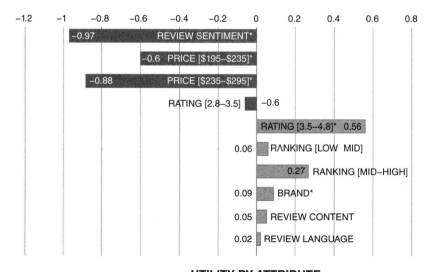

UTILITY BY ATTRIBUTE

Figure 4.6 Choice Modeling Results

value, great ratings (the second light gray bar shows the great ratings over okay ratings).

■ The same effect was true for TripAdvisor rank (the sixth and seventh bars). It was only when the TripAdvisor rank was highest that consumers placed any value on it.

■ The third bar up from the bottom represents a slight, positive value associated with a known brand over an unknown brand.

■ The last two bars, representing review content and review language, were not significant influencers of value perceptions.

Overall Value Perceptions

Once the value impacts of changes in attribute levels are established, it is then possible to look at the impact of these changes on the overall value of the hotel to the consumer. In the equations that follow, pay more attention to the way that the overall value perception changes, as opposed to trying to interpret the number itself.

In our study, the combination of attributes that resulted in the highest overall consumer value was:

Positive Review + Low Price + High Rating + High Trip Advisor Rank + Known Brand = 1.95

To understand how changes in the attribute levels impact overall value, we can change the level of the attribute and compare the overall value to the baseline as shown above.

First, we will raise the price from lowest to highest:

Positive Review + **High Price** *+ High TripAdvisor Rank + High Rating + Known Brand =* **0.46**

The value drops significantly with the higher price, with the option losing nearly three-quarters of its value, as compared to the baseline. Clearly, leisure travelers are price sensitive, so raising the price decreases the value.

Now, notice what happens when you hold everything constant and change the most influential attribute, review sentiment, from positive to negative:

Negative Review + *Low Price* + *High TripAdvisor Rank* +
High Rating + *Known Brand* = **0.01**

The value to the consumer drops to practically nothing. This is the power of those negative reviews. Consumers see no value in a hotel with negative reviews. Negative reviews will remove a hotel from the consumers' choice set. Period.

Key Takeaways

- **Reviews and price trump all other factors.** Our research suggests that positive reviews are the primary motivators for leisure travelers' choice behavior and value perceptions, followed by lower price. To a lesser extent, leisure consumers do pay attention to aggregate ratings, TripAdvisor rank and brand name. But it appears that they are not too concerned about the content and language of reviews.

- **Negative reviews remove you from the choice set. Period.** Low price or high ratings and high ranking will not overcome the negative impact of negative reviews. Leisure travelers simply will not choose a hotel that has negative reviews.

- **Leisure travelers prefer to pay a low price.** While leisure travelers will go for a higher-priced hotel when the lower-priced hotel has negative UGC, they still prefer to pay the lowest price possible. All things being equally positive, they will look for the lowest price. Hotels need to pay attention to how their reviews compare to their competitors when setting price.

- **Leisure travelers only notice high aggregate ratings and TripAdvisor rankings.** Leisure travelers do not place any value on the comparison between low and midrange aggregate ratings and TripAdvisor rankings. They only notice, and value, a hotel that is great.

Study 3: Price, UGC, and the Business Traveler

In our next study, we wanted to look at another large and valuable segment for hotels, the business traveler. In particular, we were interested to know how the unmanaged business traveler uses UGC with price to make a purchase decision. Unmanaged business travelers are defined as those travelers who are not governed by a corporate travel policy, and so have complete control over their travel booking. Phocuswright has estimated that this group of business travelers represents up to 70 percent of all business travel, and so they comprise a valuable and impactful segment for hotels.

For this study, similar to the leisure traveler study, we recruited an online panel of a representative sample of the U.S. population who had traveled for business at least six times in the past 12 months, and who had some degree of control over their travel (i.e., not overly constrained by a corporate travel policy). We told them they were traveling to a city center for a meeting, and had to pick a hotel. The hotels they were evaluating were equally convenient locations, and all equally business friendly. They were shown three hotel options to pick from, and they repeated this exercise three times.

The framework for this study was exactly the same as the leisure study (see Table 4.1). The only difference was in the brand attribute. Frequent business travelers are eligible to achieve status and rewards from hotel loyalty programs that can be quite valuable. We anticipated that business travelers would be influenced by their ability to gather points and rewards from their loyalty memberships. To test this impact, we added another level to the hotel brand attribute to capture preferred brand. We asked the participants to tell us what loyalty programs they belonged to, and their level of loyalty in that program. We then asked them to select a preferred brand from a list of brands within these loyalty programs that met the study criteria of "business-friendly" hotel, so, for example, the Hilton HHonors brands were Hilton, Embassy Suites, and Doubletree. Note that this was not a study about loyalty program membership, so we can't really make inferences about loyalty membership to the

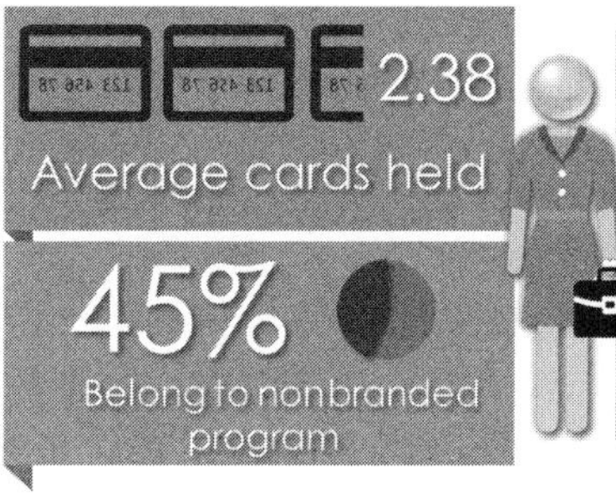

Loyalty Program Brand	% with Card	Preferred Brand
Club Carlson	15%	-
Hilton HHonors	67%	34%
Hyatt Gold Passport	38%	12%
IHG Rewards Club	21%	11%
Kimpton Hotels: InTouch Rewards	6%	2%
Marriott Rewards	59%	29%
Starwood Preferred Guest	29%	7%
Wyndham Rewards	18%	7%
I do not have any hotel rewards cards	8%	-

Average cards held: 2.38
45% Belong to nonbranded program

Figure 4.7 Business Traveler Loyalty Affiliation

general population of business travelers, but it is interesting to see how our business travelers are affiliated with common U.S. loyalty programs (Figure 4.7).

BUSINESS TRAVELERS LOYALTY AND DEMOGRAPHICS

Figure 4.7 shows the demographics of loyalty program membership. Our study participants held an average of more than two cards per person, and 45 percent of them belonged to a nonbranded loyalty program (like hotels.com or Leading Hotels of the World's loyalty program). The chart on the right shows the loyalty programs we asked about. The next-to-last column is the percent of participants who indicated that they held a card from that program, and the last column represents the percent of participants who selected a brand from that loyalty program as their preferred brand.

We also assessed our participants' loyalty behavior toward their preferred brand. Participants were asked how loyal they felt toward their identified preferred brand (using an established academic measurement scale). Over the entire study sample, the attitudinal loyalty was about 4.6 out of 7, which is not tremendously loyal. We also asked them how often they stayed with their preferred brand. The majority indicated that they stayed with their preferred brand between 25 and 75 percent of the time. Only 4 percent stayed with their preferred brand 100 percent of the time in the past 12 months (Figure 4.8).

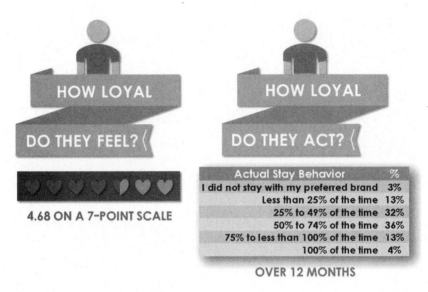

Figure 4.8 Loyalty Behavior of Sample

Finally, we collected some demographic information about our study participants (Figure 4.9). The business travelers in our study were primarily male and a bit younger than the leisure travelers. About half of them traveled between 6 and 10 times per year, and 93 percent stayed two or more nights. Interestingly, 80 percent indicated that they read reviews most or all of the time (6 or 7), and 88 percent indicated that they were highly influenced by reviews. Compare this to the leisure traveler results from Figure 4.5 and it appears that business travelers are much more likely to read reviews than leisure travelers. This result was somewhat unexpected.

Overall Attribute Importance

As with our leisure study, we first assessed the overall importance of each attribute in customers' decision making. For the business travelers, the following list of attributes were significant drivers of choice, and are presented in order of importance:

1. Review sentiment (positive, negative)
2. Brand
3. Aggregate ratings

4. Price

5. Review language (descriptive, emotional)

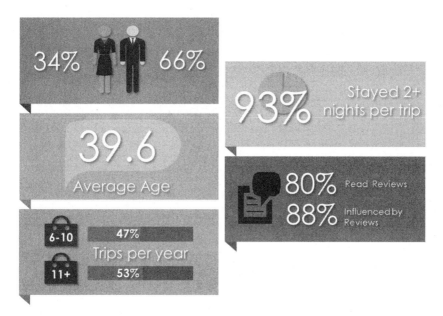

Figure 4.9 Business Traveler Study Demographics

Contrast this with the list for the leisure traveler:

1. Review sentiment (positive, negative)

2. Price

3. Aggregate ratings

4. TripAdvisor rank

5. Brand

As you can see, there are some interesting differences in how these two segments assess value and make decisions, yet review sentiment is still most influential for both segments.

Attribute Levels and Value Assessments

To understand how the attributes influenced value perceptions, we did the same analysis as with leisure travelers, taking a detailed look at the impact on value of changes in attribute levels. Figure 4.10 shows the

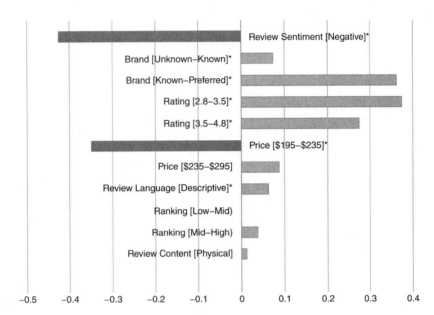

Figure 4.10 Value Impacts by Attribute Level

results of this analysis. Once again, it is more important to pay attention to the magnitude and direction of the value impacts rather than the actual number. The middle line is zero, bars that go to the left of that line represent a negative value, and bars to the right represent a positive value. The following analysis follows the bars from top to bottom, explaining how they represent value impact of changes in the levels of each attribute:

- The top dark gray bar represents the negative impact on value of a negative review. It is quite large, which explains why the attribute was so influential on choice behavior.
- The next two light gray bars represent the positive impact of brand on value perceptions. The first, smaller bar, is a slight positive value associated with a known brand over an unknown brand, and the second larger bar is the large positive value associated with a preferred brand over a known brand. Clearly, the business travelers in our study placed a lot of value on their preferred brand.

- The next set of light gray bars (fourth and fifth down) are the positive value associated with ratings. The first of the set is the positive value associated with a hotel that is okay over one that is terrible, and the second represents the value associated with a great hotel over an okay hotel. Notice that the value associated with an okay as opposed to terrible hotel is larger than that of a great hotel as opposed to an okay hotel.
- The next set of bars represents price (sixth and seventh). Interestingly, there is a significant negative impact of a midrange price over a low price, but no impact of a price change once the price is above that low price (the second bar, representing high over midrange price, is not significant). In other words, business travelers notice, and value, a deal, but do not care about any price difference other than the lowest price.
- The fourth bar up from the bottom represents the slight positive impact of a descriptive review over an emotional review.
- The final three bars show that TripAdvisor rank and review content did not contribute to business travelers' value perceptions.

Assessing Overall Value

As with leisure travelers, we can use the results of the attribute level analysis to assess how these attribute levels influence the overall value of a hotel. As with the earlier discussion, what is most important here is not to interpret the number that represents the sum of the equations, but rather, to interpret how that number changes with changes in attribute levels.

The following equation represents the most valuable option for the business travelers, in order of attribute importance.

Positive Reviews + Preferred Brand + High Rating + Low Price + Descriptive Reviews = 1.52

With this set of attribute levels as a baseline, we then manipulate the attribute levels and track their impact on overall value. For example, holding everything else constant, the next equation represents overall value when the price is raised from lowest to highest. You can see that the overall value is impacted slightly, but not by very much. This is not surprising because the price was only the fourth most important attribute to business travelers, and it was only the low price that the business travelers valued.

Positive Reviews + Preferred Brand + High Rating + **High Price** +
Descriptive Reviews = **1.25**

Contrast this result with the leisure traveler study, where price was the second most important attribute. As we described earlier, the first equation below is the most valuable option for the leisure traveler, and the second shows the impact of raising the price from low to high. Leisure travelers are clearly highly price sensitive. The overall value drops significantly when the price goes from low to high.

Leisure baseline: Positive Reviews + Low Price + High Rating +
High TA Rank + Known Brand = 1.95

Leisure high price: Positive Reviews + **High Price** + *High Rating +*
High TA Rank + Known Brand = **0.46**

Now look at what happens when the most important attribute for each traveler segment changes. Holding everything constant from the baseline, the first equation below demonstrates the impact of negative reviews on overall value for business travelers, and the second for leisure travelers. You can see here that the impact on value for business travelers over the baseline was quite significant, as nearly half of the value is lost when the reviews are negative as opposed to positive. However, for the leisure travelers, all of the value is lost when reviews are negative. Business travelers clearly pay attention to reviews, but they are willing to balance that against other attributes like, as we describe next, brand and rating. Leisure travelers simply won't consider the hotel if the reviews are negative.

Business: **Negative Reviews** + *Preferred Brand + High Rating +*
Low Price + Descriptive Reviews = **0.69**

> *Leisure:* **Negative Reviews** + *Low Price* + *High Rating* +
> *High TA Rank* + *Known Brand* = **0.01**

For leisure travelers, review sentiment and price were by far the most significant influencers on choice and value. The other three variables, while significant, were much less so. For the business travelers, sentiment, brand, and ratings were the most significant, with price and review language much less so.

The following equations represent the impact on value of the unknown brand over the preferred brand and the lowest ratings over the highest ratings. For reference, the baseline option (with the highest overall value) is also included.

> *Business baseline: Positive Reviews + Preferred Brand + High Rating +*
> *Low Price + Descriptive Reviews = 1.52*

> *Brand: Positive +* **Unknown Brand** + *High Ratings + Low Price +*
> *Descriptive Reviews* = **0.91**

> *Ratings: Positive + Preferred Brand +* **Low Ratings** + *Low Price +*
> *Descriptive Reviews* = **0.87**

Interestingly, the impact of brand and ratings is nearly equivalent. Combining these results with the aggregate rating results from Figure 4.10 suggests that it is more important to business travelers that the hotel is okay than great. It can be inferred that business travelers will assess what the experience will be like (by reading the reviews, especially descriptive ones), and as long as they feel it will be okay (and they can get points), they will book. This doesn't mean they don't appreciate a great hotel, but in the balance between staying with their preferred brand that is either terrible (as earlier) or even just okay, and a hotel with a great reputation, they are just as likely to choose the preferred brand as the great hotel.

This is, however, good news for hotels that might be in that "unknown brand" position in a market with brands that have robust loyalty programs. If you are in a better reputation position than the brands with loyalty programs, you might be able to entice some business travelers to try your hotel, particularly if you are able to offer them a lower price. Obviously, you would want to assess the impact of such a pricing strategy on your other demand streams, but the point is that there are opportunities to counter the influence of a well-established loyalty program.

Key Takeaways from the Business Traveler Study

There are a few key takeaways from this study:

- **Reviews matter.** Business travelers look to the reviews to assess what their experience will be like. If the review is positive or negative they want to know why. This is why they seem to prefer reviews that describe the experience.
- **Loyalty matters.** Business travelers will put up with "good enough" or okay if they can get their points. The preferred brand was a powerful driver of value and choice in this study. Business travelers are clearly driven by this membership, but not exclusively. Remember, the majority of the participants stayed only 25 to 75 percent of the time with their preferred hotels. You can't rest on your loyalty program, but it will make a difference.
- **Price matters.** Business travelers still recognize a deal, but it's only the lowest price that entices them. They are relatively insensitive beyond that.
- **Okay is okay.** Unlike with leisure travelers, "Okay" is okay for business travelers. Other factors are equally important, like loyalty program membership. After all, with enough okay stays, the business traveler can take her family on a great vacation! With leisure travelers, the hotel has to be great, period.

This research has really only scratched the surface of what we need to know. When we talk about our research in the revenue management community, we get many questions about different impacts of UGC. As we developed our studies, we looked to other empirical research to determine what insights had already been uncovered. The next section summarizes the current body of work in this area, according to the questions that we are most frequently asked.

USER-GENERATED CONTENT AND LODGING PERFORMANCE

As I mentioned, we surveyed the research literature to understand how all aspects of reputation impact consumer behavior and lodging performance, which formed the basis for my guidance to revenue managers below. There are also many studies available in the popular press about these impacts. Many of them are very well researched, but it is more difficult to assess the methodology or rigor of these because they are conducted on proprietary data sets or by the providers of reputation metrics. The studies I reference here were peer reviewed for inclusion in academic journals, and therefore, the authors had to be transparent about the methodology and limitations of their analysis. This is why I only included these studies as opposed to a broader list, including research from the popular press.

Ratings and Performance

A study from the Cornell Center for Hospitality Research (Anderson 2012) suggested a positive relationship between UGC and firm performance. The hotel's reputation score (as measured by ReviewPro's GRI™ index) was positively related to average daily rate, room occupancy and RevPAR. The study also found that a 1 point increase in user review score (GRI) would allow a hotel to raise its price by 11.2 percent and maintain the same purchase probability or market share. Remember that our earlier results suggest that hotels with a primarily leisure market will only get this pricing power as they move from okay to great. The move from terrible to okay will not influence pricing power.

Responses to Reviews

Many hotels have invested a good deal of resources in responding to reviews—both positive and negative. I have seen one study so far that looked at "response to negative reviews" in the context of hotel performance.

There seemed to be a relationship such that hotels that responded to negative reviews had better performance (ADR, RevPAR, Occupancy). There is plenty of anecdotal evidence as well. My own opinion—this comes down to service recovery. You would address a problem if it were brought to you in person or via letter, so responding to negative reviews is a good idea. I suspect that "over-responding," or not being genuine, however, can do as much damage as that negative review, so I'd say be careful. More research needs to be done in this area.

TripAdvisor Rank

I have heard plenty of stories from industry about improvements in TripAdvisor rank correlating with more bookings. In our research, TripAdvisor rank was marginally influential only for leisure travelers, and only when it was high. However, in our studies, we specifically looked at the end of the search process, when consumers had presumably already narrowed their choices down to a final set. TripAdvisor rank likely plays a different role earlier in the search process.

There are two aspects of TripAdvisor rank—the absolute number itself and the positioning that the rank gives you in search results. In our study, we just presented the number (x out of 217 in the market). Consumers may not be focused on the number itself, but being higher on TripAdvisor gets you noticed more because you will show up sooner in the search results. There has been plenty of research on how many pages consumers will search through before making a decision, and it isn't many. Despite what our results say, I'd still recommend working to get the best rank on TripAdvisor that you can so that you show up as early as possible in the search. Consumers may not use this information to assess value, but they may use it to find the hotel to begin with. See the revenue management perspectives section at the end of this chapter for more discussion on this.

Number of Reviews

I have seen a study that shows that consumer confidence increases with the number of reviews (Park, Lee, and Han 2007). Consumers "believe" the UGC more when there is more of it. I would definitely recommend that hotels work to increase the number of reviews posted across all types of review sites. According to Brian Payea from TripAdvisor, whom I interviewed in the perspective section, more of recent reviews also help to improve your rank.

There is one exception to this. I saw one study where increased number of reviews actually had a negative relationship with RevPAR at the luxury level only. The researchers hypothesized that as the number of reviews increased for luxury properties, the perceptions of exclusivity decreased, which left some consumers thinking "I don't want to pay this much to stay where everyone is staying" (Blal and Sturman 2014). Their study showed that the volume of reviews had a greater effect at the lower end of the market, whereas the valence (positive/negative) had a greater impact at the luxury end.

Quality of Reviews

I have seen some research indicating that consumers "trust" a review more if the review quality (length, grammar, etc.) is good (Pan and Zhang 2011). While there isn't much that a hotel can do about this, you can feel secure that a badly written, negative review will not be as impactful as a well-written positive review.

Images

An exploratory research project into the consumer research and booking process uncovered the importance of images in consumer decision making (Noone and Robson 2014; Robson and Noone 2014). In a leisure context, using eye-tracking software and retrospective think-aloud interviews, these researchers found that images may constitute an influential attribute in attracting consumers to making a hotel purchase.

CONCLUSIONS FROM THIS RESEARCH

Pricing has not gotten any easier in the past few years. Increasing influence of nonprice information on the pricing decisions means that revenue managers must pay attention not only to their price and the competitors' price, but also their reputation as compared to the market. They also need to consider the business mix and their market strategy. Of course, the challenge here is that reputation is not directly under the control of the hotel—despite some ability to manipulate certain elements—or just to delivery of good service with a quality product. Revenue managers should take the following conclusions from this research:

1. **Revenue managers need to carefully evaluate pricing opportunities.** If your hotel has positive UGC, it would be easy to interpret the research findings as a license to raise price. While our research, and that of others, supports a relationship between positive UGC and pricing power, raising price may not be the best answer for an individual hotel. Instead, revenue managers should consider their market position and their long-term business strategy and goals. Are you at the same "reputation position" as your competitors? Are there loyalty implications to a price change? How does the price change affect the brand strategy? Does the hotel have a market share strategy it's trying to execute? How would a price increase influence plans for qualified business?

2. **Revenue managers need to have a sound understanding of their own price, demand, reputation, and value proposition—and that of the competition.** Some of the data we included in this study is not traditionally tracked or stored by the revenue management department or by revenue management systems (although this is changing). With all of the new factors that can influence demand patterns and consumer reaction to price, **revenue managers must begin to collaborate with counterparts in other departments like marketing and operations** (as I discuss in Chapter 5, "Integrated Revenue Management and Marketing"). Revenue managers should take an active role not just in setting prices, but also in determining how those prices are presented to the consumer as part of the overall value proposition of the hotel stay (I will talk a bit more about this in Chapter 8, "The Path to Personalization").

There is more work to be done to gain a complete understanding of the mechanisms that underlie consumer buying behavior in today's social world. Our research was conducted in the U.S. market only, so there may be regional, cultural, or geographic differences. Most researchers are addressing either the leisure or business traveler markets, so meeting planners, groups or wholesalers might react differently as well. All of these recommendations should be taken in context and carefully considered in light of the market opportunities.

It is clear that competing on price alone is not an effective strategy for hotels that want to continue to boost revenue and share. Consumers are turning to user-generated content, and reviews in particular, to inform their hotel purchase decisions. To compete effectively, hoteliers must understand how their prices and reputations compare to the competitive set, focusing on review sentiment. Segment mix must also be considered, and everything evaluated in the light of the hotel's overall business strategy. In an era of value transparency, hotels simply must understand their value proposition from the consumer perspective.

REPUTATION AND REVENUE MANAGEMENT SYSTEMS

The evidence in the studies described earlier provides a strong suggestion that reputation should be considered in the tactical day-to-day pricing decision generated by the revenue management system. In fact, most of the revenue management vendors in today's market are exploring this opportunity. While incorporating these metrics into pricing and revenue management algorithms seems very logical, there are challenges associated with this, as with any new data source. I describe these challenges and leave it to you to determine whether you, or your chosen vendor, are approaching this in the right way.

Challenge 1: Understanding Where the Data Comes From

Many revenue management vendors have chosen to approach the data problem by forming partnerships with the major reputation vendors in the market and incorporating those vendors' metrics into the revenue management system. Presumably, reputation vendors have become experts at understanding this kind of data, and incorporating data from the same system marketing is using for reputation analysis ensures internal consistency between departments. However, there are some challenges with this approach.

First, the data itself is challenging. The hotel revenue management problem is by its nature a structured problem. Therefore, any data that is incorporated into the problem needs to be structured according to the problem formulation. Reputation data, and in particular, review data, is unstructured. Therefore, some structure must be imposed before it can be used in the revenue management algorithms. Ratings data is easier to structure, as it is a quantitative measure, but as we've seen from this chapter, it is not the most influential piece of user-generated content. Therefore, it is important to consider what type of data is being gathered to assess reputation and how that data is being analyzed. The quality of the output will be only as good as the quality of the input, as with any other analysis.

Second, analytic results can always be tuned to the conditions of the business problems they are designed to address. Remember that, in general, reputation management systems have been designed to identify problem areas and opportunities for improvement. These systems are more effective when the analytics are tuned to be "critical" of review sentiment, and "nitpick" issues from the reviews. After all, if they didn't identify any problems for the hotel to address, what value would they provide? While this is well suited for operations, the sentiment output might not reflect the actual impact on value perceptions that influence a consumer's likelihood to purchase the hotel. Over time, the revenue management system should be able to learn from, and adjust to, this impact, but it is worth thinking about whether the reputation metrics that are being fed into the revenue management system are truly reflective of the impact on a buying decision.

One aspect of this problem that I have found interesting to think about is consumer reactions to review content. The attributes that we studied in terms of content were not impactful on value perceptions (physical property versus service). However, there might be certain clues that could turn off a reader, even in a positive review. For example, the statement "my kids loved the pool" is great for a family reading the review, but perhaps not for a couple looking for a romantic getaway or for a solo traveler wanting some peace and quiet. This is an example where positive reviews, but with the wrong target market (or at the wrong time of year), will actually not result in increased bookings or pricing power. Hotels have an interesting opportunity to mine the content of the reviews for segment-level value discussions, and then leverage this information in marketing and pricing efforts. I hope to see more of this as hotels become more sophisticated in their use of text analytics.

Challenge 2: Making Apples to Apples Comparisons

As with any new data source, it is crucially important to understand how the new data relates to the existing data and ensure it matches appropriately. Remember that reputation data today influences bookings across the booking horizon into the future. Today's performance data, RevPAR, Occupancy, and ADR are the result of decisions made in the past up to last night. It is not appropriate to correlate "today's" reputation with "today's" performance. At a more macro level, it is perhaps all right to do this (year-over-year comparisons, for example), but the influence happens at the point of booking, not at the point of stay, which is when performance metrics are calculated.

This presents an important challenge when calculating the impact of reputation on lodging performance, but also when incorporating reputation metrics into a revenue management decision. Even if you feed the reputation metrics into the system today, calculate pricing, and push them out for tomorrow and the rest of the booking horizon, if reputation is updated (and evaluated by potential bookers) in real time, reputation changes over the period until the next price recalculation could impact consumer decisions. This "real-time" aspect of reviews and ratings will always challenge accurate reputation-based pricing.

Consumers evaluate value by comparing a hotel to available options in the market (the elusive competitive set). This means that the hotel needs to be collecting pricing and reputation metrics for the entire competitive set (and has defined the right competitive set, which we have already established can be a problem). I have found that the competitive set that revenue management has defined as influencing pricing decisions is not always exactly the same set that marketing is evaluating in terms of the reputation management system. If metrics managed by a different department are to be incorporated into the revenue management system, all departments need to work together to define the competitive set.

Challenge 3: Deciding on Tactical versus Strategic Usage

The last element to consider is the appropriate place for reputation metrics. Clearly, if consumers are using these metrics to make buying decisions, they belong somewhere in the revenue management process. Something as simple as plotting reputation versus pricing for you and the competitive set on a quadrant graph can be very illuminating to identify opportunities to adjust your pricing strategy based on your position in the market (Figure 4.11).

The tactical, day-to-day decision of what price to charge is a different analysis. For the math to work such that you would change your pricing decision, the reputation of the hotels in the market must change with enough frequency and complexity to warrant incorporating this metric into the pricing decision. If changes to reputation metrics are relatively constant over time, you are just adding a constant to the equation that probably doesn't change the answer.

We have to start somewhere, and I am encouraged to see all of the experimentation that's happening in this area. I suspect, however, that at some point the more advanced revenue management vendors will build their own text analytics to derive an "RM" appropriate sentiment analysis, purpose-built for the pricing algorithm. Alternatively, the reputation vendors may expand the scope of the problems they solve, and address this issue themselves. In the meantime, with appropriate caution for appreciating the unique characteristics of this problem, it is important to keep working with what we have today. I suspect that of all the chapters in this book, this one will become dated the fastest! To help you get started thinking about how to incorporate reputation data in your decision making, I've included a framework for decision

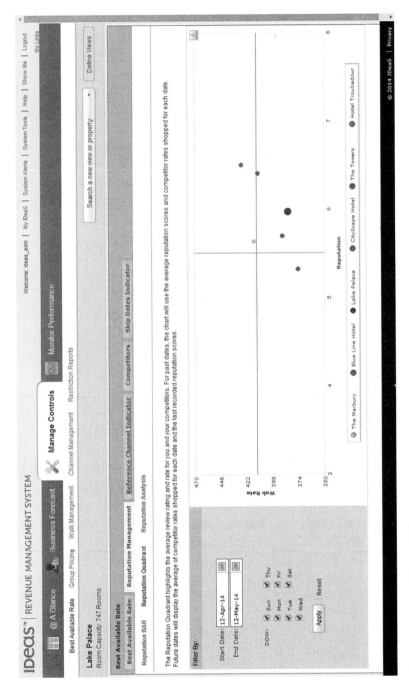

Figure 4.11 Reputation and Price.

Our hotel is Lake Palace, the largest dot in the lower right quadrant. This graph plots reputation score versus price. The lines represent the average price and reputation in the market. Given the reputation position of our hotel, it appears as though we have the opportunity to be more aggressive on our rates for this period. This screen shot is taken from the Reputation Management Module from IDeaS G2 RMS™.

making and some practical tips to guide your thinking about how to identify opportunities to incorporate social data and social channels in your existing analyses. You can find this in the appendix.

REPUTATION AND REVENUE AT LOEWS HOTELS

CASE STUDY

Loews Hotels & Resorts is a midsize hotel chain that operates 23 hotels in the United States and Canada, mostly in city centers and resort destinations. Loews is an upscale chain and tends to compete for both leisure and business travel with the higher-end brands from major U.S. chains as well as the luxury independents.

Monica Xuereb, Chief Revenue Officer, recognizes that her hotels are all located in highly competitive markets, frequently crowded by big brands with robust loyalty programs. "We have an excellent product at Loews, and we strive to provide excellent customer service and maintain high levels of satisfaction. However, we are a smaller, lesser-known brand compared to some of our nationally branded competitors. Research has proven time and time again what a significant impact a positive hotel review versus a negative can have on the guest decision. Considering how smaller brands have a hard time competing against strong loyalty programs from the bigger brands, online reputation can level the playing field."

Loews actively monitors online reputation at all of its properties using ReviewPro, which publishes the Guest Review Index, or GRI. Monica recognized an opportunity to enhance revenue management decision making when she was asked to be a charter customer on the IDeaS Reputation Influenced Pricing Module, which incorporates reputation into the pricing algorithms.

"I think it's important for us to step out of our revenue management roles and look at pricing through the eyes of the customer. The customer doesn't really care what our budgets or our forecasts are. They don't really care what the hotel's demand is. They just really care about the price that they want to pay and what they expect to get for that price," she says.

A large majority of Loews Hotels & Resorts perform very well in the GRI and Loews found that several of their hotels were potentially underpricing themselves when online reputation metrics were taken into account. "The teams that drive the revenue strategy became more confident pushing higher rates because they easily correlate our positioning against our competitor hotels in both reputation and price. At a number of hotels, when prices were raised, we maintained our GRI and drove higher revenues."

Because the revenue management team has been paying closer attention to reputation impacts on pricing, Monica has noticed that the team is more comfortable when they need to get more aggressive with retail pricing. "We have vital and relevant reputation information to verify our pricing decisions, right in the system that the revenue managers use every day. Research has indicated that consumers value reputation when they are assessing value, and we see that as an opportunity to drive our financial performance," she says.

CONCLUSION

Today's social world introduces a whole new set of challenges and opportunities for revenue management. While all of the impacts are not well understood quite yet, it is clear that revenue management needs to be paying attention to more than just their price relative to the competition. A hotel's reputation is equally, if not more, influential in the consumer decision-making process. Leaving this valuable piece of the equation out will result in a missed opportunity, and likely have a huge revenue impact.

Until recently, reputation management, monitoring, and responding to reviews, understanding branding implications and engaging guests through social channels was considered to be squarely the responsibility of the marketing department. As discussed in this chapter, there are broader implications. In fact, reputation is not the only information held by marketing that could benefit revenue management decision making. Particularly after the economic downturn in 2008, hotels have begun to realize that the demand generation activities traditionally the responsibility of marketing need to be better synchronized with the demand control activities associated with revenue management. In the next chapter, I talk about the benefits of integrating revenue management and marketing decision making, so that, much like with reputation data, the hotel as a whole can benefit from thinking holistically about the data and analytics overseen by these two departments.

ADDITIONAL READING

C. K. Anderson, "The Impact of Social Media on Lodging Performance," *Cornell Hospitality Report,* 12, no. 15 (2012): 4–11.

B. Noone, K. McGuire, and K. Rohlfs, "Social Media Meets Hotel Revenue Management: Opportunities, Issues and Unanswered Questions," *Journal of Revenue and Pricing Management,* 10 (2011): 293–305. Published online May 6, 2011.

Video of the researchers presenting the choice modeling study: http://blogs.sas.com/content/hospitality/2014/10/06/chrs_pricingsocial.

REVENUE MANAGEMENT PERSPECTIVES: A CASE FOR TRIPADVISOR RANK

Despite the results of our research that seem to indicate that TripAdvisor rank is not very influential for leisure travelers' choice and value perceptions, and not at all influential for business travelers, many revenue managers I have talked to have seen significant increases in high-value bookings as their hotel TripAdvisor rank increases. As I described earlier, I think that TripAdvisor rank is much more impactful than just the number that we tested in our study. I reconcile the conflicting results from my study with the stories I heard from revenue managers in two ways:

1. TripAdvisor rank determines where your hotel shows up on the search page. Research has shown that the higher your hotel appears in the search rankings, the more likely consumers are to notice it and book.

2. Our studies were conducted at the point of purchase, as opposed to the research phase. It is possible that consumers use TripAdvisor to narrow down their options during the research

phase, but when they are selecting which hotel to book among a fixed set of choices, this metric becomes less important.

To validate my thinking, I spoke to a hotelier who has experimented with TripAdvisor rank and I also got a perspective from TripAdvisor. Their responses follow.

Stefan Wolf, Senior Vice President, Revenue and Distribution Strategy, Onyx Hospitality Group

Onyx Hospitality Group is an Asian hotel management company offering a wide portfolio of hospitality brands, including the luxury Saffron portfolio, the market-leading Amari brand of hotels and resorts, Shama, serviced apartments and the all-new select service OZO.

I spoke with Stefan Wolf of Onyx Hospitality Group about how he leverages TripAdvisor in his overall pricing strategy. A few years ago, Stefan did an interview with Eye for Travel where he provided a case study in which he talked about the impact of a strategy to improve TripAdvisor rank they deployed at one of the independents they manage in Bangkok (www.eyefortravel.com/social-media-and-marketing/revenue-management-and-reviews-perfect-match-pricing-it-right). They took the hotel, which had just opened, from last to first in TripAdvisor in six months, and generated a good deal of incremental revenue along the way. This case study became the inspiration and justification for us including TripAdvisor rank as an attribute in our study.

Onyx's portfolio competes with global brands and the well-known regional brands in Asia. Particularly with their independents, TripAdvisor rank is a good way for Onyx properties to get noticed by consumers and compete against the larger marketing budgets and greater reach of the bigger brands.

Stefan told me that they are continuing to work to maintain and improve their TripAdvisor rank. "TripAdvisor ranking in view of price optimization continues to be a topic of discussion in our weekly revenue strategy meetings," he told me. One interesting outcome of the focus on TripAdvisor rank, as they have continued with this program, is access to new and diversified markets. "For the Oriental Residence in Bangkok, we have seen an improvement in performance for the U.S. market via various channels including the GDS (global distribution system). The property did not engage in any kind of marketing activity in that particular market, so we assume that it was TripAdvisor rank that is generating this increased interest from this new market."

Of course, I was interested to know if they felt like they had more pricing power as the TripAdvisor rank increased. From the case study in the Eye for Travel article, once the hotel was ranked between one and three in the market, they could increase price without sacrificing occupancy. This result comes with a very important caution from Stefan: "It should be noted that price elasticity can be influenced by TripAdvisor rating, but only to a certain degree. If the value proposition drops below a certain point because the price becomes 'too high' from a guest perspective consumers would look for alternatives despite a very high TripAdvisor ranking." It is really important for hoteliers to keep this in mind. According to my research, consumers always prefer to pay a lower price, so good performance on nonprice measures can only go so far.

So, for Stefan's hotels, improving TripAdvisor rank is a strategy that results in increased bookings and drives revenue for the hotel—which sounds very much like a revenue management mandate. However, achieving this higher rank is not at all under the control of revenue management. Operations has to deliver an excellent guest experience and guests need to be encouraged to write about it. This requires coordination across functional areas and between corporate and the properties. I asked Stefan how he worked with operations to ensure they were buying into the TripAdvisor rank program.

He told me that the operations team are a part of the revenue strategy meetings, where the strong correlation between TripAdvisor rank and performance was discussed. This was compelling to operations, and the revenue director made sure to point out that only with collaboration from operations would the hotel be able to keep the ranking high and continue to benefit financially.

Interestingly, understanding the relationship between TripAdvisor rank and performance was enough to continue to motivate the operations teams to focus on the service execution that keeps reviews good and rank high. Stefan does see the benefit of providing direct incentives to the overall operations team that are associated with maintaining TripAdvisor rank.

It would seem from Stefan's experience that a hotel-wide initiative to get and maintain a high TripAdvisor rank does result in improved revenue performance, and can even drive business from new or alternative sources, even without the support of a broader marketing initiative. In order to achieve this, operations must be brought on board, but if they are made part of the analysis and decision making, it's not hard to achieve their buy-in.

Brian Payea, Head of Industry Relations, TripAdvisor

TripAdvisor is the world's largest travel site, enabling travelers to plan and book the perfect trip. TripAdvisor offers advice from millions of travelers and a wide variety of travel choices and planning features with seamless links to booking tools that check hundreds of websites to find the best hotel prices. TripAdvisor-branded sites make up the largest travel community in the world, reaching 340 million unique monthly visitors and more than 225 million reviews and opinions covering more than 4.9 million accommodations, restaurants, and attractions. The sites operate in 45 countries worldwide. TripAdvisor also includes TripAdvisor for Business, a dedicated division that provides the tourism industry access to millions of monthly TripAdvisor visitors.

Based on your experience with your hotel partners, how important do you think rank on TripAdvisor is for the hotel to get noticed and drive bookings?

Ranking is a reflection of guest satisfaction and has an important impact on the size of the audience that will engage with a hotel's listing. For many years, the TripAdvisor Popularity Index has provided travelers with a ranking of popular hotels based on the quality, quantity, and recency of reviews on the site. Our Popularity Index is incredibly powerful in recognizing properties that deliver great hospitality experiences according to the wisdom of the crowds. But the hotels that are at the top of the list may or may not be the best hotel for a particular trip for a variety of reasons—such as budget, location, hotel style, availability, or amenities. So in October 2014, we launched a personalized hotel ranking called Just for You as our default setting to help each user find the ideal hotel for their individual preferences and needs that they selected. The Popularity Index is still relevant—it helps users understand the relative ranking of each hotel—while Just for You helps narrow the consideration set to the best properties that are right for you.

What are some strategies you have seen hotels employ that have helped them to improve rank?

To improve ranking on TripAdvisor, the absolutely most important tactic is delivering a great guest experience. A hotel manager also wants to ensure that he or she is setting the guest expectations accurately, to allow for the outstanding reviews that result from an experience that exceeds expectations. If you oversell your property and can't live up to expectations, then it's very difficult to "wow" a guest. Be transparent, then wow the guest, then ask for the review. It's the process we've seen when we talk to hoteliers around the world who've done very well on TripAdvisor.

How is TripAdvisor rank calculated? Are there certain types of reviews or feedback that hotels should be focusing on to improve their scores?

The TripAdvisor Popularity Index dynamically ranks hospitality businesses worldwide based on the popularity of a given business, as measured by factors such as the quality, quantity, and recency of the reviews written about the property on TripAdvisor. The exact calculation or algorithm is confidential, but properties can help improve their ranking by delivering a fantastic guest experience and requesting reviews from their recent guests to ensure that prospective guests have fresh content to use in their evaluation.

As for our Just for You feature, we leverage a number of different approaches to deliver personalization, including TripAdvisor research history, proprietary algorithms, and users' preference inputs. No one of these technologies individually is the key to personalized results, but together they combine to deliver a set of hotel recommendations tailored to a user based on their past preferences and current travel needs.

Many hotels spend a good deal of time responding to reviews on TripAdvisor. What is your advice in this area? How important do you think responding to reviews is in terms of consumer perceptions?

Data from surveys, and from empirical analysis, absolutely show a correlation between management responses and guest satisfaction. Well-done management responses demonstrate the level of hospitality a prospective guest can expect at the property, and, importantly, also give reassurance that any negative experiences described in earlier reviews will not be repeated in a future stay. Management responses that do not provide reassurance, that are merely "checking a box," are unlikely to have that same positive impact. If you are going to do it, it's best to do it well. The key is to make responding to traveler reviews a habit and to respond to both negative and positive reviews. This shows travelers that the hotelier cares about guest service.

What new travel technology innovation are you keeping your eye on? What upcoming technology trend do you think will have the biggest impact on the travel industry and how should we be preparing to deal with it?

Travel technology innovations continue to accelerate. Interesting trends to watch are growth in mobile usage and all the benefits and challenges that come with that, as well as the ability to deliver a much more personalized recommendation, such as the "Just for You" sort I mentioned earlier.

CHAPTER 5

Integrating Revenue Management and Marketing*

Integrating revenue management and marketing is a logical step toward the ultimate goal of an integrated revenue culture. Remember the early days of revenue management? We had to work closely with reservations and front desk to ensure they understood to the importance of executing our pricing, overbooking, and restriction decisions. We need to keep moving through all the functions within the hotel to ensure everyone is aligned with the goal of driving profitable revenue.

—Neal Fegan, Executive Director, Revenue Management, FRHI Hotels and Resorts

From the previous chapter on reputation and price, it is clear that the lines between revenue management and marketing are blurring. As consumers become increasingly empowered throughout the buying process, revenue management can no longer ignore the consumer when calculating and deploying price. This means developing a closer relationship with counterparts in the marketing organization.

At times, the disciplines of revenue management and marketing have seemed diametrically opposed. Traditionally, revenue management has been responsible for demand control through setting rate and availability controls. They own the rooms' inventory and hold information about price sensitivity and demand by property, market segment, date, and rates. They know when and where demand is expected and needed. Marketing, on the other hand, has been responsible for demand generation, including campaign strategies, guest relationship management, and loyalty programs. They own the guest, and hold information about preferences, purchase behavior, and guest value. They know who the guest is and what offers they are most likely to respond to. Revenue management complains that marketing dilutes revenue by generating too much demand from discount promotions. Marketing complains that revenue management's overly restrictive rate and availability controls are keeping out their best guests.

Thinking holistically, it could be said that revenue management and marketing are really two sides of the same coin. Each department holds key pieces of information about demand that, when integrated, result in critical insight about demand patterns, product preferences, and purchase behavior. Unfortunately, as described earlier, due to misaligned goals and poor communication, employees in these two closely related functions do not always work well together. Acting with the best of intentions, marketers, with a goal of generating demand, send out discount promotions that dilute rates during peak periods. Meanwhile, revenue managers, trying to maximize revenue, close off promotional rates meant to encourage stays from the most loyal guests. These conflicting activities damage revenue performance and guest relationships.

During the economic downturn that started in 2008, traditional playbooks were thrown out the window. Without excess demand to control, all departments in the hotel were forced toward demand generation, working closely to understand where demand could be sourced and building pricing strategies designed to encourage bookings (or at least that's what should have happened). Weekly demand planning meetings, where marketers and revenue managers sit down to strategize, became the norm for many hotels. This type of communication is equally important during good times. When demand is high, it is important that all functions across the hotel protect rates from dilution from misplaced promotions or unnecessary discounts.

The role of the revenue manager is evolving from tactical inventory management to a more strategic demand management focus. As this evolution happens, marketing data and analytics become even more critical to maximizing revenue while maintaining price and value position in the market. Whether taking a longer-term view or trying to generate shorter-term demand, the complexity of the market makes manual processes and waiting for a weekly meeting unsustainable. These two departments must regularly share key information. Both functions need access to critical information held by the other to make routine decisions independently, so that meetings can be reserved for deeper discussions. This ultimately will require the hotel to move toward an automated, integrated environment, where data is shared efficiently in the formats and level of detail dictated by the business function, and analytics from one department are influenced automatically by the actions of the other.

It is not news to hoteliers that there are advantages to revenue management and marketing working more closely together. When decisions are synchronized, more revenue opportunities are uncovered. As an industry, we've been talking about opportunities in this area for a while, and with the growing focus on digital marketing and personalization initiatives, it's only become more important for these two groups to work together. Technology can be the glue that binds these departments together, but technology alone will not solve this problem. Organizations need to realign their goals, incentives, and organizational structures to encourage this level of integrated thinking.

In this chapter, I talk about emerging opportunities to synchronize demand generation and demand control activities with the goal of driving more profitable revenue through intelligent demand management. As digital marketing initiatives expand and hotels consider how to leverage digital data and channels to improve the guest experience, the tight integration of revenue management and marketing will ensure that these initiatives are executed profitably. I discuss this further in Chapter 8, where I talk about how revenue management should participate in personalization initiatives.

A VISION FOR INTEGRATED MARKETING AND REVENUE MANAGEMENT

The idea of integrating decisions from the revenue management and marketing departments is not new. Most hotels have organized weekly or monthly meetings to bring both sides to the table. But is that really enough? In today's fast-moving social world, weekly status meetings may not be sufficient. Instead of bringing spreadsheets to weekly meetings to trade routine information and compare notes, revenue managers and marketers need to be able to access the information they need, when they need it, in the systems they use every day, and in the format they prefer.

When routine decision making is automated, revenue managers and marketers can spend the weekly meetings working together to address events that require more rigorous analysis and carefully planned strategy.

LARGE ECONOMY HOTEL CHAIN

CASE STUDY

The revenue management department needed a mechanism to communicate demand patterns to the marketing department on a more regular basis than the weekly meeting. Revenue management wanted marketing to be able to design programs to generate demand during need periods. They started by sending over revenue management forecast reports with rows and columns of data. Marketing had a hard time interpreting the reports, and so they weren't really using them. The teams finally sat down together to determine what information marketing really needed, and what they didn't. After this discussion, the report was dramatically simplified to a bar chart with the number of rooms left to fill and the revenue management system's price recommendation. The bars were color coded based on thresholds set to correspond with the degree of need. The report was built in the company's business intelligence system so that marketing could access the report whenever they needed it.

"Working together on the report format was eye-opening for us. It was really interesting to learn how marketing looks at things. Now we work together much more efficiently in the weekly meetings, especially because we don't have to discuss the routine stuff anymore," says the vice president of revenue management.

In a truly integrated system, all decisions are synchronized through easy access to integrated data and analytics. Revenue management forecasts and pricing decisions are transmitted to campaign management, so better decisions can be made about the design, content, timing, and contact strategy of promotions. Guest analytics uncover which guests are most likely to respond to what kinds of offers, and marketing optimization algorithms select the best set of offers, prices, and contact lists that maximize the profitability of each campaign, while operating within the constraints of the revenue management forecast—protecting against dilution. The revenue management system incorporates promotional information into the demand forecast, improving accuracy and resulting in better pricing decisions. Consider the diagram in Figure 5.1, which describes this integrated vision for revenue management and marketing data and analytics.

Operating off a "single version of the truth" database with common definitions of key data points and metrics, four key capabilities unite by leveraging each area's data and analytics:

1. At the intersection of **customer analytics** and **revenue management**, the value of each known guest is combined with demand forecasts and optimal pricing recommendations for guest-centric pricing—a price that balances the value of the guest against the value of the inventory they wish to consume.

2. At the intersection of **revenue management** and **campaign management**, revenue management forecasts are incorporated into promotion planning so the promotions are placed in need periods, protecting the firm from dilution. Expected demand from campaigns is incorporated into the revenue management forecasts, improving forecast accuracy and pricing decisions.

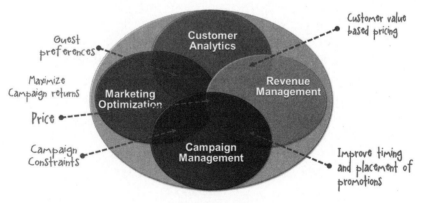

Figure 5.1 The Vision: Integrating for Better Decisions

3. At the intersection of **campaign management** and **marketing optimization**, available campaigns are compared with eligible guests in the database, generating a list for each campaign that will maximize overall response rates and revenue while respecting constraints like remaining rooms to sell and prevailing rates.

4. At the intersection of **marketing optimization** and **customer analytics**, the preferences of each guest are included in the promotion planning activities, respecting guests' expressed contact preferences and previous interests.

At the intersection of guest analytics, revenue management, marketing optimization, and marketing automation is intelligent demand management (Figure 5.2). At this intersection, campaigns are created that stimulate exactly the right amount of demand during need periods, ensuring that discounts do not drop below the expected value of the room inventory established by the revenue management system. These campaigns are sent to the guests most likely to respond, according to a contact plan that maximizes overall response rate and revenue goals (see also Anderson and Carroll 2007).

Figure 5.2 Intelligent Demand Management

This evolution can happen by establishing a common technology framework, where each department has access to the other's data and analytics in the solutions they use every day. However, technology alone will not suffice to bring these functions together. Deeper cultural and organizational changes will be required. Departmental goals and incentives need to be aligned. Business processes need to be defined across departmental silos and reporting structures adjusted to reduce conflict. The analytics culture grows as data-driven learning is encouraged by leaders across the organization. Any organizational change can be complicated, but the reward is better pricing decisions, ultimately leading to increased revenue and profits. While the organizational structure is being discussed and implemented, departments can get started with the process of integrating data and decisions. In the following sections, I describe the data and analytics each department uses, and how these analytics might be valuable to the other department.

LIMITATIONS OF THE REVENUE MANAGEMENT APPROACH

To identify the opportunities associated with integrating revenue management and marketing, it is important to first understand the goals, business processes, data, and analytics used by each department. Revenue management has traditionally been less concerned about who the individual guest is and more concerned about demand for the hotel rooms. The primary focus is careful analysis of demand patterns by location, date, room type, length of stay, segment, channel, and rate, as well as competitor price and positioning, which, taken together, provide a comprehensive view of demand. While this approach has resulted in increased revenue, there are some limitations that working more closely with marketing can help overcome.

Whether using the price sensitivity of demand to calculate optimal price or an inventory optimization model to set availability controls, revenue management carefully manages the limited capacity of hotel rooms in order to increase property-wide revenue and profits. Revenue management is also branching into other areas of the hotel, like function space and food and beverage (as I discuss in the next chapter). All of this activity is very much focused on the revenue-generating potential of the inventory, not the needs, preferences, or value of the guests. In the revenue management world, as long as a potential guest is willing to pay the rate determined to be "optimal" based on demand, revenue management doesn't care who they are or what their long-term relationship with the hotel might be.

Although this process has been very successful at maximizing revenue across the booking horizon, it is by nature a short-term view. When demand is strong and the hotel can afford to be choosy, it ensures that only the highest-value demand has access to the hotel rooms, and therefore, maximizes revenue. However, when demand weakens, or new competition enters the market, a strong, loyal customer base helps to sustain the hotel. Revenue management has been missing this perspective on sustainable, long-term revenue generation, with consideration for the characteristics of the guest segments.

Revenue management systems are very good at predicting demand levels and setting prices that can maximize the revenue potential of the demand to come. They do not provide recommendations of how to generate demand.

When comprehensive information about guest behavior (described later) is integrated with demand patterns and price sensitivity analysis from revenue management, proactive demand sourcing becomes a reality. Revenue managers and marketers working together can synchronize promotion and pricing decisions to increase overall revenue and profits. This results in a longer-term, sustainable revenue stream, as opposed to simply maximizing revenues in the short term.

> Understanding what would improve my value proposition by segment and geo source would allow a much more granular approach to revenue optimization. For example, if I knew that guests from my top performing market, traveling on leisure, place a higher value on upgrades versus breakfast, I could amend

my offers to reflect that. At the same or even a higher price, conversion would improve and more revenue would be generated from that market.

—*Stefan Wolf, Senior Vice President of Revenue and Distribution Strategy, Onyx Hospitality Group*

UNDERSTANDING MARKETING DATA AND ANALYTICS

Marketers collect and manage a robust set of information about guests (or hopefully they do!), typically through the hotel's loyalty program. This information includes stay patterns, booking channels, room types, demographics, on-property activities, travel purpose, and geographic preferences. Lately, marketers have also had access to social media and social network activity as guests begin to share their social credentials.

Once this information is collected, it contributes to advanced marketing analytics, including:

- **Microsegmentation** to identify statistically significant subsets of guests with similar preferences and purchase behavior: for example, eco-conscious families with children under 10 that travel in the summer and prefer to stay in the West or Southwest.

- **Market basket analysis** to identify "missing" products: for example, guests who stay with you as a business traveler but never for leisure.

- **Social network analysis** to find guests who influence other travelers' behavior: for example, every time a certain corporate guest stays at your property, he or she brings three other guests from the same company.

- **Likelihood to respond** provides the probability that a guest will respond to a certain offer, which helps marketing determine how much demand will be generated from which offers.

- **Lifetime value calculations** to identify the most valuable guests, and identify how to cultivate and grow that value over time.

- **Cross-sell/up-sell** to determine which add-ons or upgrades to offer to which guests.

INTEGRATING REVENUE MANAGEMENT AND MARKETING DECISIONS

Deep insight about guest behavior combined with strong analysis of demand patterns across the system provides the opportunity to:

- **Incorporate total guest value in the revenue management decision.** Optimize property-wide revenue by considering the total guest spend profile beyond the room rate (or gaming revenue).

- **Forecast promotion demand.** Incorporate expected lift from promotional activities into demand forecasts for an accurate picture of the impact of incentivizing demand.

- **Create dynamic packages.** Allow the guest to choose the elements of the package, and then price the entire package appropriately based on forecasted demand for all components. Suggest alternate times and dates, which would push demand to slower periods while providing a lower-cost option for the guest.

- **Next best offer.** While guests are exploring your website or speaking with your agents, using the guest profile and searching behavior combined with pricing from the revenue management system, you can encourage conversion by creating an offer designed just for them. For unknown guests, browsing behavior on the website compared with experience with similar guests can provide the basis for an offer that they are most likely to accept, at revenue management's revenue-maximizing price.

- **Cross-sell/up-sell.** Find opportunities to cross-sell or up-sell products based on guest preferences and the optimal price for those products based on demand.

Consider this scenario: Revenue management alerts marketing that demand is soft during weekends in February for leisure travelers for suites at the city center hotel in Philadelphia. The system has determined that up to a 20 percent discount off the weekend rate would still maximize revenue for those weekends. Marketing reacts by developing a promotion that targets guests who are likely to book at that price during that time period, and stimulates just enough demand to fill the empty rooms. Promotional details are sent back to the revenue management system, which automatically incorporates the expected lift into the revenue management forecast.

Without accurate intelligence from each department, this scenario is not possible. Working together, marketing and revenue management can transform the organization from reactive to proactive, forming deep and lasting relationships with guests while maximizing property-wide profits.

INCORPORATING CUSTOMER VALUE INTO THE RM DECISION

CASE STUDY

Hotels can look to casino companies for inspiration on how to incorporate customer value into the pricing decision. For casinos, the largest and most profitable revenue source is the gaming floor. Casino managers use the other outlets, including the rooms, to drive revenue on the casino floor, through discounting and other special promotions. Player loyalty cards help casinos track patron play behavior, and this information is used to calculate theoretical player value—the patrons' expected spend per visit. Casino managers use that player value to assess how the patron qualifies for promotions and offers. The goal is to profitably incentivize patrons to come and spend more at the casino.

"We make the most money when no one is paying for a room. If we've done it right, the casino is full of our highest-value gamers, spending on the casino floor," says the vice president of revenue management for a major U.S. casino company.

Casino revenue management follows a slightly different process from hotel revenue management. Casinos segment their known gamers based on their predicted value, and forecast demand by these gaming segments along with the other segments of "unknown" patrons, which include retail and group demand. This forecast by segment is then used for two purposes: determining what level of discount to offer each known patron segment, and setting the retail rate for the rooms.

There are a couple of different ways that current revenue management systems handle this in the forecast and optimization. As you could imagine, some segments get huge discounts or even complimentary rooms. The room rate for these segments is artificially low, so using those rates as a forecast rate segment would discriminate against rather than reward that segment. To account for this, the revenue management system supplements the gaming segments with their player value as an input to the optimization.

Following the optimization, either the optimization outputs are matched to a rate plan that provides the appropriate discounts by gaming segment, or the selling system uses the *threshold price* from the RM system output to derive the per-patron rate (Metters et al. 2008). The threshold price, or hurdle rate, is an output from the optimization. It represents the value of the hotel having one additional room to sell, and therefore is the minimum that the hotel should accept for a room. When a patron calls to reserve a room, if they are a known player, the system subtracts the hurdle rate from their forecasted player value. The amount remaining is the rate they pay. If their player value is higher than the threshold rate, the room is free. Unknown patrons are quoted the BAR or retail rate derived by the RM system. This pricing method works because known gamers book through private channels, like behind a login on the website, call center, or hosts, so no rate parity or fairness perceptions are violated.

Most recently, casinos are attempting to build a 360-degree view of patron value. They are aggregating patron spend across the organization and augmenting the patron's gaming value with their nongaming spend. Obviously, the revenue streams have to be adjusted for contribution, as not all revenue streams have the same profit margin. This value is then incorporated into the forecast and optimization the same way that the gaming value is used.

One of the downsides to rewarding patron spend this way is that casino patrons become trained to expect discounted or free rooms. This became particularly problematic during the recent economic downturn, when casinos were struggling to attract any demand by deeply discounting rooms or offering other services at drastically reduced rates. The deep discount offered over time became the patron's reference price (I discuss this

(*Continued*)

> **(*Continued*)**
>
> further in Chapter 7), and it was difficult to recover price when demand recovered. A better understanding of price sensitivity by casino segment will help casinos generate additional incremental revenue, while reducing the negative impact of consistent deep discounting.

ACHIEVING THE VISION

The intelligent demand management vision is achievable in small steps. Ensuring that the foundational technologies are available, and utilized, by each department provides short-term benefits. Automated exchange of key data (even without analytics) gets each group used to working with the other's data before it is incorporated into the analytics. This data share also facilitates communication between the groups, and helps to break down organizational and cultural boundaries. Small steps in analytics can be taken as well. Start with incorporating expected response rates to promotions in the revenue management forecast, for example.

Technology can be the glue that binds departments together, but, while a well-planned technology strategy is essential, it is only an enabler. Goals and incentives need to be aligned, and there must be buy-in from everyone from top corporate executives to property level analysts. The best way to obtain buy-in is to demonstrate success. Success doesn't have to mean sweeping change, but it does need to be significant enough to demonstrate potential.

To get your hotel started, build a cross-functional task force:

1. Select motivated and open-minded folks from the revenue management and marketing departments.
2. Ask these representatives to share their daily activities so they can better understand the details of each other's jobs.
3. Have the team investigate the available data and metrics from each department. Determine what data should be shared, align

metric definitions to improve communication, and identify missing information.

4. Ensure the team evaluates business processes and the technology you are using to support them. Determine whether you are leveraging all available functionality, and build a business case for augmenting where necessary.

A carefully planned, phased approach to a technology implementation ensures success (Figure 5.3). Think of a four-step process:

1. First, **establish** enabling technologies and evaluate the organizational structure. If you don't have a revenue management system or marketing analytics, this is the phase to implement them and get the departmental users comfortable with the system and the output. Meanwhile, the organization needs to identify any potential blocks caused by the organizational structure, like misaligned incentives or reporting structures that create conflicts with marketing and revenue management working together.

2. Next, in the **integrate phase**, there is a period of manual exchange of data between departments. Users get used to the format and impact of data from other departments. They understand where and how to incorporate it into their business process and become comfortable with how the results look. This is the phase in which organizational and cultural changes can be put in place to facilitate a more automated process.

3. After that comes the **optimize phase**, where automation adds speed and accuracy to decisions. Departmental decision making is synchronized, based on a common platform of data and analytic processes.

Figure 5.3 A Phased Approach to Integrated Marketing and Revenue Management

4. Finally, at the **innovate phase**, once the decision making is automated and synchronized, it's time to incorporate new data sources or launch new initiatives (which may then return you to the establish phase).

Following a process like this ensures buy-in from the organization and a sustainable business process moving forward. Most important, careful integration of these two departments should help you move the hotel away from out-of-sync demand generation and demand control efforts and toward intelligent demand management.

CASE STUDY

MARKETING AND REVENUE MANAGEMENT AT LAS VEGAS SANDS

Las Vegas Sands is a casino and resort operating company based in Nevada. They operate large integrated resorts worldwide, with two properties in Las Vegas (the Venetian and the Palazzo), one in Bethlehem, Pennsylvania (Sands Resort Bethlehem), the Marina Bay Sands in Singapore, and the Venetian Macao, the Sands Macao, and the Sands Cotai Central development in Macao. This portfolio consists of more than 17,000 rooms and millions of square feet of retail and meeting space.

"Our business is very complex. We need to balance demand from casino players with retail and group business, thinking about the impact not only on room revenue, but also revenue from the casino floor and the function space. The bottom line is that we need to fill thousands of rooms at each property, profitably, every night," says Mark Molinari, Corporate Vice President of Revenue Management and Distribution. "If we didn't work closely with our counterparts in marketing and sales, we'd never get that done."

Las Vegas Sands was one of the first companies to recognize that the crucial step to getting marketing and revenue management to work more closely together was to ensure that the organizational structure and incentives were aligned. Corporate revenue management and marketing report to the global chief marketing officer (CMO). This greatly facilitates synchronized decision making.

"At every property, revenue management knows exactly how many rooms are left to sell over the booking horizon, and we sit down with marketing to figure out how we are going to accomplish that. Marketing learns when our busy periods are, and understands to preserve revenue during those times. This is much easier to do when we aren't working against conflicting performance metrics or departmental goals. We communicate often with casino marketing to understand how the casino blocks are performing and work closely with sales for function demand. The point is, the entire team needs to communicate for this to happen profitably," says Mark.

His prediction? "Today, revenue managers often have a seat in the marketing meetings and are helping to develop promotions, packages, and offers. In the future, the line between revenue management and marketing will become more blurred. Revenue managers are more frequently becoming involved in all areas of distribution, including group sales, OTA and tour operator sales, and ecommerce. They are working with sales to negotiate contracts, and working with marketing on developing strategy. Because of their exposure to sales and distribution, it's likely that many of today's revenue managers will become tomorrow's CMOs."

A WORD OF CAUTION

There will be significant organization and cultural changes required to achieve this vision. Departmental incentives will have to be aligned, and reporting structures may need to be adjusted. Marketers and revenue managers will need to get used to working with new data types and data sources. A cross-functional team will need to be organized both at the property level and at corporate. As these two functions become more tightly integrated, it is important not to lose sight of the core skill set of each resource at the table, particularly the unique perspective revenue management provides.

Revenue managers understand how market conditions, buying behavior, channel management decisions, marketing initiatives and operational factors impact customer value perceptions, and ultimately, pricing power. The job is getting more complex with more moving pieces. Revenue managers are crossing over into areas that were more traditionally managed and controlled by marketing, and they are having to collaborate with their counterparts in marketing or operations at a much closer level than ever before.

Despite this evolution in scope and responsibilities, revenue managers must never lose sight of their core competencies and primary charter. Someone within the organization needs to understand demand patterns and pricing strategies at a detailed level. When strategic pricing decisions are made that trade short-term revenue generation in favor of longer-term revenue potential, someone in the organization needs to analyze the tradeoff and help the group make an informed decision. When marketing initiatives are designed, someone needs to understand where and when that demand is needed and ensure that the promotion does not dilute revenue.

It is tempting to get distracted by the latest innovation or high-impact trend. Whether it's Google Analytics or Social Media Management, analytical-minded revenue managers can get carried away with analysis that starts to stray farther away from the purpose of their investigation—to determine the impact on pricing decisions. I am not suggesting that revenue management ignore everything but traditional data, forecasts and optimization algorithms. In fact, learning about these emerging areas is beneficial not only to the organization, but also to an individual's career path. I am suggesting that revenue managers remember that they are best qualified to look at these emerging areas through the lens of their impact on pricing strategies.

In other words, organizations cannot afford to have their revenue managers become generalists, part ecommerce, part digital marketer, part salesperson, and part price manager, but not deep in any of these areas. Not that revenue management doesn't belong in broader conversations, but the role should always be to provide the pricing perspective, not to become just another marketer. I describe in more detail the skill set required for the revenue manager of the future in Chapter 9.

Organizational structures have evolved to facilitate communication between demand management departments. Many organizations are bringing together marketing, sales, and revenue management under a common reporting structure. I discuss that further in Chapter 9 as well.

The discipline of revenue management has evolved and will continue to evolve. As success is demonstrated, market conditions change and new techniques emerge, the role of the revenue manager will evolve as well. However, the core focus of building profitable pricing strategies should not change. Inputs and outputs will adjust, but the fundamental need to understand and represent demand patterns, customer value perceptions, competitive effects and market conditions remains constant. Be careful getting distracted away from tried and true by new and shiny!

CONCLUSION

There are significant advantages to revenue management and marketing working more closely together. Synchronizing decision making ensures that revenue is protected during peak periods and the right demand is stimulated when it is needed. Marketing has a view to the revenue- and profit-generating potential of the hotel rooms, and revenue management better understands the drivers of demand. This concept is a bit broader than simply "revenue management," so it should be thought of as "intelligent demand management," where the right demand is nurtured throughout the sales funnel, instead of focusing only at the base where demand is controlled by price (Anderson and Carroll 2007).

Achieving this vision will require organizational and cultural changes, in addition to a supporting technology infrastructure. Many hotel companies are starting down this path, particularly after the economic downturn of 2008, when there was no demand to control through price. I discuss some organizational options that facilitate a better working relationship between marketing and revenue management in Chapter 9, "The Revenue Manager of the Future."

In the next chapter I discuss the concept of total hotel revenue management, where all revenue streams are optimized to maximize the revenue and profits from the entire property, as opposed to just the rooms. At the core of this concept is the need to build a revenue-minded culture throughout the hotel. Bringing marketing and revenue management decision making closer together is one step on the path to this goal. Similarly, a revenue culture needs to be fostered throughout all of the revenue-generating assets in the hotel. When all of the supporting functions throughout the hotel understand the importance of driving profitable revenue, decisions can be made that are optimal for the entire enterprise.

As revenue management and marketing get used to working more closely together, it becomes easier to support other strategic initiatives that span departments and functions. For example, many hotel companies are embarking on personalization initiatives, which are designed to foster engagement, loyalty, and repeat business from a greater portion of potential guests by offering an experience that is more targeted at an individual's needs and preferences. This initiative involves a coordinated effort between revenue management, marketing, and operations to uncover and deliver service according to guest preferences, guest value and operational conditions. While driven by the marketing department, without the involvement of revenue management to ensure that demand patterns and pricing opportunities are included and without operations to ensure consistent delivery this initiative will not be successful. I discuss this in more detail in Chapter 8, "The Path to Personalization."

ADDITIONAL READING

C. Anderson and B. Carroll, "Demand Management: Beyond Revenue Management," *Journal of Revenue and Pricing Management,* 6 (2007): 260–263; doi: 10.1057/palgrave.rpm.5160092.

B. Noone, S. Kimes, and L. Renaghan, "Integrating Customer Relationship Management and Revenue Management: A Hotel Perspective," *Journal of Revenue and Pricing Management,* 2, no. 1 (2003): 7–21.

S. Pinchuk, "A System Profit Optimization," *Journal of Revenue and Pricing Management,* 7 (2007): 106–109.

Revenue Management Perspectives: What about Sales?

The sales department tends to have a lot of power, both on property and at the corporate level. After all, this group is responsible for generating a huge amount of revenue for the hospitality organization. They accomplish this through building relationships with a network of clients and using those relationships to negotiate sales of room blocks, corporate deals, and group functions.

Sales is critical to the hotel's profitability through *volume* business, but they aren't always focused on or incentivized to generate *profitable* business.

> As an industry, we tend to be very much sales led. Sales will come to revenue management for information from time to time, but they tend to lead the charge. This is a bit like the tail wagging the dog, in my opinion. If hotels really want to drive profitable revenue, revenue management determines what is needed and where the opportunities are, then they go to sales (and marketing) to execute on this. Until we get all three organizations working together, we will never realize our potential.
>
> —*Chris Crenshaw, Vice President of Strategic Development, STR*

Although it is easy to agree with this statement, some feel that the job of sales could be constricted if it were overly controlled by revenue management policies. Negotiations with clients are complex, with many moving parts. Whether it's negotiating a corporate rate or a large function, sales needs different information at different times to successfully assess the piece of business and close it. When a potential client asks for a quote, sales doesn't always have time to wait for that quote to be assessed by revenue management before they accept it. They need to be able to be nimble and flexible with clients, based on their experience of what it will take to close the deal.

Some suggest that when it comes to setting parameters for sales, it's more effective to provide information to guide negotiation than to dictate policies. Letting sales know whether the group would be more profitable if they could be flexible to move a week or two, or giving a floor and ceiling rate to the negotiation, would allow sales to be creative but work within the bounds of what is good for the hotel as a whole.

The point is that sales, marketing, and revenue management need to work together to set the right business strategy for the organization, and then execute on that strategy. Revenue management can identify need periods, and the organization can determine whether sales or marketing efforts are needed to fill that gap.

> To be successful, we need to forge a joint mind-set. Sales and Revenue are two disciplines that are often at odds with each other, both approaching opportunities to generate revenue in the hotel from different perspectives. At Viceroy, we believe in being courageous and making bold moves to shake up the industry, including the long-held belief of Sales and Revenue as separate disciplines. By merging Sales and Revenue, we have a better understanding of how these two drivers of success can work together to achieve revenue optimization across our company. We continue to show great success and forward momentum, including having our Directors of Revenue cross-train with our sales team and participating in sales calls and closing business. Sales managers are becoming active in strategy setting for hotels and understanding the impact of pricing and inventory decisions. Blending Sales and Revenue may seem a bit unusual, but I believe it is the future of our industry as we apply a quantitative approach to commercial sales.
>
> —*Scott Pusillo, Vice President, Market Strategy,*
> *Viceroy Hotel Group*

Fabian Bartnick, Director, Revenue Generation, Tune Hotel Group

Tune Hotels is a Malaysia-based hotel company operating 45 hotels across nine countries. Tune Hotels' core proposition is to offer a great night's sleep at a great price.

I met up with Fabian Bartnick from Tune Hotel Group when I was traveling in Asia. I immediately noticed a difference in his title from other revenue leaders I have interacted with, so I asked him about it. "My title is director, revenue generation. I have responsibility for revenue management, business analytics (includes feasibility and pre-opening), voice and channel optimization (central reservations office, customer service handling, distribution) and traditional offline sales," he said.

I asked him about the advantages of that title over a more traditional revenue management title. "When I started in RM we always used four stages: Create demand, forecast demand, manage demand, and retain demand. Traditional revenue management roles have direct impact on two of those. My role at Tune allows direct control across all four of those areas," he explained.

Fabian continued, "A traditional DORM works in the here and now—using pricing, forecasting, et cetera, to drive the business. Yet the DORM looks only after one or two portions of the overall picture and therefore relies on other departments to support or drive forward. There is a lot of impacting and influencing required and sometimes other departments have other priorities and you end up 'fighting' for your place. The beauty about my role is that I control the levers themselves. I can decide and steer all of my departments in the same direction with limited impacting or influencing required, as there is a common goal, not just virtually but also hierarchy-wise, because it all comes back to one decision maker. Of course, there are always discussions with marketing and operations, but the benefit is that all revenue-generating departments work as one and are seen as one.

"One key benefit of our role is also the aspect of *when* RM gets involved. My role gets involved at the construction or conversion stage of development. RM decides on the room breakdown—twins, doubles, et cetera, the meeting rooms, signs off on revenue projections for the first 10 years and once the hotel comes into preopening we take over the positioning and then of course the managing going forward. So essentially I am part of the active decision-making process before the hotel is actually built. This rarely happens in a traditional revenue management role."

Fabian makes some good points here about the benefits associated with a demand generation approach to revenue management. Though I do hope that Tune decides to roll marketing into his responsibility soon to round out the picture.

CHAPTER 6

Total Hotel Revenue Management

To get to total hotel revenue management, hotels can start by thinking about optimizing what they currently have outlet by outlet, but should quickly move to using that information to figure out how to find the optimal space mix for the hotel overall. This requires understanding the hotel's optimal profit per square foot (or meter), and finding the right outlets mix and business mix to achieve that.

—Neal Fegan, Executive Director, Revenue Management, FRHI Hotels and Resorts

After the discussions in the last chapter about synchronizing decisions about demand generation and demand control, it is natural to extend that thinking to the decisions being made across all revenue-generating assets throughout the organization. If revenue management has been successful in hotel rooms, surely it can benefit other areas of the hotel. Much like price optimization, as I mentioned in Chapter 2, this concept of applying revenue management broadly across the hotel has been widely discussed across the industry but not very widely implemented, and, much like price optimization, it has also fallen prey to overuse and incorrect interpretations. In this chapter, I discuss the opportunities and challenges associated with expanding revenue management beyond hotel rooms and provide advice about how to move the organization toward a more holistic perspective on generating revenue and profits.

Based on the success of hotel room revenue management, expanding revenue management outside of the hotel rooms to other revenue-generating assets at the hotel seems to be the next opportunity for hotel revenue management to make a big impact on revenue. Some companies have experimented with applying revenue management to function space, food and beverage, or spa. Others, most commonly in the casino industry, have talked about a more guest-centric approach, evolving the pricing approach to optimizing the revenue potential of each guest as an individual across their entire set of interactions with the hotel.

The term most commonly used to describe this collection of opportunities is *total hotel revenue management*. Despite how much the industry speaks about this term, we still have not quite managed to agree on exactly what it is or how to achieve it.

For example, revenue management system vendors use different terms that mean approximately (but not quite) the same thing:

- Rainmaker (www.letitrain.com) uses the term *profit optimization*, implying that the decision needs to be about profits, not just revenue, because once you incorporate more than one revenue stream, you are not comparing apples to apples in terms of the profit margins. This definition works well, particularly when your most profitable revenue source is not the hotel rooms. For example, in casinos where the gaming floor is the revenue generator, hotel rooms are used to capture high-value gamers through discounting or comps, so you need to think about the profit associated with gaming revenue versus hotel rooms and other services when pricing each aspect of the guest experience.

- Duetto (www.duettoresearch.com) has started using the term *revenue strategy*, implying a more holistic view of revenue generation that includes more data sources and more involvement from departments across the hotel enterprise. The benefit of this concept is that it seeks to overcome the traditional weakness of revenue management systems, which is a short-term focus on revenue maximization, and it incorporates both demand generation and demand management.

- IDeaS (www.ideas.com) uses the phrase *total revenue performance*, implying that there are both good and bad revenue opportunities, so it is important to assess the overall performance of the revenue generation across the property. Focusing on revenue performance ensures that revenue managers are thinking strategically and understanding the role that each piece of business, and each outlet, plays in the overall revenue-generating potential of the hotel.

If the industry could come to agreement on what total hotel revenue management (THRM) means, there probably wouldn't be space for vendors and consultants to attempt to redefine the terms to suit their approach. We also might have an easier time communicating longer-term vision and strategy to owners and asset managers, who care a lot about the "revenue-generating potential" of their entire hotel asset.

I can see why we have gotten ourselves into this situation. Applying revenue management principles to any outlet that exhibits the right characteristics can increase revenue. However, there is a danger in "locally" optimizing outlets without considering the impact on the profitability of the entire enterprise. For example, booking out all the function space with local events when the hotel needs group room demand might be profitable for banquets and catering, but not for the hotel as a whole. Trying to determine how the pieces fit together into a profitable whole results in throwing around terms like "profit" and "strategy" and "performance."

Although most discussion of total hotel revenue management centers on optimizing the revenue from all revenue-generating assets, it is also important to consider the role of the guest and the business mix. As hotels consider overall hotel revenue generation, would we rather have a guest who goes to the spa and eats in the restaurant, or one who just pays a high room rate? What business mix results in the most profitable revenue generation for the hotel? This answer will vary depending on the characteristics, strategy and goals of the hotel company, of course.

Others in the community have been advocating for adding distribution channel costs to pricing algorithms, allocation decisions, and strategy discussion. As the distribution landscape becomes more complex and distribution costs start to rise, channel mix can have a huge impact on overall hotel profitability. Finding the right mix of business, both from a segment and a channel perspective, must, therefore, be considered in the THRM decision.

So, what is the right answer to THRM? Is it the outlets? The guests? The channel mix?

In my opinion, what we are actually striving for is a responsible and holistic combination of all of these factors—simple enough, right? The reality is that the levers that you pull to execute THRM could look very different depending on hotel type, region, business mix, or size. It is crucial to educate yourself on the opportunities you have for your specific operating conditions before embarking on any type of holistic revenue management program. No matter what opportunities you take advantage of toward the goal of THRM, at the core of successful execution is fostering a revenue culture throughout the hotel. From marketing through operations, all functions need to be aligned toward maximizing the revenue-generating potential of the entire asset.

In this chapter, I describe a process for applying revenue management to assets outside of rooms. I then address the concept of guest-centric revenue management as it relates to the goal of THRM. Finally, I lay out my perception of what the goal of THRM should be, and how hotels should start working toward that goal.

REVENUE MANAGEMENT BEYOND ROOMS: A PROCESS[*]

As hotel room revenue management matures, the law of diminishing returns begins to apply. After the initial implementation of a good revenue management system and solid revenue management business practices, more and more effort is required to squeeze out fewer and fewer incremental dollars from hotel rooms. Experienced revenue managers are turning to revenue-generating assets outside of the hotel room as the next low-hanging fruit for driving incremental revenue, such as:

- Function space (Kimes and McGuire 2001)
- Restaurants (Kimes et al. 1998)
- Golf courses (Kimes and Schruben 2002)
- Spas (Kimes and Singh 2009)

Hotel room revenue management is a fairly well-established discipline with researched and tested technology, analytics, and business

---

[*]Portions of this section are taken from www.hotelexecutive.com/business_review/2642/revenue-management-beyond-hotel-rooms-five-tips-to-get-started. HotelExecutive.com retains the copyright to the articles published in the *Hotel Business Review*. Articles cannot be republished without prior written consent by HotelExecutive.com.

processes. While some opportunity for innovation remains, most hotels have some systems and processes in place to manage rooms revenue, which are based on research and experience. Outside of rooms revenue management, however, there is little infrastructure, practically no business process, and few technology options. There has been some preliminary research into the opportunities (see previous list), which I refer to during this section and have listed at the end of the chapter. There are also some vendors that are building preliminary solutions to address opportunities outside of rooms (for example, Avero is pulling together food and beverage data, and IDeaS has released a function space revenue management solution). Applying revenue management to new areas is ripe for innovation, and has the potential to help you make a real difference in your organization.

I suggest the following framework for the application of revenue management to new areas within the hotel.

1. Understand the theory.
2. Follow a formal process.
3. Involve the operations.
4. Look for low-hanging fruit.
5. Publicize your successes.

These five suggestions are based on revenue management research, conversations with managers who are implementing nontraditional revenue management programs, and my own experiences in this area. They help managers take full advantage of the opportunities to apply revenue management beyond hotel rooms while also working within the constraints of the existing operations. Let's explore how this works in a bit more detail.

Understand the Theory

There are a few basic concepts that will help you to identify the right area to focus on and to identify the opportunity within that area. First, as we discussed earlier in the book, in order to take advantage of revenue management, an industry must meet the following five necessary conditions (Kimes 1989).

1. **Relatively fixed capacity** means that it is expensive or impossible to add more capacity to meet demand, so you have to get the most out of what you have. For example, a hotel might have 300 rooms or an airplane only 150 seats. You can't just add more when there is more demand for them.

2. **Time perishable inventory** refers to the concept that the product cannot be sold after a certain time. For example, if the morning spa appointment is not booked, you can't sell that same appointment in the afternoon, or if a plane takes off with an empty seat, you lose the chance to sell that seat.

3. When the business has peak and off-peak periods, or **time-variable demand,** there is an opportunity to keep prices high when demand is high, and discount to fill space when demand is low. For example, a resort in the Northeast may be busier in the summer when the weather is nice but have trouble filling rooms in the winter.

4. **Segmentable markets** refers to the concept that there are different customers who value access to the inventory differently. For example, more price-sensitive leisure customers will book earlier or move their trip to pay a lower price, whereas business travelers will pay more for guaranteed access to the inventory when they need it.

5. Finally, **high fixed and low variable costs** means that it costs relatively little to sell another unit of the product, so you are willing to discount to generate some revenue to offset the fixed costs. For example, it costs relatively little to occupy one more hotel room (electricity, amenities, housekeeper to clean), compared to the cost of operating the hotel, or to add one more passenger to a plane (extra can of soda), compared to the cost of staffing the plane and filling it with fuel.

To illustrate how this works, let's look at golf. There are a limited number of tee times available, and it is difficult to add more without redesigning the course. If the 7 A.M. Tuesday tee time is not sold by 7:01 A.M. on Tuesday, you can't sell it later in the day. Most golfers prefer to start in the morning in order to have ample time for 18 holes. Weekdays can be slower than weekends. Golfers could be segmented based on their willingness to pay for a desirable tee time, or on their skill level—assuming that more experienced golfers play faster, and therefore one could move more of them through the course in the same amount of time. Finally, compared with the cost of maintaining the course and the clubhouse, the cost of selling one additional tee time is relatively minimal. As you can see, golf matches the necessary conditions for revenue management.

If you have multiple revenue-generating assets that meet these characteristics, the next step is to understand the strategic impact of each on the business. For most traditional hotels, rooms are the largest and most profitable revenue stream. A logical next step is to select the revenue-generating asset that has the highest impact on, or relationship with, sales of hotel rooms. For example, while a hotel's function space might not be the largest or most profitable revenue source, room sales are generally highly dependent on function space sales, so that could be a good place to start. In resort hotels, the same might be true for golf courses, food and beverage, or spa.

There are two strategic levers for revenue management: price and duration (Kimes and Chase 1998). The goal of any revenue management program is to move price from fixed to variable and duration from unpredictable to predictable. Continuing with our golf example, golf courses typically charge a set price for a certain number of holes, so an opportunity for golf is to move toward variable pricing where different prices may be charged based, for example, on time of day or day of week. Duration in golf is unpredictable. Unlike in hotels, where guests reserve rooms for a set number of nights, golfers reserve a "round" without specifying the time it will take to complete that round. If golf duration were more predictable, managers could schedule tee times at more frequent intervals, potentially increasing the number of available tee times, and hence revenue.

Kimes has recently argued that there is actually a third strategic lever for revenue management—space. As revenue management moved beyond airlines and hotels, applications began to extend to industries where space (or inventory) was more flexible. For example, in function space, function rooms can be divided and configured in different ways (i.e., classroom or banquet). For restaurants, there are different table configurations, and in rental cars, cars can be moved from location to location should inventory be needed elsewhere.

As you are evaluating opportunities to apply revenue management, the degree of flexibility in the space, or inventory, also influences how you might implement the program or measure success. For example, classroom setups in function space can hold more guests than banquet rounds. Should you charge more to use the room for a banquet? How you book rooms with dividers also matters, depending on the sound-proofing or accessibility of the room. Would you need to charge more if the party wants a section of the room that blocks other people from using the other part of the room? In restaurants, larger parties tend to take longer for the dining experience and spend less per person. If you knew that there was enough demand for smaller party sizes, would you decide not to take a larger group, or charge more for that group? In rental cars, understanding the value of one more car at a certain location based on demand patterns helps with deciding whether to take on the cost of moving vehicles. When space is flexible, the right performance metric to manage against becomes critical to the revenue management decision.

Understanding Performance Metrics

The performance metric that is used for all revenue management programs is an efficiency metric that measures how well the capacity constrained, time-based inventory is generating revenue (Revenue Per Available Time-based Inventory Unit or RevPATI) (Kimes 1989). Revenue Per Available Room (RevPAR) is the ubiquitous metric used for measuring the efficiency of hotel operations and the success of hotel room revenue management (equation follows). RevPAR is calculated by multiplying average daily rate by occupancy. In this way, revenue (ADR) is adjusted for how many of the capacity-constrained inventory units (room nights) are sold.

If you think about how this measure is calculated (revenue divided by room nights sold) multiplied by (room nights sold divided by number of available room nights), it accounts for all of the strategic levers: price (room rate), duration (a night), and space (a room).

$$RevPAR = ADR \times Occupancy$$

Or
$$\left(\frac{Revenue}{Room\ Nights\ Sold} \right) \times \left(\frac{Room\ Nights\ Sold}{Room\ Nights\ Available} \right)$$

Or
$$\frac{Revenue}{Room\ Nights\ Available}$$

In the case of hotel rooms, the space is fixed (it's a hotel room), but hotels have an opportunity to make price more variable and duration more predictable (forecasting and optimizing by length of stay considering price sensitivity of demand). Measuring RevPAR helps to define and manage the goal of the hotel room revenue management program, identifying and rewarding the successful manipulation of the levers that can be pulled to increase revenue. For example, hotels could raise prices, increasing ADR, or lower prices, increasing occupancy. They could deploy an overbooking strategy to hedge against no-shows, which will increase occupancy, or they can price by length of stay, which may lower ADR on one peak night but generates more revenue by selling more rooms on the adjacent days, or shoulder periods. Each of these revenue management strategies has proven successful in generating incremental revenue from hotel rooms.

When bringing revenue management to another revenue-generating outlet, the first step is to understand whether that outlet meets the necessary conditions (see earlier). Next, you need to define the revenue metric (usually easy), capacity-constrained inventory unit/space (can be challenging), and time (can also be challenging). These factors represent your opportunity to apply revenue management. I give two examples that describe how to derive these metrics using two assets that tend to represent a large portion of hotel revenue outside of rooms, restaurants, and function space.

A Restaurant Revenue Management Performance Metric

For restaurants, revenue is the average check per person (total nightly revenue divided by the number of people served). The capacity constrained inventory unit is the number of seats in the restaurant—you can't add more space for seats, so you can only serve as many customers as there are seats. Next, consider how long people use the seats (time). Generally, you can use a seat more than once per day, so a daily measure is not going to uncover the full extent of your opportunities. The same goes for a meal period, as it is likely you could turn the tables more than once during a meal period. Most applications of restaurant revenue management use hour as the time measure, which represents the dining duration (how long a particular party uses the table), as well as the time variability of demand (at 5 P.M., there are fewer diners than at 7 P.M.). The metric that is commonly used for revenue management is RevPASH—Revenue Per Available Seat-Hour (Kimes et al. 1998).

Function Space Revenue Management Performance Metric

Some RevPATI definitions are very straightforward, but others are a bit tricky. When we first tried to apply revenue management theory to function space (Kimes and McGuire 2001), we ran into some problems. Function space met the necessary conditions—fixed capacity (only so much function space to sell), time-variable demand (peak and off-peak periods for function demand), high fixed costs and low variable costs (compared to the cost of operating a hotel, the cost of booking an additional function was small), and segmentable demand (different groups want to use the space for different purposes). The next step was to understand how to evaluate the effectiveness of the pricing and use of the space, and determine which of the strategic levers would be most effective in increasing function space revenue.

Starting with the price lever, revenue in function space is a combination of room rental, per person food and beverage charges, and AV/equipment rental. Each of these revenue sources has a different profit margin. Additionally, the different types of events (weddings versus conventions, for example), had different profit margins based on the number of staff and required setup time. Since we weren't comparing apples to apples, we determined we needed to use "contribution," not revenue. This means that we needed to have a contribution margin percent that could be applied to each of the revenue streams. As you probably know, determining contribution margin isn't always a straightforward activity. However, we were able to determine at least an estimate of contribution margin by revenue stream and function type that the entire team could agree on.

Defining capacity was also tricky. The number of customers that each function room could hold depended on the configuration and setup of the space. This meant that a "per person" measure—like a number of seats or a maximum occupancy (as for restaurants) would not work. Since some rooms could be divided, and portions of events could be held in the foyers, hallways, or patios of the function space, a "per room" metric (as with hotel rooms) also did not really work well. We realized that in this problem, given the configuration flexibility, the hotel was really selling the "space" itself, to be used as dictated by the function, so a square foot or square meter as the "inventory unit for sale" would work to measure how efficiently the hotel was using the function area.

Finally, we needed a time definition. Function space is typically sold by "chunks of time" (as opposed to an entire day at a time, or by hour). One determining factor for how often the space can be resold in a day is the setup time for the next function. For example, if you have a complicated wedding setup on a Friday night, it might not be possible to sell the room for a breakfast meeting on Friday, because there will not be enough time to flip the room. However, a break area could be sold multiple times per day because all that needs to be done is to clean the high-top tables and pull in a refreshed snack and beverage cart.

The first thought was to use hours, as in the restaurant problem. I argued that this definition was not actually the way that time was "sold" in the function space problem. Most of the salespeople I talked to said that they sold by day part, so perhaps that time frame would be a more accessible metric for the sales team. Sherri Kimes, my coauthor, argued that an hourly measure would help the hotel team account for the revenue impact of operational improvements like shrinking setup time. In the end, I'm not sure that we ever really agreed on whether the function space metric should be ConPASf(m)H (contribution per available square meter or foot-hour) or ConPASf(m)DP (contribution per available square foot/meter-day part). (Either way, it does not seem to roll off the tongue like RevPAR or RevPASH.)

As you can tell from this discussion, the application of revenue management requires a good understanding of the operation and the ability to adapt the core theory to a new problem with a slightly different operational condition. In order to be successful, you will need to spend time with the operators, fully understand how the operation works, and then socialize the revenue management theory with them. Revenue management at its best is a new way of thinking about an existing problem, but it should also be intuitively in tune with operations such that a savvy manager can easily understand and implement it.

OPTIMAL TABLE MIX ANALYSIS

CASE STUDY

Early in my career, I had the opportunity to do a consulting project with a 400-seat seafood-focused buffet restaurant. During certain meal periods, there was significantly more demand than supply, so there were long waits for tables. Customers were (understandably) upset about the long waits. We were called in to apply revenue management techniques to increase throughput and revenue. In our discovery and planning meetings, as we asked questions and observed the operations, we started to brainstorm techniques we might eventually apply. One option we brought up was to conduct an *optimal table mix analysis* (Kimes and Thompson 2004).

As I discussed earlier, seats are the constrained inventory unit in restaurants, but the seats are typically arranged around a table—and only one party at a time will use that table. This means that if the mix of party sizes does not match the mix of table sizes well, there will be empty seats—representing a lost revenue opportunity. In an extreme example, if a restaurant has 100 seats, arranged in 25 tables of 4, but the demand is only for tables of 2, at any given point every table might be full, but only 50 percent of the seats will be occupied. If the restaurant instead configured the seats into 50 tables of 2, they would have the opportunity to serve 50 additional customers per turn (assuming the demand exists, of course).

Optimal table mix is generally calculated using an optimization algorithm (as I described in Chapter 2), which mathematically matches the typical

(Continued)

(*Continued*)

mix of party sizes to a table mix configuration, accounting for uncertainty, configuration issues and demand patterns. The output of the optimization algorithm is the best possible table mix considering all operational constraints. When we left the meeting, we had decided that our next step would be to see if the data the restaurant had provided us was sufficient to conduct this analysis and, if so, we would start developing the model.

About a month later, when we were back, the buffet manager pulled me aside. "Kelly," he said, "I heard what you said last time about the table mix, and it made sense to me, so I went ahead and switched out a bunch of four tops for deuces in the dining room." "That's great, Bob!" I said. "What happened?" "Well, we're getting about 36 additional covers per hour during our peak periods. That reduced wait time, satisfaction is up slightly, and we're making more money. This revenue management is really great stuff!"

It turned out that the optimal mix derived from the optimization recommended a few more tables for two than Bob initially added. However, the technique, while not something that Bob had considered previously, was intuitively logical to him enough that he was willing to experiment on his own. Although he did not come up with the exact right answer, he still was able to make an improvement in the short term, and became a strong internal advocate for our future recommendations.

Expect that in order to be successful in implementing revenue management to new outlets, savvy revenue management professionals will have to spend a good amount of time understanding the unique operating conditions at the target outlet. Only then can you really understand what the opportunities will be. Following the process as outlined in the following section will help guide you to the right answer, but you must be willing to partner closely with the business. During the process of understanding the operations, you also have the opportunity to begin to develop a revenue culture in the outlets, so that the operators can actually assist you in identifying and executing on opportunities.

Follow a Formal Process

Kimes and her colleagues (1998) recommend a five-step process for implementing a revenue management program at a new outlet.

1. **Establish the baseline of performance.** Thorough analysis of the existing operation is essential as a first step. Different from the traditional financial or cost analysis that outlet managers or finance might conduct, this analysis establishes the baseline performance of the key strategic revenue management levers: price, duration, and space. A full investigation of pricing strategies, demand patterns, and usage of the inventory is required so the RevPATI metric can be developed. This will certainly involve pulling data from the selling system, reservation information, cancellations, and no-shows. For those industries where duration is uncertain (like golf and restaurants), time studies of the service process to understand usage patterns is also helpful (Kimes et al. 1998).

2. **Understand the drivers of that performance.** Sit down with the team and discuss the results of the baseline analysis. Look carefully at demand patterns and see if you can segment out customers with different needs. Investigate low- and high-demand periods and see if you can figure out why those periods are popular or slow. Look at utilization patterns and see if there are any operational issues like staffing levels, job functions or technology issues that might be driving suboptimal performance.

3. **Develop a revenue management strategy.** Once you understand the drivers of performance, look for opportunities to apply the levers of revenue management: price, duration, and space (Kimes and Chase 1998). Are there opportunities to vary prices to stimulate or restrict demand? Would duration management techniques such as increased staffing, service process changes or technology upgrades improve utilization? Do high no-show rates provide an opportunity for overbooking? Are pricing or reservation policies restricting revenue-generating opportunities, or are stricter policies needed?

4. **Apply that strategy**. Working closely with all key stakehold-ers will ensure success. Although some strategies may be simple, buy-in from the staff that will execute these strategies is essen-tial for success. Make sure line-level staff are fully trained on the "whys" of your new policies, and ensure that their incentives are aligned with your desired outcome.

5. **Monitor the outcome**. Although this step may seem obvi-ous, it is often overlooked. Continual monitoring of outcomes is essential not only to prove success, but also to identify op-portunities for continuous improvement. Set up a revenue committee—or invite the outlet managers to your regular rev-enue meeting. Review performance and identify opportunities to improve. Establish training and development procedures to ensure that the revenue management program will continue through staff turnover.

Look for Low-Hanging Fruit

As you are working through step three of the process outlined previ-ously, remember that small changes can have a big impact on revenues. Hotel revenue management has advanced to the point that automated software with advanced analytics is now essential to achieve incremen-tal revenue gains, but in the early days, operational changes made a big difference. Credit card guarantees for advanced reservations can reduce no-shows. Marshals on the golf course can speed up rounds, resulting in more capacity for tee times (Kimes and Schruben 2002). Adjusting the restaurant table mix so that it better matches the customer mix will increase utilization and revenue by filling more seats with paying cus-tomers (Kimes and Thompson 2004). "Easy" operational changes will result in an early success you can point to as justification to continue. Encourage the staff to get creative about identifying opportunities to drive incremental revenue.

I heard a story from a revenue management executive friend of mine who said that after going through a revenue management pro-gram implementation with the F&B outlets in one of their hotels, the bar manager found a very old bottle of French liquor in the basement.

The price tag on the bottle indicated that it had been purchased in the early 1900s for about 29 cents. Clearly it had not sold. They decided to market it in the upscale hotel's bar for a pretty high price per portion, positioning it as a chance to try something that was more than 100 years old (it was designed to age, by the way). After seeing the first few orders (and presumably the associated tips), the entire staff took it on as a competition with each other to see who could sell the most. They sold out of the bottle in just a couple of months. All of that incremental revenue on an item that was already in stock and not selling!! The bar manager was just sorry he couldn't find another bottle to continue the program.

Involve the Operations

Participation from the unit managers and line-level staff is essential to the success of any revenue management program. Not only can these folks provide valuable insight about operations, but they will ultimately be responsible for executing the strategy. As I described in the case study, operations managers can be great partners in proving out the concepts, and revenue management programs can ultimately help these managers be more successful, driving revenue, profits, guest counts, and even satisfaction scores.

The same revenue management executive who inspired the creative liquor selling told me that when they arrived at that hotel for the final debrief session, they got a standing ovation from the entire food and beverage team, managers through chefs down to the line-level employees. When was the last time that happened in one of your hotels? The revenue team had worked hard not only to design a program that could be successful, but also to involve the operations to the degree that they felt a part of the solution as opposed to this being just another corporate initiative they had to manage. Oh, and everyone was making more money, which certainly helps!

Neal Fegan, executive director of revenue management for FHRI Hotels and Resorts, gave me a great example of the importance of involving operations in revenue management programs. This example relates to rooms revenue management, but it is an important example of how interconnected revenue management initiatives can be. In the early days of rooms revenue management, when he was director of revenue management for one of Fairmont's city center hotels, they were trying to implement an up-sell program for club rooms at the front desk. These rooms frequently went empty on nights where the hotel didn't sell out, so they were willing to offer a "day of" discount on an upgrade to drive incremental revenue from existing demand. "This was a great way to drive incremental revenue, and we were providing a really attractive discount for the guests, but the program just wasn't taking off. It wasn't until I went down to the front desk to investigate that I figured out why. Housekeeping was cleaning these rooms last, since they were supposed to be empty. This was a standard (and logical) practice for housekeeping. However, when the front desk was ready to offer an upgrade to a guest standing at the front desk, there weren't any club rooms available to put them in, so they couldn't make the upgrade offer. We hadn't communicated the program to housekeeping, so they hadn't changed their behavior to align with our plan. It was then that I realized how important a fully integrated revenue culture was. Everyone from revenue management through front desk and housekeeping has a part to play in our ultimate success. You can't leave any department out of the revenue management strategy."

Publicize Your Successes

You had better believe that we used the buffet manager's success resulting from splitting tables in all of our future conversations with our clients (and I'm still using it today, obviously). In fact, optimal table mix analysis turned out to be essential to the success of the entire buffet revenue management project I spoke about in the case study. The "real-world" story became a much more powerful marketing tool than the results from the mathematical models we use to predict revenue increases. Well-publicized successes will ensure that your efforts can continue. Developing success metrics and communication strategies is as important a component of the revenue management strategy as the pricing and duration controls. Use regular team meetings to highlight successes (and praise the efforts of team members who assist you along the way). Make sure everyone from the general manager to the owners to the managers of other outlets knows about your program. There is nothing like a solid win to inspire the team to continue, and to think bigger.

At SAS and IDeaS, one of our first clients on our brand-new hotel revenue management software did such a good job publicizing the success of the pilot properties and reinforcing that during the rollout that every time I showed up at a conference, as soon as people from that company saw my company name, they would run over and ask when they were getting the new system. For an industry where technology implementations are notorious for being difficult and change is, at times, not a positive word, this was a major accomplishment of the hotel company's change management team and contributed significantly to their successful rollout.

The five steps in the process of applying revenue management to nonroom assets described in this section should ensure that you position yourself for success, no matter which asset you decide to start with. There has been a good deal of research into applying revenue management outside of hotel rooms. If you would like more information about applying revenue management to a specific asset, start with the additional reading at the end of this chapter, and use that as a jumping off point to identify other sources of information. They should provide a good "shortcut" to establishing the baseline and identifying opportunities.

GUEST-CENTRIC REVENUE MANAGEMENT

Applying revenue management to revenue-generating assets across the hotel is one component of THRM. Hotels are also starting to recognize the importance of attracting guests who will use the other revenue-generating outlets during their stay. Guest- (or customer-) centric revenue management has therefore been held up as the holy grail for many hotel companies—or maybe just held up as the next big evolution in hotel revenue management. The concept here is to incorporate some indication of the total guest spend in the revenue management algorithm, favoring guests who spend freely and profitably across the enterprise (as opposed to just paying the room rate). Obviously, this relates to THRM in that if you are favoring guests who bring in a significant amount of ancillary revenue in addition to the room rate, revenue across the entire hotel will increase.

There are a couple of different ways to think about how to calculate guest value. Casinos track gaming behavior through their player value card, and derive a "Player Theo," or an estimate of the amount a "known gamer" is likely to spend per visit, or per day, on the casino floor. Many casino operators are expanding that value to include spending on other outlets in the casino as well. The translation of this for hotels would be to track spending across the hotel for each guest, perhaps using their loyalty card, and derive a measure of what they are likely to spend per visit on ancillary services. The revenue management algorithm could be tuned to favor guests according to their value per stay, either reserving inventory for higher-valued guests, or providing access to discounts, packages or special services that encourage them to book and spend.

Another option is to consider guest lifetime value, which is the aggregate of all of their interactions with the hotel through the duration of the relationship. Again, those guests with higher lifetime value are favored in the revenue management decision. One benefit of this approach is that it overcomes, to a certain extent, the short-term view of traditional revenue management (maximizing revenue over the booking horizon with no consideration for longer-term implications like restricting access to loyal or frequent guests who pay lower room rates but spend more or stay more often—I provide an interesting case study from citizenM on this in Chapter 7). There is a significant amount of research on the best approaches for calculating lifetime value from experience across many industries, including retail and financial services. At a simple level, the process involves calculating guest profitability, projecting it into the future, adjusting for retention probability, discounting to present value and summing across the future values to come up with an overall figure.

The first challenge with calculating per-visit spend or lifetime value is the data. There has to be a way to collect and aggregate spend data both across the hotel property and through the estate. This requires guests to either charge back to a central location (like the folio) or identify themselves somehow at every interaction. Many property management systems are not set up to capture or retain guest information at the right level of detail for this type of analysis. Even if they were, this information would also have to be collected across the disparate systems and integrated into a centralized database. The various revenue streams need to be adjusted for margins, which can be challenging, as not every outlet may truly understand their cost structure. Naturally, this methodology can only be applied to guests who are willing to identify themselves consistently. Unknown guests would not have a value associated with them, and therefore may be discriminated against in revenue management decision making (which could be good or bad depending on their potential).

If any guest-centric methodology is implemented without considering how to grow the guest value over time, revenue is ultimately eroded. It is tempting (as some casinos do) to provide discounts based on guest value (if you have a higher ancillary value, you get a lower room rate), but applying this as a straight discount does not account for willingness to pay, and ultimately results in training guests to expect a discount, lowering, rather than raising, their value. Further, the primary and most profitable revenue source at casinos is the gaming revenue, so it makes sense to discount all other services to encourage more spend on the casino floor. Hotels' primary revenue source is rooms. Does it make sense to start discounting your primary and most profitable revenue source? How much incremental revenue do you expect on the hotel room side from discounting other ancillary services?

Guest-centric pricing has to be deployed in a private channel, or risk violating fairness perceptions or rate parity restrictions. If you have a relatively small percentage of known guests, or your loyalty program members account for a relatively small portion of overall revenue, cultivating this group through guest-centric methods might not move the needle enough to make the investment in the development of private channels worthwhile.

Many hotels are finding it easier and more feasible to think about value at the level of a market or rate segment. Room rate, ancillary spend, and channel preferences can be combined to get a view of overall segment profitability. Price and availability can be set at this segment level to attract the most valuable mix of business. At the individual level, unknown guests can be matched to segments based on demographic, behavioral or channel criteria, so the hotel doesn't miss out on an opportunity to acquire a new, potentially high-value guest. Known guests can be treated according to their individual value either while on property or during booking if they are logged into their loyalty account, but the hotel is setting strategy based on the desired business mix at the segment level.

Regardless of how this is ultimately implemented, revenue management like this will require a dramatic change both to the business process and the systems that support it. Many companies are talking about this, but as of the publication of this book, I have not seen any companies truly implement it. Casino companies are coming close but still are not quite capturing all the patron value across the enterprise, and are not executing on the 1–1 pricing (which also requires participation from the selling systems).

WHAT IS THE GOAL OF TOTAL HOTEL REVENUE MANAGEMENT?

Clearly there are many ways to think about total hotel revenue management, and perhaps a one-size-fits-all approach is not reasonable. Thinking about driving revenue at the hotel level as opposed to the individual department level will require synchronized decision making and good communication between departments. There may be cases where optimizing overall revenue requires sacrificing revenue in an outlet or area. For example, the hotel may need to give up room revenue for a group that will spend in the spa, or accept that the restaurant will do less business from resident guests because there is a large function in-house.

I've done a lot of thinking on this topic, and I firmly believe that there are two facts about THRM that cannot be ignored.

1. THRM will be customer-focused as opposed to asset-focused. It's about a profitable mix of business, considering profit generation across the enterprise, based on how the segments use all of the elements of the asset.

2. THRM requires integrated marketing and revenue management, as these two departments, acting together, can direct sales and reservations toward strategies that generate the right mix of business.

So, THRM is all about attracting the right mix of business to your property that will profitably generate revenue across the enterprise. Defining that profitable mix of business is up to revenue management, attracting it is up to marketing, and taking advantage of it is up to operations. This means that integrated revenue management and marketing can be considered an essential component of THRM.

Many thought leaders talk about optimizing across all revenue streams in the property. In order to actually do the math, there has to be a common element among the revenue streams. That common element has to be demand: the guest, the business mix. You need to understand the characteristics of the hotel's demand, the way the guest segments use the hotel and how they spend across the property. This is why it's about business mix (market segment, customer segment, however you define it), rather than synchronizing asset revenue streams. For those properties that attract "outside" demand, those nonrooms segments must also be evaluated against rooms-related demand.

The bottom line is that the entire organization needs to organize itself around this optimal business mix. Whether serving this mix is "optimal" for an individual location or not, the entire enterprise needs to make room for that optimal business mix. However, each outlet, schooled in the revenue culture, then can fill in around this core business mix according to available capacity and pricing opportunities. It is only with this common goal that the organization can build a sustainable core revenue stream and generate incremental revenue around it, thus maximizing the revenue potential of the entire asset.

I believe that the guest-centric revenue management programs we have been talking about for years should be thought of as part of THRM, as opposed to being considered as a separate initiative. It will be more profitable for the hotel in the long run to invest in optimizing each asset and then bring the program together by attracting the most profitable mix of guests and encouraging those guests to spend freely across the property, incentivizing them based on their needs, preferences, and value.

> The concept of Total Revenue Management [RM] is not a new notion; hotels have always endeavored to maximize the entire asset. The difference today is the desire by hotels and resorts to sophisticate their approach to profit maximization. In essence, Total RM is simply about optimizing revenues and profits from all revenue streams (rooms, F&B, parking, spa, golf, retail, other activities, etc.). The crux of the issue, however, is that the revenue management discipline as it is structured today and with the tools available is not set up for success when it comes to optimizing profitability. From the revenue manager's job description to the structure of a P&L, there are no "building blocks" in place to make Total RM happen. From the departmental organizational structure of most hotels to the systems used to optimize demand, once again the integration of the component parts needed for practicing Total RM is not in place. Until the industry fully addresses these disparate and often conflicting pieces of the puzzle, the practice of Total RM is destined to evolve very slowly in hospitality.
>
> —*Bonine Buckheister, President, Buckheister Management, Ltd.*

Once the demand is on property, it is up to the outlets to be set up to take advantage of that demand. It is crucial that all outlets have a revenue management program in place so they are prepared to understand the organizational mind-set of THRM and participate in strategy development. They should know when they need to reserve space for hotel guests, and when they need to try to stimulate demand that's not related to the rooms. They should be thinking of strategies to drive truly incremental revenue (like the expensive drink add-on I described earlier, which had basically no cost associated). You will only be successful in THRM if the team has individually understood how revenue management applies to each outlet, and then thinks holistically about the optimal business mix for the hotel and how each asset contributes to attracting that mix. Understanding the profitability, popularity, and potential of each asset relative to the others will likely cause the hotel to rethink operating hours, price points, and the allocation of space itself. Longer-term renovation strategy could (and probably should) be impacted by proper application of THRM principles.

How any organization decides to deploy this is up to the business strategy. It could be through loyalty programs, personalized pricing, or strategic sales efforts. Cultivating customer value will also be key. It's not sufficient to just attract that business mix, but you need to continually cultivate that value by providing "the right" opportunity for your guest to spend more or stay more with you.

PUTTING IT ALL TOGETHER

To me, THRM is a strategy as opposed to a system. Systems may, in the long run, be able to support THRM across all revenue-generating assets. More likely, there will be incremental additions to technology, but programs will be run across departments through conversations, data sharing, and business process changes. Frankly, I think that efforts to integrate marketing, sales, and revenue management decision making will have as much impact as any one outlet's revenue management program, as these functions are ultimately responsible for ensuring that the hotel attracts and captures the right business mix.

In order to successfully instill a THRM mind-set throughout the hotel and ensure you are successful in your THRM implementation, there are several guiding principles to keep in mind.

■ THRM will require educating the entire organization on the principles of revenue management. It will also require educating revenue management on the unique operating conditions of the other hotel departments, and on demand-generating techniques commonly used by marketing and sales. In other words, departments will have to work together much more closely than ever before.

- Incentives and goals must be aligned across departments so that the organization can act holistically instead of locally.

- Every opportunity to generate incremental revenue or profits should be evaluated. For example, carefully evaluating how upgrades are managed or finding opportunities to drive local business in the restaurant or spa (assuming this does not conflict with the rooms demand, of course).

- Communication mechanisms should be set up and incentives provided to encourage profitable revenue as opposed to just volume of business. Departments that are responsible for generating demand need to pay attention to the profitability of that demand and work cross-functionally to ensure that they understand what that means for the organization.

This example, from Linda Gulrajani, Vice President, Revenue Strategy & Distribution, Marcus Hotels and Resorts, demonstrates how important it is to involve the whole organization and to think holistically about revenue opportunities, instead of department by department. If the organization were not aligned, this scenario would not have been possible, and the hotel would have suffered over time.

> We have had some nontraditional THRM success at our resort where we have had guest dissatisfaction issues on summer weekends because our pool and public areas were so crowded. We strategically decided to take more wedding business on weekends with sleeping rooms at a lower rate. Although this has hurt our ADR, we made up some of the revenue in catering, and more importantly our guest satisfaction scores are much higher because more of our guests have a planned wedding event to attend and are

not using the resort facilities. We believe that higher guest satisfaction scores and TripAdvisor ratings will ultimately help us grow our business and overall rate in the long run.

—*Linda Gulrajani, Vice President, Revenue Strategy & Distribution,*
Marcus Hotels and Resorts

CASE STUDY

TOTAL HOTEL REVENUE MANAGEMENT AT FAIRMONT

FRHI Hotels and Resorts has been working toward the goal of total hotel revenue management for several years. It has applied revenue management to nontraditional outlets like function space, restaurants and spa, as well as put a focus on attracting and nurturing the most profitable business mix for each hotel. Neal Fegan, Executive Director, Revenue Management, has been overseeing these programs for the company.

"Building a revenue management culture within these new outlets is the first crucial step to the ultimate success of a program. It can involve introducing some unintuitive new concepts. We start each program with some education about what revenue management is, and then we brainstorm with the teams about ways to increase revenue. I get some of my best ideas from this interaction," says Neal.

Neal reminded me that traditional revenue management always happens around busy times, where you need to think about pricing and access for peak and shoulder periods. While this is still important, revenue management today has started moving into the nonbusy periods.

"There are really only two things you can do to generate revenue when you aren't busy," he says. "First, you can get more guests, and second, you can get more money from the guests that are already there." These activities sound a lot more like marketing than revenue management, but it's all part of the same effort.

Neal first points out how the staff should be acting during busy periods. "Our biggest challenge is overcoming the strong 'service' mind-set of the operators. They are (justifiably) unwilling to do anything that might upset guests. It's a lot like overbooking at the front desk. It took a lot to

(Continued)

(*Continued*)

overcome the mind-set that overbooking at all was too risky, because the front desk just hated walking guests. After a while, when the front desk saw that revenue was increasing without increasing the number of walks, everyone started to feel more comfortable. It's the same here, the operators become more comfortable as they see the success of the program, and gauge guest reactions."

Neal's favorite part of about any new implementation is when he brainstorms with the team around revenue management concepts and about generating revenue during nonbusy periods. "Some staff can get really creative, which gives me great ideas. More important, it makes everyone feel involved in the process and really helps people understand what we mean by incremental revenue."

The goal of any of these implementations is to help the staff understand how to optimize their own operation, but also to help them build a revenue mind-set so they can extend that thinking to the enterprise as a whole. "There will be times when outlets need to sacrifice revenue opportunity for the good of the whole enterprise. If they understand revenue management concepts (and are incentivized properly, of course), they are more willing to participate, and even generate ideas on their own."

CONCLUSION

While rooms typically generate the most, and most profitable, revenue for hotels, other outlets can contribute significantly to overall hotel revenue. The success of revenue management for hotel rooms has generated interest in applying revenue management techniques to other ancillary outlets within the hotel. Now that room revenue management has become mainstream, and there are systems and business processes to support it, it is becoming more difficult to generate significant additional incremental revenue solely from a rooms program. Therefore, hotels are turning to applying revenue management techniques to generate incremental revenue from other assets. As these programs spread throughout the hotel, the hotel moves closer to THRM, where revenue and profits are optimized at the hotel level, as opposed to outlet by outlet or only at the rooms level.

The most important component of applying revenue management to other revenue-generating assets is to instill a revenue culture throughout the operation. Once each outlet has implemented a revenue management program and begun to think in terms of profitable revenue generation, it becomes much easier to think about how each outlet can contribute to overall hotel revenue and profit maximization. In this chapter, I outlined a process for designing a revenue management program at these alternative outlets. Involving the operations in the design and execution of these programs will not only ensure a successful implementation, but will also help to instill that revenue mind-set across the organization.

The concept of THRM is the intersection of revenue management applied to each outlet and the optimal business mix for the hotel overall that can take advantage of all of the offerings across the property. As the potential for each outlet is explored, the organization can get a sense of how each outlet contributes to the overall profitability of the hotel, and can use this understanding to determine the right mix of business that drives overall profitability. When all outlets are revenue managed and acting with a revenue mind-set, the hotel is set up to take full advantage of that optimal business mix, and can then fill in around that mix according to the needs and operating characteristics of each of the outlets. Sales and marketing will have a crucial role in attracting and cultivating that business mix, as well as in filling in with alternatives if sufficient demand is not available in the target segments.

The previous three chapters have illustrated the potential to expand and elevate the revenue management discipline within the hotel. Many hotel companies are already innovating in one or many of these areas. Whether it's incorporating reputation into pricing strategies, integrating revenue management and marketing for a holistic demand management strategy or applying revenue management techniques to other revenue-generating assets, expanding into these areas provides more exposure for revenue management and also more revenue-generating opportunities. The important first step is to carefully evaluate the business to identify high-impact opportunities. All of these areas require involving new stakeholders, understanding business impacts more broadly, and taking the time to educate the organization on general revenue management principles. It is only when you build an enterprise-wide revenue culture that the goal of THRM becomes achievable and the organization is set up to continue to innovate and drive revenue.

In the next chapters, I describe some upcoming opportunities for revenue management to participate at a more strategic level within the organization. Revenue management will be better positioned to take advantage of these opportunities if the foundation of an integrated revenue culture through revenue management, marketing, and operations is already in place in the organization. The goals of integrated revenue management and marketing and total hotel revenue management not only support more profitable revenue generation in the short term, but also position hotels to be able to take advantage of strategic or longer-term opportunities.

In Chapter 7, I talk about the importance of considering pricing as a lever that can support an overall business strategy as well as a revenue-generating tool. If the organization is set up with an integrated revenue culture, contributing to overall business strategy is much easier.

In Chapter 8, I discuss personalization, which is the strategic initiative that I hear the most about in the market today. This initiative is typically driven by marketing, but requires the participation of revenue management and operations to be successful. Personalization is the execution of a guest-centric strategy that includes accounting for guest value, guest needs and preferences, and operational conditions at the hotel. The total hotel revenue management foundation, supported by a close relationship between revenue management and marketing, will make this type of initiative successful.

In the final chapter, Chapter 9, I describe in more detail how to align the skill sets and organizational structure of revenue management departments to be able to successfully support all of the opportunities I describe in this book.

ADDITIONAL READING

S. E. Kimes, R. B. Chase, S. Choi, P. Y. Lee, and E. N. Ngonzi, "Restaurant RM: Applying Yield Management to the Restaurant Industry," *Cornell Hotel and Restaurant Administration Quarterly*, 39, no. 3 (1998): 32–39.

S. E. Kimes and K. A. McGuire, "Function-Space RM: A Case Study from Singapore," *Cornell Hotel and Restaurant Administration Quarterly* (December 2001): 33–46.

S. E. Kimes and Lee W. Schruben, "Golf Course RM: A Study of Tee-times," *Journal of Revenue and Pricing Management*, 1, no. 2 (2002): 111–120.

S. E. Kimes and S. Singh, "Spa Revenue Management," *Cornell Hospitality Quarterly*, 50, no. 1 (2009): 82–95.

Calculating Guest Lifetime Value, http://blogs.sas.com/content/hospitality/2012/02/29/customer-lifetime-value-analytics-the-holy-grail-for-hotels-and-casinos.

REVENUE MANAGEMENT PERSPECTIVES: DISTRIBUTION CHANNEL MANAGEMENT

After the optimal business mix for the hotel is identified, hotels need to source that business mix through all available channels. Therefore, an aspect of THRM is to consider the channels to source demand, the cost of acquisition for each piece of business, and how that contributes to the profitability of that segment. The relationship between hotels and their distribution partners, particularly the online travel agents (OTAs), has been rocky over the years. In fact, distribution management and the distribution landscape in general could be the subject of an entire book on its own. For this book, I decided to provide an industry perspective on two issues that are top of mind for revenue management these days: the rising cost of distribution and rate parity agreements.

The issue of rising distribution costs has been hotly debated in the hotel industry recently. Third-party distribution companies have huge marketing budgets and the ability to generate incremental demand, which they bring to bear on behalf of their hotel clients. However, the commissions that hotels pay for these reservations are rising, making it a very expensive way for hotels to generate business. Many hotels now think of these third-party distribution channels from a cost perspective, but there can be opportunities to use them to drive incremental revenue or to support a business mix strategy.

Another hot issue in the distribution space is the rate parity agreements that the OTAs forced hotels to make as the OTAs gained power and reach. Basically, hotels are required to offer the same rate they give to the OTAs through any publicly available channel, including their own brand.com sites. Requiring pricing to be the same through every publicly available channel is a big barrier to guest-centric revenue management and to attracting an optimal business mix. As of the publication of this book, several courts in Europe were testing the legality of these agreements, contending that they could violate antitrust or fair trade agreements (www.hotelnewsnow.com/Article/15696/Bookingcom-to-amend-rate-parity-in-Europe).

Because of these factors, the relationship between hotels and third-party distribution channels has always been controversial in the industry. It is also one of the faster moving areas in hotel management, with innovation generating new entrants and new opportunities. No one can predict at this point how this relationship will evolve, particularly in the face of rate parity potentially going away in Europe and the entrance of new major players like Google and Amazon. Since this area impacts hotels so much, particularly in their ability to attract an optimal business mix through pricing and positioning strategies, I interviewed an experienced hotel distribution channel manager and an executive at Hotels.com to get their perspectives on the current opportunities to leverage third-party distribution channels and what the future of this relationship might be.

Chinmai Sharma, Vice President, Revenue Management and Distribution, Louvre Hotels Group

Louvre Hotels is the second-largest European hotel group and is in the top 10 hotel groups worldwide, with more than 1,100 hotels in 43 countries. It operates six hotel brands ranging from one to five stars.

Chinmai is responsible for the revenue management, distribution, and ecommerce functions for the hotel group. He was previously vice president of revenue management at Wyndham Hotel Group, and has experience in revenue management and distribution roles for mid- to large companies like Joie de Vivre (now Commune Hotels) and also Expedia. Chinmai is based in Paris, and his hotels will be front and center of the rate parity debate. Given his experience with distribution management and his perspective from his current role, I thought he would have a good view on the current issues in distribution management.

Between when I asked Chinmai these questions and the publication of this book, he took a new role as chief revenue officer at Taj Hotel Group in India. I look forward to his new perspective from his new region in the second edition of this book!

What is your general philosophy about the role of third-party distribution channels in your overall selling strategy?

I think the third-party partners add a significant value to our overall distribution strategy. While I do not fully agree to the "billboard effect" (as the overall market occupancies with strong OTA contribution have stayed relatively flat, which shouldn't be the case if there was a 1:1 billboard effect), I do believe that they bring new customers to our hotels from markets we cannot reach. We assign different value to our OTA partners based on the type of business they bring (international points of sale versus domestic, booking window, length of stay, and on-property spend, etc.). Overall, my personal belief is that they do add incremental RevPAR if managed properly.

Where do you think the biggest pressure on hotels in the distribution landscape will come from in the next three to five years (in terms of new entrants, new agreements, etc.)? What are the biggest opportunities?

I think there are two main pressure points in play currently. One is the fact that hotel companies feel that OTAs have become too dominant in the customer journey, and so they are finally investing in their own digital infrastructure to ensure they get their fair share of the Internet/mobile channel. This investment will result in a win-win scenario for customers and suppliers and improve overall ecommerce. The hotels and hotel companies who stay on top of this digital investment will be the only ones with a healthy and profitable distribution mix.

The other big thing going on right now is the online market mutation resulting from online companies like Google, TripAdvisor, and Amazon getting serious about monetizing their customer base. In a way, these entrants, along with newer metasearch models, diversify the mix for the hoteliers, so that they don't have to put all their eggs into the same large OTA basket.

I think the biggest opportunities for hotel suppliers are in ensuring they have a unique product with good service for guest retention (and resulting positive feedback); a strong distribution platform to attain fair distribution share; and optimal pricing strategies to avoid cannibalization from some of the emerging business models. These factors also put pressure on hotel companies to hire and retain skilled executives and to reorganize their organization structures in order to stay on top of these changing trends.

What are some of the biggest challenges you find in working with your distribution partners? How do you manage these challenges?

Our endeavor is to find and retain a few key partners that not only represent our hotels and policies correctly but also bring incremental business when we need it most. Our main challenges arise when partners either represent our pricing strategy or policies incorrectly or sometimes operate out of the contractual boundaries. For example, running paid search campaigns on our brand or hotel terms if the contract restricts this type of marketing. We have also had some issues in the past with a few rogue affiliate partners not following the same policies that we have outlined with our main OTA partners.

Additionally, the process of building and maintaining connectivity with our distribution partners continues to be a labor-intensive process, as our needs with our CRS and connectivity partners continue to grow.

Many suggest that the OTAs have too much power, and that hotels are always at a disadvantage when negotiating contracts. What is your advice for hotels to level the playing field?

My advice is for hotels to first understand their business really well. I am still amazed when investors and hotels complain about rising costs of OTAs without understanding their own distribution mix in the context of their overall business mix. Distribution managers need to understand the value being provided by each channel. Only then does it become easy to decide which partners to work with and how. As an example, some analysis around distribution mix on constrained dates, coupled with geographic mix of OTAs, can lead to some good inferences on whether a hotel should work with an OTA or not, and at what cost.

However, as I mentioned before, there is no substitute for running good, clean hotels with great service, so customers have a reason to find the hotel and to return. Couple that with a good distribution and pricing strategy and—thanks to the Internet—the hotels have an absolutely level playing field.

What do you think will happen to hotel pricing if the courts decide that rate parity is illegal?

I personally don't think this is going to change the overall dynamics a lot. While it will give the hotels the option to price their channels differently on the cost versus value of each channel, it will also give the option to intermediaries to play with their cost structure and offer discounts and value-adds to customers, especially in closed groups. These dynamics could result in revenue dilution for both hotels and third-party partners if they are not managed properly. In addition, the OTAs will probably merchandize only those hotels where the pricing offers are attractive, or at least the same, as compared to other channels. Of course, in this case, hotels who need the business might do what's best to get the business.

Lack of rate parity might also give rise to more robust net rate models, where hotels just give their lowest net rates to their third-party partners and allow the partners to decide how much to mark up to the end customer.

If hotels do get the opportunity to price by channel, then it will definitely give rise to more complex pricing structures that incorporate additional factors like cost and total value by channel. This will make operational pricing more multidimensional to include product (for example, room type), market segment, and channel.

From the online travel agent perspective.

Hari Nair, Vice President of North America, Expedia, Inc.

Expedia, Inc. is the world's leading online travel company and operates localized websites for travelers in the United States, Canada, France, Germany, Italy, Denmark, Austria, Belgium, Ireland, The Netherlands, Norway, Spain, Sweden, United Kingdom, Australia, New Zealand, Japan, India, China (through a controlling investment in eLong), and Singapore.

Hari has been with Expedia in various roles across their brands and geographies since 2002. Prior to joining Expedia, he worked for the Oberoi Hotel Group. Hari is very passionate about the value that a strong partnership between a hotel and their distribution partner can provide both the hotel and the partner. I asked him some similar questions to Chinmai, and here are his responses.

Since the OTAs came on the scene, there have been lots of new entrants in the distribution space. Where are you feeling increased competitive pressure, and how are you preparing to compete?

The global travel marketplace is a $1.3 trillion market, which is a pretty massive marketplace. Travel is also a fun space to be in and therefore by design, you are naturally going to have many enterprises that have and will continue to demonstrate deep interest in this category. Travel is also very broad, and one is already seeing that to be a global player, one needs scale, technology, and sales infrastructure to stay efficient and profitable. We find increased competitive pressures across many levels; regional OTAs going hard after the regionally based customers, niche players in the mobile segment, and hotel direct websites that are becoming more sophisticated with their offerings and pricing. Expedia's approach to stay relevant is to stay true to our operating principles: that is, to have a scientific and data-driven approach to the way we do things, err on the side of simplicity, and make planning travel simple for our customers and have a test/learn approach in refining and constantly tweaking our website for improved performance and conversion.

How do you see this space evolving in the next three to five years?

There is likely going to be a big evolution in harnessing the "Power of Now," which involves taking and examining data in real time and converting it into observations and learnings. This is going to be of immense interest to both the consumers and to the supplier community. A recent example of this is real-time reviews, where customers are sent a quick survey upon checking in, and their response is instantly fed to the hotel, which allows them to do service recovery while the guest is still in-house. Other examples include providing customers with a view of the general price trends in a market and whether it is going up or down, much like a stock exchange ticker symbol tracker. The other segment set to evolve is the space of alternate lodging, with consumers searching for hotel-like accommodations, yet has a degree of a "touch of home."

Many suggest that the OTAs have too much power, and that hotels are always at a disadvantage when negotiating contracts. What is your advice for hotels to level the playing field?

In truth, OTAs are nothing more than distributors and partners of the industry, with the sole objective of matching a customer's needs with an accommodation choice that is right for them, to the extent that the hotel wants access to a specific type of customer. Hotels set their own pricing and inventory approaches, and they, in part, are part of a larger marketplace comprising of all hotels within a defined area. The advice to the hotels would be to take advantage of the global reach of the OTAs, who can bring in customers from the deepest corners of the world in a manner that is most cost-effective. Apart from being competitive, providing the customers with an unparalleled service so that they can tell about it to the rest of the world through online reviews is a great way to drive higher conversion and ADRs while also attracting more customers to come to the hotel direct site.

Both Chinmai and Hari emphasize that there are opportunities to drive incremental revenue and profits through distribution channels, provided that hotels understand the value of the demand generated through these channels. Incorporating channel into the evaluation of optimal business mix, and then understanding how to best position the hotel through these various channels, will make the investment in increased commissions worthwhile. Most important, as I discussed in Chapter 4, both Chinmai and Hari brought up the importance of a good service experience, which not only encourages repeat business but also generates positive reputation scores, further driving business. This is a crucial point. Don't forget to run your hotel well while you are strategizing how to sell it!

PART THREE

The Future of Revenue Management: Pricing as a Business Strategy

CHAPTER **7**

Pricing as a
Strategic Tool*

*[Strategic revenue management is] . . . the ability to
influence a company's bottom line, driving profitability
using basic revenue management principles but
integrating them into a broader business context.*

—Craig Eister, Senior Vice President, Global Revenue Management and Systems,
Intercontinental Hotel Group, from The Analytic Hospitality Executive *blog*

The initiatives I describe in the previous chapters represent an opportunity for revenue management to expand the reach and influence of discipline within the hotel. As success is demonstrated, for example, through better integration with marketing or building a revenue-generating culture throughout the hotel, revenue management will gain the visibility required to participate in more strategic initiatives, earning a seat at the business strategy table. In many hotels, this transition is already occurring, whether through organizational changes or mind-set changes, or both. Other hotels will follow in the future, as organizations recognize the value of a revenue-oriented approach to strategic planning.

In these last three chapters of the book, I describe how revenue management should be leveraging its expanding role to position itself for the future, aligning to take advantage of opportunities that will come up in revenue management and also in the hospitality organization as a whole. In this chapter, I discuss the opportunity to think about pricing as a lever to support an overall business strategy. In the next chapter, I describe how revenue management should be involved in designing the new guest experience by supporting personalization initiatives, which are rapidly becoming a key strategy for most hotel companies. In the final chapter, I talk about how revenue management should organize itself for the future to be prepared to meet the challenges and take advantage of the opportunities that are coming fast.

---

*Portions of this chapter were taken from www.hotelexecutive.com/business_review/3631/ pricing-as-a-strategic-tool-how-revenue-management-can-support-business-strategy. HotelExecutive.com retains the copyright to the articles published in the *Hotel Business Review*. Articles cannot be republished without prior written consent by HotelExecutive.com.

Widespread adoption of revenue management systems has enabled much of the evolution of revenue management from a tactical "open and close rates" to a more strategic role both at the property level and at the corporate level. Once systems took over the process of calculating and delivering analytic-based pricing recommendations, revenue managers were freed from the manual tasks of data extraction, data analysis, and selling system updates. With revenue management systems bearing the burden of day-to-day pricing, revenue managers are now tasked with developing the strategy for deploying price, as well as performing more ad hoc or longer-term analysis to support the broader pricing strategy. For example, as I previously described, revenue management is expanding into revenue managing other revenue-generating assets, coordinating with marketing counterparts, or monitoring competitive movements in both price and reputation. With all of this activity, the temptation is to simply let the revenue management system do its primary job without much intervention—deliver revenue maximizing daily pricing decisions while the revenue manager moves on to other activities.

However, by blindly following system recommendations, hoteliers might be missing out on some important opportunities to leverage price as a strategic tool to support longer-term business strategy. Revenue management systems are set up to achieve only one objective—to maximize revenue across the booking horizon. This is effective in the short term, but does not necessarily consider longer-term goals like driving market share, increasing customer loyalty, or reinforcing branding. Nor does it help in defining how the pricing recommendations should be delivered to the consumers in a way that makes them most likely to book (for example, the format of the price, the framing of the price, or the perceptions of fairness of the price).

The next big opportunity for revenue management to elevate themselves within the broader hotel organization is to help the organization think about price more broadly. Revenue management needs to structure the deployment of the system's pricing recommendations in context of an overall business strategy. This can include where prices are deployed, how they are presented, how the price presentation strategy is communicated to the customer and to the frontline sales staff, and whether the system recommendations should be overridden to support some other business goal.

In this chapter, I discuss why pricing is an important strategic lever. I describe the importance of considering consumer reaction to the deployment of price recommendations and pricing strategies, and discuss how hotels can configure and position pricing to avoid negative consumer reaction to revenue management pricing practices. I then describe how revenue management practice and systems can be integrated into broader business strategy, and provide some case studies and examples of how organizations align price with their business strategy. Finally, I provide some practical tips for strategic pricing.

STRATEGY CONSIDERATIONS

By now, most are familiar with the McKinsey report (Marn and Rosiello 1992) that showed that a 1 percent increase in price (overall) resulted in 11 percent improvement in profits (for the target companies in the study). This is because price increases on their own do not increase costs—in other words, it's a very easy way to drive profits (if you can raise price without a negative impact on demand, of course). This is exactly why the revenue management function is so important, and why companies put so much focus on the data, analytics, and technology I described in the first part of this book. However, price also provides other opportunities that can support longer-term company goals.

In addition to price being an important driver of profits, pricing can also represent a business strategy or support a brand promise. Walmart, for example, has successfully built their business on their "Everyday Low Price" strategy. Every facet of their operations, from marketing to supply chain, has to be lined up to deliver on this promise. Walmart is well known for driving every penny out of their supply chain. Their marketing focuses on making customers aware that they will always find the lowest prices at Walmart. In fact, the phrase "everyday low pricing" is as strongly associated with Walmart as classic marketing tag lines like "Where's the beef?" and "Can you hear me now?" are associated with Wendy's and Verizon, respectively. Their success with everyday low pricing is a direct result of driving this business strategy through their entire operation.

Southwest has a similar strategy with their pricing. After the major carriers started charging fees for things like baggage, onboard meals or preferred seating, Southwest publicly announced that "bags fly free." The ancillary fee pricing strategy resulted in billions in profit for the major carriers, but irritated the customer base. Southwest took the opportunity to reinforce their business strategy of being the "friendly" carrier for the leisure traveler. A pricing strategy contributed to their brand promise.

Price can also be a signal of quality. There is research in the restaurant and retail industries that shows that whole dollar pricing (prices that end in a 0) signal quality, whereas those that end in a 9 signal value (Naipaul and Parsa 2001). This is evidence to suggest that how you present your price needs to be aligned with your business strategy as well.

This price presentation is particularly important to think about as the industry moves toward price optimization.[1] Some in the industry are advocating for continuous price optimization, to let the system select the exact rate in dollars and cents that represents the optimal price. This means that you may end up with a price that is $53.24 or $635.82. How might the customer perceive these prices? Maybe if you are pricing a Motel 6, the dollars and cents pricing makes sense, but what about at a mid- or higher-range scale? Does this price create the brand perception you are hoping for? Is the extra $0.82 per reservation worth a hit in quality perceptions?[2]

I have heard some in industry (particularly at the luxury level) talk about the importance of the expectation associated with brand and price. Revenue management (and owners) can be tempted to decouple brand and price, particularly in an economic downturn, when the owners become desperate to generate cash flow. While a few percentage points up or down in price may be acceptable to customers, pricing, for example, an upscale product at a mass market level can violate consumer expectations and create conflicting signals. Customers might be confused enough to not buy the product because the price doesn't make sense to them. Instead of generating demand with the lower price, you might actually reduce demand, or cause long-term damage to the brand.

Price and Brand: The Importance of Consistency

A revenue management executive for a luxury boutique hotel chain told me, "We have found what seemed to be a completely contradictory effect, particularly in more competitive markets. We have a newer hotel that is quite large and in a very competitive market, so as we introduced the hotel, we tried to generate awareness and drive demand by offering a lower price. When we lowered price too much, closer to the mass market level, we actually generated less demand than at a higher price point. This didn't make sense to us until we realized that we were sending contradictory signals to the consumers. We were advertising a luxury experience but at a near mass market price. The price didn't match the promise, and consumers got confused, so they just didn't book us. When we brought the price back up, bookings increased. This really highlighted for us that price is an important signal of the brand promise, and we have to be mindful of that as we use price to generate demand."

This can happen when the price is higher than what the customer expects as well, even when it is aligned with the market. I recently spoke with a revenue manager of a midscale chain hotel, which was flagged as a well-known brand from a global hotel company. It was located in a compressed market, and the price, while aligned with the market, was frequently higher than what consumers might have typically paid for that brand. "I noticed a direct correlation between higher prices and negative consumer reviews. Even though the rest of the market was priced at that level, our guests who were very familiar with the brand weren't expecting a price that high, so they held the hotel to higher standards, and punished us more because of it. When the pricing got out of alignment with the brand promise and consumer expectations, the value proposition suffered."

Because consumers have access to all prices in the market, as well as other signals of quality and value like reviews and ratings (Noone and McGuire 2013a), it is becoming increasingly important to ensure alignment with expectations. In fact, brand expectations are just one factor that consumers consider when evaluating a price. When hotels adjust prices according to demand patterns and market conditions, it is also important to consider fairness perceptions.

Price Fairness

Revenue management works for the hotel industry because hotels have the flexibility to adjust price frequently according to demand, both technologically and practically. This flexibility to vary price does raise some concerns about how consumers will react. Hotel managers have good reason to be concerned about negative consumer reaction to demand-based pricing. Research has shown that consumers have become accustomed to fluctuations in hotel room pricing (Kimes and Noone 2002), and consider demand-based fluctuations to be fair. This is good news for revenue management, but research has also shown that in some circumstances, like raising the price of snow shovels in a storm, consumers will punish firms that they perceive to be acting unfairly in their pricing strategies by refusing to patronize them in the future (Kahneman et al. 1986; Thaler 1985). Revenue managers should be aware of pricing practices that risk negative reactions so they can continue to take advantage of variable pricing opportunities, without risking alienating the customer base.

The underlying theory about consumers' reactions to pricing practices comes from behavioral economics, which is a branch of economics where researchers use social, cognitive, and emotional factors to understand the economic decisions of individuals and institutions. These economists have determined the factors that influence consumer reaction to pricing practices and developed theories to explain consumer behavior in financial decision making. These theories can be easily translated into the revenue management context to ensure you are implementing your price strategies without generating negative customer perceptions.

Principle of Dual Entitlement

Consumers believe that they are entitled to a reasonable price, but they also believe that firms are entitled to a reasonable profit (Kahneman et al. 1986; Thaler 1985). They understand that the airlines may have to raise ticket prices when fuel prices increase or restaurants may have to charge more for lettuce when there is a drought in California. However, consumers react negatively to firms that try to take actions that result in "unreasonable" profits, seeing these firms as unfairly taking advantage of consumers. For example, raising the price of a Coke as the outdoor temperature rises could be considered "unreasonable" profit seeking. Remember how much trouble Amazon got into when they were caught charging different prices for the same book to different customers?

This concept of dual entitlement is perhaps the most salient to keep in mind for hoteliers who are looking to maximize revenue. Any unexplainable price increases run the risk of violating consumers' sense of a "fair profit," resulting in perceptions of price gouging. As I mentioned earlier, research has shown that consumers find demand-variable pricing acceptable (Kimes and Noone 2002), but revenue managers need to be careful not to carry this too far into "unreasonable." It is important to provide a reasonable justification for any price that the consumer is asked to pay. In revenue management terms, one way to accomplish this is by creating rate fences, which offer consumers discounted prices but impose rules and regulations at each level of discount to balance the perceived value for the different market segments (Hanks, Noland, and Cross 1992). For example, the ability to cancel without penalty has value for a business traveler, but not for a leisure traveler who is less likely to cancel. The leisure traveler pays a lower price, but must pay ahead. To be perceived as fair, the fences need to be logical, transparent, up-front, and fixed so that they cannot be circumvented.[3]

▮ CITIZENM CASE STUDY 1

CASE STUDY

citizenM is a small hotel chain, as they say "driven by one desire: to create affordable luxury for the people." It is targeted at a "new breed of international traveler, one who crosses continents like others cross streets—The Mobile Citizen of the World." It currently has seven properties, six in Europe and one near Times Square in New York City.

As the commercial team was planning for New Year's Eve in Times Square—one of the most popular events in the world—they realized they had a problem. Even three-star hotels around Times Square on New Year's Eve sell for $800 to $1,200, when they are normally priced in the $250 to $300 per night range. However, the chairman of citizenM specifically said he would not ever want to price any higher than their normal price range, for fear of appearing to be gouging their best customers and going against their stated brand promise of "affordable luxury." The commercial team knew if they offered a price that was so much lower than the market, they would attract a customer who was not in their target market, which could result in both online reputation impacts and making their core customer base uncomfortable. They considered minimum length of stay restrictions, but that didn't seem to be working either.

"I realized that there was just no way we could sell any rooms on New Year's Eve without impacting our brand promise," Lennert de Jong, Commercial Director, citizenM Hotels, told me. "So we decided to do something completely counterintuitive, and give them away." citizenM started a lottery for their best customers and gave away 50 rooms in Times Square for New Year's Eve. "We liked that idea so much, we decided to give away rooms in Amsterdam and Paris, too." citizenM turned a case where they might have been accused of violating the principle of dual entitlement and risk backlash from their target market, to an opportunity to foster longer-term loyalty to the brand.

Reference Price

A reference price is what consumers expect to pay for a product or service, based on their own experience or what they hear from other consumers. The reference price is not based on any objective measures, simply what they consider "normal" (Kahneman, Knetch, and Thaler 1986; Thaler 1985). They will compare any future prices they see to this reference price. If the current price is too high when compared to the reference price, they will consider the price unfair. While reference prices can change over time, the more exposure the consumer has to a price, the stronger that price as a reference becomes. This is one of the reasons why the revenue manager of that midscale chain hotel described earlier had so many problems with reputation when the hotel was priced high. Even if it was aligned with pricing in the market, the reference price in consumers' mind was lower, so they were more critical of the value of the purchase.

The concept of reference price is one reason hotels find it so difficult to raise prices after long periods of deep discounting. The discounted price becomes the consumers' reference price over time, so they will compare all future prices to that reference. If hotels raise prices too drastically, or too quickly, the consumers' reference price expectation is violated, and they feel the firm is trying to take advantage of them. They will book with a competitor whose pricing is closer to their expectations, or complain about value through social channels.

Hotels need to be very careful about how and where they publish discounted rates, as the longer and more widely available these rates, the more likely they are to become the reference price. Rate fences and private rates can help maintain the reference price while generating needed revenue. Another way to get around the reference price is to obscure it by packaging the product with add-on services whose prices might not be as familiar to the consumer. This could be spa treatments, meals, in-room amenities, theater tickets, or Internet access. These elements change the basic product such that consumers cannot rely as heavily on their previous experience for value judgments. Another great technique is the buy two nights, get one free promotion. This is actually a 33 percent discount across three nights, but instead of exposing consumers to a discounted rate for each of three nights, they are exposed to the regular rate for two nights. This results in a deal that will drive demand but maintains the reference price when the deal is no longer necessary.

Prospect Theory

Prospect theory describes decisions between alternatives when the decisions involve some risk (like financial decisions) (Kahneman and Tversky 1979). Researchers in this area evaluated how consumers make these risky decisions, and found that they don't always behave rationally (in pure economic terms). One aspect of prospect theory is that consumers always respond more positively to a gain over a loss, even when the economic value is exactly the same. Consider the scenario where the rate for advanced purchase is $150 and the rate for last minute is $200. Consumers who book at the last minute will feel worse if they are told they are being charged $50 extra (loss) for last-minute booking (advance purchase is the base price) than if they were told they would have "saved" $50 (gain) for booking earlier (last minute is the base price)—the result is the same, there is a $50 difference in price between the two rates. It's all about which price is *framed* as the baseline, and how the pricing strategy is applied from there.

In simple terms for revenue management, price differences for the same product should always be framed as a discount as opposed to a surcharge (think about how you would react to a young person's surcharge as opposed to a senior citizen's discount). This goes back to the fencing discussion from earlier: always set up a fencing condition under which the consumer can get a discount as opposed to a condition in which the consumer must pay more—even if the value is exactly the same.

Familiarity

Perceived fairness of pricing practices increases as consumers become more familiar with these practices (Campbell 1999). Practices that initially seem unfair may become more acceptable over time because consumers become accustomed to them.

As I mentioned earlier, the good news for hoteliers is that consumers are becoming quite familiar with revenue management pricing practices and consider them to be fair and acceptable (Kimes and Noone 2002). As revenue management has become commonplace in hotels, consumers are becoming well educated in variable pricing practices. Of course, this has led to the deal-seeking behavior that has been giving us so many headaches these days.

This concept leads to the notion that hotels should be transparent in their reasoning behind pricing practices and policies. I discuss this further in the context of the study I describe in the next section, but it doesn't hurt to remind the consumer why they are receiving a particular price. If your fences are set up properly, and fairness concerns are considered, there should be no reason for the consumer to have a negative reaction to the information.

Familiarity, Brand Class, and Information

Taylor and Kimes's 2010 study on perceived fairness in hotel pricing reinforced that familiarity was the most important factor supporting the perceived fairness of pricing practices. They looked at the role of brand class (three-, four-, or five-star), and found that class did not influence perceived fairness of variable pricing at all. This is great news for luxury hotel managers who have been concerned that variable pricing might damage their brand perception. Remember, of course, from the earlier discussion, that going too far outside of the thresholds that consumers expect from the brand may risk confusing customers and ultimately impact demand. (It's not easy, is it?)

The final finding from that study was that providing information about why the rates varied increased fairness perceptions. However, other research has found that it is not enough to just let customers know that hotel rates will vary. Information on the factors that will influence the rate changes (such as day of week, length of stay, advance purchase) increases fairness perceptions the most (Choi and Matilla 2005).

So, based on this brief lesson in behavioral economics, here are six tips that hoteliers can use to ensure their pricing strategies do not generate negative consumer reactions:

1. **Have confidence.** All signs are pointing to consumers accepting variable pricing practices in hotels without negative consequences, so routine revenue management actions are likely very safe. You should be careful about how you introduce dramatic changes or new programs, however. Make sure your marketing department reads this section before they put out their next promotion. It could also be a good topic of discussion for your next revenue meeting.

2. **Use discounts, not surcharges.** Whenever possible, frame pricing as discounts rather than surcharges. For example, you get a reduced rate if you book ahead of time, take a room without a view, or pay in advance. You never "pay more" for last-minute access or an ocean view.

3. **Build logical rate fences.** Rate fences help you ensure limited access to discounts, but also protect you from unfairness perceptions; 21-day advance purchase, association memberships, room locations, or amenities are all good ways to build incremental business without risking negative reactions.

4. **Protect the reference price.** Avoid making deep discounts widely available, or publishing them widely for long durations.

The more exposure the general public has to a discount, the more likely it will become the reference price, and you'll have difficulty raising your price when conditions warrant. Use rate fences, such as private channels, to help protect the reference price. Another good trick is providing a night free with the purchase of several nights at full price. For a three-night stay, it's the same as offering 33 percent off, but consumers see the full price for the room, not a discounted price.

5. **Hide the price of the core product.** If you fear damage to the reference price, you can always bundle the core product with add-on services that provide value but change the offering. The actual price of each element is masked, so the reference price is preserved.

6. **Be transparent.** Provide as much information as possible to your consumers about your pricing strategy. Train your staff to remind the consumers why they are paying the price they are paying. This will help not only with fairness perceptions in the short term, but to build familiarity over time, leading to even greater acceptance. It could be a great sales tactic. For example, "This is a particularly busy weekend for us, but if you wanted to book the following weekend, the price will be less" shifts demand where you need it and/or helps the consumer understand why they are paying what they pay.

I strongly encourage you to learn more about behavioral economic theory and how it applies to revenue management. All of the articles I have referenced here are good for this, albeit a bit academic. I have a few more references at the end of the chapter that are written in a more business-oriented language.

PRICING TO SUPPORT BUSINESS STRATEGIES

How the price is presented to consumers, including the format and framing, is one way to ensure a sustainable long-term revenue stream for the hotel. Using price to support longer-term business strategies is another. While revenue management systems have been very effective in maximizing revenue potential by delivering an optimal pricing recommendation, there may be situations where you choose to forgo short-term revenue in favor of longer-term business strategy.

Jeff Bezos, founder and CEO of Amazon.com, once famously said, "Profits kill growth." At the early stages in his company's history, it was more important to move product than to hold onto inventory with the hopes of making a couple more dollars on the sale. His goal was to ensure he was still around 5 or 10 years in the future, which meant metrics like cash flow, revenue, and market share were more important in the short term than profits. Driving traffic to the website through attractive pricing and product availability helped establish Amazon.com as the leader in ecommerce—a position it arguably still holds today, nearly 20 years after the company was founded. (I know, scary to think Amazon has been around that long, and that there are college students today who have never lived in a world where you had to go to a store if you wanted to buy anything! By the way, this also means that there are a lot of revenue managers who have never revenue managed in a world where OTAs didn't exist, either.)

For hotels, price can be a useful lever for manipulating demand, attracting certain market segments, driving bookings, or stealing share. You may lower price in the short term to drive growth, and gradually gain back your price position as your goals are achieved. On the other hand, you may raise price to slow bookings for transient customers or close off certain channels so that you can reserve availability for specific segments—loyal customers or corporate bookings, for example, in order to win their long-term business. Mobile might not be a profitable channel for you now, but given growth forecasts, it might be worth forgoing some profits in the short term to encourage bookings through the channel in order to set yourself up as a market leader in the future. As your hotel company enters emerging markets, your pricing strategy may be aggressive in the short term. You can keep the competition out, establish yourself as the market leader, and make up for loss in profits after you've shut out the competition.

Recently, I worked with a multibrand company in the travel space that was investing in new pricing and revenue management analytics. They were planning for improvements in their forecasting and price optimization, but wanted their pricing efforts to align with their brand strategy—keeping the brands, and their brands' customers, distinct. To them, this translated to maintaining a specified price alignment between the brands, and across locations, even if their revenue management system would have recommended that one brand should be priced higher than another in one market, and the reverse in another. While the "optimal" recommendation would have resulted in short-term, incremental revenue, they were focused on the long-term goal of strong brands as a method of sustaining revenue and profits. The company wanted to know the trade-offs they were making in short-term revenue to achieve this longer-term goal, so the pricing analytics provided detailed and optimal recommendations, which were then interpreted and adjusted according to their business strategy for the selling systems. The revenue analysts could use the detailed analytic results to continue to refine the pricing strategy and understand the trade-offs the company was making to support the branding strategy.

Leveraging Your Revenue Management System in Price Strategy

This example leads to a discussion about the role of the revenue management system in strategic pricing. Incorporating a business strategy or deploying recommendations in alternate formats systematically will require implementing a new "strategic" wrapper around existing revenue management technology. Pricing decisions must be based on the core analytic revenue management process of demand modeling, unconstraining, forecasting, and optimization. However, the implementation of the recommendations can be adjusted based on strategic constraints, business rules, or even preferred pricing formats. The revenue management system needs to continue to provide detailed forecasts and price recommendations, but how those recommendations are deployed might change.

For example, you may employ a strategic constraint that adds a market subsidy to properties in a certain area—so the price recommendations for that area are adjusted slightly to drive market share. The adjustment is based on the pricing analytics, so you always know the revenue trade-off, and can ensure you are not trading too much in favor of market share increases. Similarly, you may add a business rule that specifies that loyalty members of a certain level are always granted access to rooms, no matter what the current availability restrictions are.

Another way to think about deploying pricing recommendations as part of a pricing strategy is to consider them in the context of all the selling actions that should be taken at that time, as opposed to the price recommendation itself. Revenue management forecasts or pricing recommendations could be translated postprocessing to a signal (red, yellow, green) that indicates a set of selling actions the frontline should take, in addition to the pricing that should be offered. The color coding represents a strategy, letting agents or sales managers know how and what they should sell.

In order to capture full potential and to maintain the flexibility to change strategy over time, it is important to maintain the complexity and level of detail of the analytics in the revenue management system. Robust demand modeling, forecasting, and optimization models at the core of a strategy provide the insight into the impact and trade-offs of your pricing decisions as well as the option to adjust your strategy and deployment as business conditions change. A "rules-based" pricing system alone is not going to provide a sustainable foundation over time. However, these rules can be layered over the revenue management system recommendations.

HOW TO BE MORE STRATEGIC IN PRICING

Revenue managers must work hand in hand with their counterparts across the organization to ensure that business strategy is incorporated into the application of revenue management pricing recommendations. The revenue management system is the cornerstone of this approach, as it holds the data that will help to analyze the trade-offs you make between strategy and short-term revenue. The strategy and process around the revenue management system will be what moves the organization's strategy forward.

In the following sections I describe three important actions you can take to move to a more strategic view of pricing:

1. Back up your strategy with analytics.
2. Analyze your rate spectrum.
3. Build a selling strategy around the system recommendations.

Back Up Your Strategy with Analytics

Strategic pricing is not a license to throw away your revenue management system and its analytics, or an excuse not to modernize your system to take advantage of the latest and greatest analytics. In fact, these strategic pricing decisions require even more careful analysis than a tactical day-to-day price. It is crucial to understand the trade-offs you'll be making when you decide to use price as a strategic lever. You'll need to understand how much revenue or profit you'll either gain or give up in exchange for meeting your strategic goal. Using data from the revenue management system, you can evaluate the trade-offs until you come up with a workable solution. Your revenue management system can forecast the demand captured at the recommended price. If you take an alternate price, you can use this demand relationship to determine what you might be giving up. For example, in a market share strategy, you may be able to fill the hotel at a really low price, but if you settled for 70 or 80 percent occupancy, you could still meet your share or segment goals, but give up less profits.

Analyze Your Rate Spectrum

Most hotel companies need to have preestablished rate plans that are turned on and off according to expected demand patterns, due to the limitations of the selling systems or those of the third-party distributors. These rate spectrums represent all of the available pricing you can push out into the market, and as such, they serve two main purposes.

First, they represent your ability to generate revenue from your limited capacity of sleeping rooms. Thus, it is imperative that there is sufficient variety in available rates to capture the price sensitivity of the market. This means considering the number of price points, the highest and lowest rates you are willing to offer and the spread between room types, if you have to deploy pricing according to a fixed spectrum. Careful analysis of demand patterns, market conditions and competition will help to set the right spectrum to adequately capture market demand.

The same type of analysis can be conducted throughout all revenue streams for the property. For example, many restaurants are using the Boston Consulting Group's matrix to help with menu engineering. You plot the menu items on a two-by-two matrix according to their popularity and contribution margin. So, for example, high popularity and high contribution margin items are "stars," and should stay on the menu, whereas low popularity and low margin items are "dogs," which are candidates for removal. The other two categories are candidates for price changes or marketing efforts. Similar methodologies could be followed for spa treatments or retail items.

Second, the rates themselves can influence consumer perception of your brand, as I described earlier. The way you present rates in the market sends a branding signal. For example, your price position relative to the market—do you stay at the top of the market, or try to position yourself relative to a competitor? Each sends a different message. Even the rates themselves matter. Research has clearly shown that price presentation methodologies influence consumer perceptions of the brand (Naipaul and Parsa 2001; Yang, Kimes, and Sessarego 2009). Do you use "whole number pricing" ($200 or $150 versus $189 or $147)? Do you price on the "99s" ($199, $99, $49.99)? This is true of hotel rooms, restaurant menu items, and retail items as well.

Build a Selling Strategy around System Recommendations

You need to set rules about how the pricing recommendations from the revenue management system are implemented, once you have them. This can be done through the "wrapper" system I described earlier, or through your selling process, price presentation, or distribution strategy.

For example, you may want to foster relationships with loyal customers or build up business from particular market segments. You might have a selling strategy that favors these customers, even operating within the revenue management price recommendations. For example, you can close down channels that are not popular with loyal customers first as the hotel starts to fill, or offer last room availability to loyalty program members (at the risk of a walk).

The recommendations from revenue management systems can be very complex. As I describe earlier, using the output from the revenue management system to provide directional guidance to sales managers or frontline employees, rather than presenting them with the detailed information, can be a way to enforce pricing discipline without over-burdening operational managers. For example, there could be different strategies associated with "green, yellow, or red" periods. This approach could be useful for sales teams in the hotel. For example, during periods of low demand, the "green" strategy could include offering special discounts to key strategic groups, free sell of function space or accepting groups without additional evaluation. It could point sales teams to a rate spectrum they should use, or provide suggestions of floor and ceiling rates to use in negotiations. There are two advantages here: First, this is an easy-to-communicate strategy, which allows users to consume only a color instead of complex numerical recommendations. Second, it allows a much richer set of actions than simply recommending one price over another. This could also work really well in limited service hotels or other hotel properties where there is not a dedicated on-site revenue manager.

As revenue management moves into nontraditional areas, as I discussed in Chapter 6, this kind of methodology is also a good way to get teams used to implementing revenue management techniques. For example, the restaurant could identify hot and cold periods according to historical RevPASH figures and then implement strategies to sell more to each customer during cold periods and turn tables faster during hot periods.

BENEFITS OF STRATEGIC PRICING

Pricing strategically, as illustrated in this chapter, is a very complex process, requiring a deep understanding of business strategy, consumer behavior, market complexities, and operational constraints.

However, this longer-term focus enables organizations to build a long-term, sustainable revenue stream.

To conclude this chapter, and inspire some thinking about options, I present several examples that demonstrate how a more strategic approach to pricing could benefit a hotel.

Lodging Performance

The first example comes from the pricing strategy research I mentioned earlier. Cathy Enz, Linda Canina, and their various coauthors have done extensive research using STR data into the impact of pricing strategies on lodging performance. All of the references are included at the end of the chapter, but I review the findings briefly here.

Cathy Enz and Linda Canina (with various colleagues) have been studying pricing strategies and performance through the last two recessions. Their findings overwhelmingly indicate that hotels that are able to drive price (ADR), as opposed to chasing occupancy by lowering price, achieve higher RevPAR than the competitive set. These results hold through good economic conditions and bad ones. Their study, "Strategic RM and the Role of Competitive Price Shifting," conducted with Breffni Noone, showed that during the period of 2007–2009, those hotels that consistently raised or held prices stable, as compared to their competitive set, experienced a less negative RevPAR impact than the competitive set—regardless of whether they were priced above or below the market. Their 2004 study "Why Discounting Doesn't Work," with Mark Lomanno, showed that demand, particularly in the United States, is relatively inelastic. These findings raise important points for revenue managers:

- Being aggressive with prices is the strategy that will be most likely to improve RevPAR. Occupancy is the weaker lever in the RevPAR equation. Don't get spooked by demand patterns. (Of course, this assumes that your value proposition supports the level of pricing that you want to charge.)

■ Demand is relatively inelastic. This means that you can shift share in the market by lowering price relative to the competitors, but no new demand is created when prices are lowered. All you are doing is bringing the market down with you.

When Enz and Canina (2010) studied European hotels they found that in that market as well, hotels that offer ADR at the top of the competitive set consistently have a higher RevPAR.

Consumer perception studies support this finding. In a study of American travelers conducted by Maritz in 2009, it was revealed that only 13 percent of respondents had even noticed that hotel rates had decreased, and only 3 percent said that lowered prices made them more likely to stay at particular hotels (Garlik 2009).

Short-Term versus Long-Term: citizenM Hotel Glasgow

As described earlier, citizenM is a small hotel chain, whose brand promise is to provide "affordable luxury" to the international traveler. They have a hotel in Glasgow, Scotland. In 2014, Glasgow hosted the Commonwealth Games, which ran from June 23 to August 3, among several other special events that dramatically impacted demand in that market. As a result of this activity, STR reported that RevPAR was up in Glasgow by more than 23 percent, making it the highest growth market in that region. CitizenM has a 200-room hotel in Glasgow, which is a market served by a high amount of repeat business in normal years. In 2014, citizenM was one of the few hotels in the market that did not achieve this level of RevPAR growth. When most hotels were increasing their rates from £60 or £80 to £200, citizenM held its rates at its "normal" levels, and did not tap into the groups coming in around the Commonwealth Games.

"We had a short-term opportunity to drive revenue, but in normal years, Glasgow is a market with a high level of repeat business," says Lennert de Jong, Commercial Director, citizenM. "We didn't want to risk angering those repeat customers in the short term by asking them to pay a higher rate, or risk them not being able to stay with us because we were out of their per diem range. Instead, we decided to take a longer-term view, and keep our loyal customers happy by offering the price they were used to paying. They will be back next year when there aren't any games, and we probably gained a few new repeat customers along the way, who didn't want to pay the high special event prices offered in the market."

This is a great example of a hotel taking a longer-term, strategic view of sustainable revenue generation from their best customers, as opposed to short-term revenue maximization. This required some creative thinking, expert market knowledge and good commercial discipline from the team.

Back to the Basics at Red Roof Inns

The example that follows demonstrates the impact of putting a solid revenue management strategy, focused on the basics, in place even before you consider implementing technology. As I describe, the brand transformation at Red Roof needed to be supported by a pricing strategy, and there was pressure on the company to generate results after that investment. This case demonstrates as well that while it is easy to get distracted by new data or new technology, the basic tenets of revenue management remain effective, even if implemented in a relatively manual environment.

Red Roof Inns is an economy chain with more than 400 locations in the Americas. They are owned by Westmont Hospitality. When Timothy Wiersma, Vice President, Revenue Management, took over the revenue management function, the entire brand was in the midst of a transformation, with ongoing upgrades to the product and a new brand strategy focused on providing a caring and comfortable environment for all their guests. Red Roof Inns are mostly roadside inns, and demand tends to materialize within 48 hours prior to arrival. Forecasting demand with economy scale properties is challenging because of the booking patterns and other complex variables that can change on an hourly basis. This has presented a unique set of challenges for Tim's team as they must always be very active in managing quickly changing demand patterns. Red Roof has a core team of dedicated revenue managers who each handle their own portfolio of properties.

"When I took over this function, I realized that in order to be successful we were going to have to start with the basics and build from there. There are many constraints in the economy space, including resources and technology. In order for us to be successful, we needed to teach the owners and franchisees the basics of revenue management, since they were probably going to be the ones executing the programs for their hotels. We wanted our hotels to focus on understanding demand patterns so they knew when to raise price to drive revenue or keep price lower to stimulate demand," Tim says. "Oftentimes managers, owners, and franchisees think they understand what it means to revenue manage their property but when we sit down and discuss overarching strategy on any given day we get varied answers from the team members. Understanding basic demand principles and the cause and effect of strategic initiatives is important in building a winning strategy on any given night. We focus a lot of our time and effort training the general managers in the ideologies of revenue management to ensure we optimize each property's potential. We encouraged our franchisees to evaluate every piece of business to understand whether it would be profitable, or displace better revenue. Just the basics, but many in the community had never thought of their business this way."

This focus on the basics has been successful for Red Roof. While the segment was at about 9 percent RevPAR growth in the first half of 2015, when I talked to Tim, Red Roof has consistently exceeded the economy segment performance by a significant margin. "Obviously, the new branding and renovated properties have helped us, but the focus on revenue discipline has gone a long way toward improving performance. When the owners and franchisees can see results like this, they are encouraged to continue with this line of thinking."

I have also included a case study on market share shifting in the airlines in the appendix. The network problem in airlines from the hub and spoke system creates some unique challenges. Although it doesn't have direct application to the hotel industry, I thought some might be interested in reading about how airlines manage through the process of opening up markets when they have the challenge of working through their hubs.

CONCLUSION

As the revenue management discipline gains visibility and expands the area of responsibility in hotels, there are emerging opportunities to focus on a longer-term pricing strategy, as well as to use price to support the hotels' business strategy. Revenue management systems are designed to provide revenue maximizing pricing decisions at a detailed level across all products through the booking horizon. It is up to the revenue management function to determine how these prices should be deployed in the market. There is more to a pricing strategy than simply accepting the revenue management system recommendations. Consumer perception of the presentation of pricing can influence booking behavior, so hotels need to ensure they are being transparent about the reasoning behind variable pricing practices, and be careful about how they present discounts. As well as supporting revenue maximization, the rate spectrum itself can be a strategic tool to signal quality and room type differentiation.

Revenue management system recommendations can be a part of a larger pricing or selling strategy. Some organizations, particularly those with highly disparate operations, strong branding considerations, or a large sales force might see benefit from translating revenue management system recommendations into a simpler format (like color coding or lettering). The detail from the revenue management system is maintained, but the translation either becomes easier for the frontline to consume, or becomes part of a larger set of actions that should be taken. For example, the signal for a low-demand period in the restaurant tells the waitstaff to try to up-sell more courses or more expensive menu items, whereas a high-demand period requires turning the tables faster to increase cover counts.

Finally, pricing can support a larger business strategy. A hotel might decide to lower prices to support a market share strategy that blocks new entrants, or change availability controls (like a minimum length of stay) to provide access for high-status loyalty members. Some companies make price a part of their brand promise, like citizenM in this chapter. Others build strategic initiatives that need to be supported by well-aligned pricing.

The next chapter describes just such an initiative. As of the publication of this book, one of the most prevalent strategic initiatives across the hotel industry is *personalization*. There could be many names or deployment options, but most of the industry has spoken about the desire to use what they know about their guests to create a more meaningful, personalized experience, one that the guest could not get from a third-party distributor or another hotel company. The execution of these initiatives will require coordination across departments at the hotel, including revenue management. In the next chapter, I describe the implications of such initiatives and identify the role that revenue management should play.

ADDITIONAL READING

Dan Ariely, *Predictably Irrational* is my favorite book about behavioral economics. In fact, everything he writes is just fantastic and should be required reading for every revenue manager (after you finish this book, of course).

Cathy Enz, Linda Canina, and Mark Lomanno, "Competitive Hotel Pricing in Uncertain Times," *Cornell Hospitality Report*, 9, no. 10 (2009). (Unfortunately, bad times will come again; this article will help you justify staying firm through downturns to better position for recovery.)

Cathy Enz, Linda Canina, and Breffni Noone, "Strategic Revenue Management and the Role of Competitive Price Shifting," *Cornell Hospitality Report*, 12, no. 6 (2012).

Maarten Oosten, "Strategic Pricing: The Secret Sauce of Executives," SAS white paper, www.sas.com/content/dam/SAS/en_us/doc/whitepaper1/strategic-pricing-secret-sauce-executives-106561.pdf.

REVENUE MANAGEMENT PERSPECTIVES: ADR VERSUS MARKET SHARE

While research shows that those hotels that maintain an ADR higher than the market tend to have better RevPAR performance (Enz, Canina, and Lomanno 2009), executing this strategy can be difficult at the hotel level. Hotels constantly struggle between longer-term positioning goals and the short-term need to drive revenue and share. Owners and franchisees need cash flow from their assets. Brands, particularly those that are public, need to report quarterly growth to the market. All of these factors put downward pressure on ADR.

"There will always be a conflict between short- and long-term strategies. After all, as a franchisee or owner, I take my RevPAR to the bank, not the market's RevPAR. As long as brands are reporting quarterly performance, market share will continue to be crucial. If hotels can drop their rates slightly and drive share, they will. As a result, there is much more downward pressure on ADR than there is upward pressure," says Chris Crenshaw, Vice President of Strategic Development at STR.

Chris and I spent some time talking about this issue of downward pressure on ADR. Many hotels today chase an occupancy strategy. Not only is it less risky, as I describe later, but, as Nicole Young, Vice President of Revenue Management and Sales at SBE Hotels, pointed out to me, it's a strategy that owners and asset managers understand and even encourage. Raising price to improve RevPAR performance is not as easily understood and appears risky.

It is easy to signal to the market that you are going to drop rates. You just do it, and the entire market will see and probably eventually drop their rates as well. Hotels don't necessarily follow the reverse scenario (i.e., when you raise rates the market goes with you), so for the market as a whole to start to raise rates, coordination is required. But, if the entire market plans to raise rates together, that's collusion and it's illegal.

It isn't just about regulations, however. When the majority of the market raises rates, the risk is low to raise rates too. A hotel can raise rates with the market and not lose share. However, the risk is high when the majority of the market drops rates and the hotel wants to stay where it is.

Therefore, the degree to which the management can tolerate that kind of risk, or the degree to which an experienced revenue manager can explain why the risk should be taken, is an important factor in whether a hotel will chase occupancy or ADR.

It is also possible that hotels have now become a short-term investment. Owners want to generate as much revenue as possible and then flip the asset. In this case, a short-term occupancy strategy achieves that goal.

Chris and I also talked about how this type of mind-set contributes to the commoditization of the hotel industry. The move to online distribution increased consumers' perceptions of value as expressed by price, as well as increased the immediacy of purchase. It also encouraged hoteliers to compete strictly on price, creating a perception that there is little to differentiate one hotel in a class of service from another.

CitizenM, the case study in this chapter, is a wholly owned, privately held brand, so it has the opportunity to adjust pricing according to brand standards without having to answer to owners or shareholders. Most hotels don't have this flexibility. We saw this during the financial crisis of 2008, when owners, who wanted to drive occupancy and thought price was the way to do it, were bringing suit against brand management that refused to lower rates and risk compromising brand standards.

Research does show that demand in most markets, particularly in the United States, is relatively inelastic. This means that if the market as a whole lowers price, it will not generate new demand into that market. However, within the market, a lower price as compared to the competitive set, all things being equal, will drive share to the hotel. This presents a constant temptation to start price wars that end up spiraling the entire market down. Every market is at the mercy of the weakest and most desperate competitor. However, this share shifting strategy doesn't always make up for the revenue lost from dropping rate. For this to be successful, a trade-off analysis must be done to understand the impact.

Some suggest that as rate parity agreements start to get overturned by the courts, downward pressure on rates will increase, as hotels start to compete with online channels on their own rates as well as those of the market. I am not sure whether this will be the case, but it will be interesting to watch. Chris points out that rate parity makes it really easy on revenue managers. It makes sense and is intuitive as a strategy. Theoretically, with rate parity, consumers have the confidence to just book wherever they see the hotel, and there is an appeal to that level of simplicity. However, rate parity runs counter to the core revenue management strategy of segmenting customers by the value they place on the purchase, and that includes a channel component. Further, I firmly believe that consumers do not understand rate parity. They don't believe that price is the same everywhere they book, and the most price sensitive consumers will still comb the Internet to find the best deal.

Eliminating rate parity will mean that revenue managers are going to have to carefully think through their pricing strategy and their relationship with the distribution channels. It will provide an opportunity to drive more profitable revenue, but only for those who are willing to put the work in to find the opportunities. Presumably, a strategy that drives demand to owned channels, and makes the hotel more than just the price, is going to be the winner in this scenario.

Stefan Wolf, Senior Vice President of Revenue and Distribution Strategy at Onyx Hospitality Group, provided this perspective on the elimination of rate parity: "With the decision of some European countries to challenge the rate parity enforcement practice of online travel agencies comes an opportunity for revenue managers to be back in control of distribution channel pricing. By correlating price elasticity by channel and geographic source, and taking into consideration the different contribution margins, it would allow revenue managers to price much more precisely and therefore drive up conversions and reduce distribution costs. It would however require having the analytical capability to do that as well as the ability to distribute different prices seamlessly."

So, what are hotels to do? I don't think we get away from this pressure in the short term, but focusing on differentiating strategies will help. If you are more than just your price relative to the competitive set, then the right guest won't be tempted away. I'll talk more about this concept in the next chapter, "The Path to Personalization." As revenue management systems move toward price optimization (as described in Chapter 2), newly available scenario testing ("what if" analysis) will demonstrate to owners that dropping price to shift share may actually result in less revenue than holding rate and accepting lower occupancy. Revenue management will need to be able to clearly support their pricing strategy, and presenting this type of information will help convince others of the short- and long-term benefits.

NOTES

1. See Chapter 2 for a discussion of price optimization.
2. Some may find these results slightly in conflict with the results of the research from Chapter 4, where we found that consumers were not using price as an indication of quality. I see two important differences. First, in our research, we carefully selected a range of prices that were aligned with the brand and class of hotel we tested, and second, consumers had access to review and rating information, which they were using as a quality indicator. In the absence of that information, research shows that consumers do pay attention to price.
3. As I noted at the beginning of this book, the industry has been moving away from fenced rates, particularly fences that are applied to segments rather than products. Because the fencing concept is so useful in combating unfairness perceptions, it is worth keeping in mind when building pricing strategies.

CHAPTER 8

The Path to Personalization: Revenue Management's Contribution to the New Guest Experience[*]

I am fascinated with the advances in predictive analytics and location-based marketing. Whoever masters and/or finds a way to innovate in these fields will wield a powerful hammer in the distribution battle.

—Calvin Anderson, Director of Revenue, New York Hilton Midtown

On the surface, this chapter barely seems to fit into a revenue management discussion. Personalization initiatives have primarily been conceived and driven by the marketing department, as they involve some sort of effort to develop a more relevant and engaged relationship with the guest designed around their particular needs and preferences. The reason personalization is suddenly so attractive to hotel companies is the same market changes that are impacting revenue management analytics and business process. As competition for the consumer's attention in the noisy digital environment increases, hotel companies are looking for any edge that can set them apart and keep the consumer coming back.

As I described in the last chapter, price contributes to much more than profitable revenue generation—it has implications on the guest, the brand, and the business. Personalization initiatives are a great example of how profitable pricing, and a strong revenue culture, can support a broader business strategy. Personalization involves using all of the assets within the hotel to create a meaningful experience for guests. Given the strong focus on guest experience, the balance between providing engaging, guest-centric experiences, and meeting revenue and profit goals will be challenging for hotels. These initiatives must be executed with an eye to profitable revenue generation. If revenue management hasn't already developed a strong working relationship with marketing, and instilled a revenue culture across the hotel through initiatives like

*Portions of this chapter were taken from www.hotelexecutive.com/business_review/3850/ personalization-and-pricing-how-to-drive-profitability-in-web-based-booking-engines. HotelExecutive.com retains the copyright to the articles published in the *Hotel Business Review*. Articles cannot be republished without prior written consent by HotelExecutive.com and www.hospitalityupgrade.com/magazine/MagazineArticles/The-Path-to-Personalization-The-Vision.asp.

total hotel revenue management, personalization initiatives could end up not generating profits as expected. Revenue management should have a crucial role in these initiatives, ensuring that the balance between guest experience and driving revenue and profits is maintained.

In 2014, Intercontinental Hotel Group conducted a comprehensive study of their global consumer base and came to this conclusion: "Hotel brands have traditionally concentrated on being 2D—how to be both global and local. But our research shows that the rise of *personalization* means brands must be 3D [personalized, local, global] in order to build both trust and lasting relationships with guests and to win in a highly competitive global market" (Richard Solomons, CEO of Intercontinental Hotel Group, *IHG Trends Report* 2014). Arne Sorenson, CEO of Marriott International, has widely publicized his vision for the "Next Gen Traveler" (the LinkedIn article is referenced at the end of the chapter), and described how Marriott will design an experience tailored to that emerging segment. Chris Nassetta, CEO of Hilton Worldwide, in a 2014 interview with *HOTELS* magazine, acknowledged that Hilton's customers are looking for more choice and control over their hotel experience. While he uses different words, the underlying desire is the same—to have an experience more tailored, or personalized, to an individual's needs and preferences.

The theory is that in order to stand out in an increasingly commoditized environment, hotels need to provide value to the consumer, not just by offering a "deal" on their products and services, but by providing a compelling, engaging, personalized experience during every interaction across the entire guest journey.

As the momentum around these initiatives increases, revenue managers are left wondering, first, what "personalization" actually means, and second, what revenue management's role will be in achieving this vision. In order to answer the second question, it is important to understand how marketing is conceptualizing this initiative from a guest and technology perspective, and then to identify opportunities for revenue management's data and analytics to contribute to the profitable execution of this vision. First, let's understand what "personalization" means in the context of the guest experience.

Dictionary.com defines *personalize* as: "to design or tailor to meet an individual's specifications, needs or preferences." In a technology context: "Personalization technology enables the dynamic insertion, customization or suggestion of content in any format that is relevant to the individual user, based on the user's implicit behavior and preference, and explicitly given details" (Dorman 2012).

This definition mentions the individual consumer, and refers to content, preferences, and behavior, which seems to put personalization initiatives squarely in the marketing arena. Yet, I would argue that the success of any personalization initiative depends very much on the entire organization being aligned on the back end for execution. Personalization initiatives need to be delivered with an eye to demand patterns and pricing recommendations, or they will err too much on the side of guest experience and not enough on the side of generating profits.

In order to help revenue managers assist their organizations in maintaining this delicate balance between guest experience and profitability throughout the execution of personalization initiatives, I first describe a vision for personalization within a hospitality environment. I discuss the technology, data, and analytics challenges with personalization initiatives, and finally, describe revenue management's crucial role in the successful execution of these initiatives. I spend some time in this chapter speaking about these initiatives from a marketer's perspective in order to provide revenue management with a comprehensive viewpoint on the initiative and possible impacts, as well as a common language to approach their marketing counterparts with.

PERSONALIZATION, A VISION

Consumers are leaving digital trails all over the Internet—across social media platforms, review sites, travel sites, and your own web and mobile sites. The challenge for hospitality companies will be to stitch together all of this rich data about their customers, augmented by offline guest profile data, in concert with operational insights and delivered through relevant marketing messages to execute this vision of a highly personalized guest experience. Simply applying business rules derived from aggregated web analytics data will not be enough to capture the attention (and share of wallet) of today's consumer. The company that is able to leverage advanced predictive analytics in a digital environment, combine that data with offline guest data, and deliver intelligent, personalized recommendations (in real time), will win the battle for the consumer.

Hotels have two opportunities within the umbrella of personalization. First, hotels can provide content, recommendations, or experiences that match the guest's expressed or inferred needs and preferences throughout the guest lifecycle. This isn't a "new" idea—frankly, it's just good service—but with technology enablers, personalization can be infused into every interaction, and delivery can be standardized across touch points, whether digital or in-person. For example, when a guest is researching a vacation on the hotel's website, the content they see can be customized to their search patterns (pictures of Caribbean properties in the web frames if they are searching for resorts). Further, follow-on offers can be developed based on previous searches that did not result in a booking. For example, if this same researching guest did not book during the initial browsing session, marketing can follow up with an e-mail offer or awareness communication about resorts in general, or for the specific resort the guest looked at.

The second opportunity is for the hotel to give the guest control over certain key aspects of their stay—flexible packages, attributes of the room, amenities, on-property activities, or local experiences, effectively allowing them to customize their own experience. Offers and choices should be captured, so that profiles can be updated, recommendations improved, and the program can continuously evolve.

These two opportunities are linked by the common goals of making it easy to do business with the hotel, increasing engagement and loyalty, and providing value above and beyond the room rate. Guests should not have to work hard to find properties they are interested in, features of the hotel or packages they qualify for and would like to book. Once they are on property, any and all information they have given the hotel in the past should be used to improve their current stay experience, without, of course, crossing the line to creepy.

An Illustrative Example

Consider the diagram in Figure 8.1 depicting the stages of the guest experience in broad strokes. At the center, we have Ann Roberts, our loyalty program member who is planning a weekend getaway. Ann generally stays with us for business, but in this session, her search patterns are different than normal, matching more to a leisure context. The website shows her leisure-oriented properties, packages, and room types. As she narrows down the search and starts selecting parameters, analytics can predict the three packages she'd be most likely to book, using a combination of her preferences and search context with the recommendations from the revenue management system. When she arrives at the hotel, the front desk offers her a discounted upgrade to a room type that she looked at but did not select on booking based on the pricing and availability controls from the revenue management system.

During her stay, the hotel staff is able to deliver personalized recommendations whenever they encounter her, for example, inviting her to the hotel's Friday-night wine tasting. When she attends a concert on Saturday night, and tweets about what a great event it was, the hotel's social media monitoring picks up the tweet and, in real time, algorithms determine that she qualifies to be invited to a special performers' reception at the hotel. She's messaged back with the invitation. As she checks out, her profile is updated with her stay activity, and subsequent offers reflect her stay pattern and preferences.

This is one possible example of a personalized guest experience. Other opportunities to leverage online and offline behavioral data include

Figure 8.1 The Guest Journey

flagging profiles of guests who have had service problems in the past, so that staff can be aware of any existing sensitivities. Also, if you have social media identification information from the guests, you can mine their social media activity for preferences or monitor communications for opportunities to improve their experience. Even for limited service properties, guest data about room-type preferences, amenities, or local attractions can still add value to the guest's stay experience when designed and offered appropriately.

The key to successfully executing this, or any personalized guest experience, is to infuse predictive analytics throughout the journey. Guest profiles, particularly those developed from guests with a long history with the hotel, can form the basis for some simple actions, but predictive analytics help to guide the hotel to the next best offer for that guest, based on his or her behavior, that will cultivate value in the long term. Analytics not only predict the right offer or interaction for each guest, but can also calculate the impact on operations to ensure that the hotel is set up to execute (for example, forecasting how many guests are likely to take up the spa offer so the spa can be staffed appropriately). The analytic recommendations must also be wrapped in an execution plan for how to deliver them that is aligned with the brand promise, based on past guest behavior, genuinely delivered and respectful of the guests' privacy.

Unknown Guests Are an Opportunity, Too

The personalization vision as described earlier does depend to a certain extent on what is known about Ann through past interactions with her, combined with the context of her current interactions. Most hotel companies have detailed profile information on only a small percentage of guests. This means that the vast majority of visitors to the website or even to the property do not have a rich guest profile to draw on. The same processes that are used on known guests can also be leveraged with unknown guests, but the analytics become even more critical. By tracking their search patterns on the web or mobile device, unknown guests can be analytically matched back to the context of search from other guests, and content is intelligently surfaced based on what the analytics predict is their intention. Reactions to that intervention can inform future offers to similar unknown guests.

The recommendations may not be as good as the ones that were provided to Ann, but over time, and given repeated interactions with this consumer, a profile can be stitched together and augmented if the guest books and stays. All of the interactions with known and unknown guests are tracked, improving the analytic results over time. The next section describes the data and analytics to execute this vision for both known and unknown guests. The intention of this section is to expose revenue managers to the kinds of techniques available to and being considered by digital marketers today. This helps revenue managers participate actively in conversation and identify opportunities to enhance the process with pricing and availability recommendations. But first, a slight tangent.

Execution

There will be a lot of discussion over the next few years about the proper way to execute on personalized recommendations. I am often asked for advice on this front, which is difficult to give broadly, as much of this strategy will depend on the brand strategy and the way an individual hotel has decided to construct the guest journey. I can tell you that from what I have seen so far, I have a few recommendations for organizations to consider. Again, the burden of execution will be on the operations department, but it is useful for everyone to think about.

- **Take time to map out the guest journey.** Successful organizations will have taken the time to think through what they want the guest experience to be like, from research to poststay follow up, mapping alternatives, even to the segment level. This will form the basis for execution, and, therefore, the input from all of the functions across the organization should be taken into account. This way, all actions can be taken in light of an agreed-on plan.

- **Only take action on information the guests have provided to you** (or think they could have). With all the information most people put out on the Internet, you don't really even have to ask guests for personal information anymore. Many companies are advertising that they can fill out a guest profile using web searches. I suspect that guests will consider this an invasion of privacy (see the British Airways story later). It is probably best to only use information the guest provided, or easily could have.

- **If you ask for it, use it.** Preliminary research seems to indicate that guests are willing to provide personal information if they feel that the company will use that information to serve them better. If you are asking for information, be sure the guest can see that you are using it—particularly when it comes to personal identifying information or preferences.

- **Be genuine.** In the end, analytically driven personalization recommendations are supposed to be for decision support, not to replace the good instincts and service-oriented mind-set of a great employee. Give your staff enough room to be genuine and caring.

- **On that note, train!** Simply providing an output to frontline staff to execute on is not going to make the guest feel cared for and appreciated. Front-line staff should be trained in how they should use the provided information. You can't rely on everyone to make the right decision on their own, and the stakes are pretty high when mistakes will be widely broadcast on social media.

With the operational considerations in mind let's get back to how the data and technology can support this personalized experience.

MOVING PAST TRADITIONAL WEB ANALYTICS TO DIGITAL INTELLIGENCE[1]

Data is collected at every stage of the guest journey in a variety of systems and formats. The biggest challenge to deliver on this vision of integrated, personalized marketing is to stitch together these fragmented sources of data, which come from online, offline, and even third-party sources. The data needs to be pulled together in a format useful for both analytics and reporting. There are challenges associated with integrating this data, cleansing it and ensuring it is analytics-ready, particularly because the data can be in some nontraditional formats.

Data-driven marketers use advanced analytics to perform sophisticated analyses, like regression, decision trees, or clustering, but they have traditionally been limited to using *offline data* (data collected through on-property interactions, or through reservation systems), primarily due to restrictions on access rights to online data from third-party technology vendors. Even if hotels get access to online data, commonly available web and digital analytics tools primarily aggregate and report on historical information and thus are not well suited to perform predictive analysis. In this aggregated environment, obtaining an omni-channel, integrated view of a single guest across the fragmented digital ecosphere has been extremely difficult. As a result, it has been practically impossible to get a data-centric, comprehensive view of the guest that could feed integrated marketing analytics, or more specifically, provide prescriptive recommendations for marketers. Enter digital intelligence.

Digital intelligence is defined as: "The capture, management and analysis of customer data to deliver a holistic view of the digital customer experience that drives the measurement, optimization and execution of digital customer interactions."[2]

This requires that marketers focus on understanding the "who," "what," "where," "when," and "why" of digital experiences, collecting detailed 1:1 data across channels, as opposed to aggregated snapshots channel by channel. As with any data project, it's also important to consider the downstream activities and use cases you wish to support.

For example:

- Predictive analysis to identify what unique behaviors or attributes in a visitor's digital journey are closely correlated with revenue-generating events (like a conversion or up-sell). These behaviors and attributes can then be identified and fostered for future visitors.

- Analytically forecasting website visitation by traffic source, and identifying which ad-centric channels have the largest effect in increasing overall traffic (attribution modeling). The ad strategy can be adjusted based on which channels are most productive.

- Predicting online and offline behavioral drivers of digital conversions using analytically driven segmentation techniques, and improving outbound and inbound targeting rules for future marketing communication and personalization efforts.

To support the opportunities outlined here, web and mobile data, if collected and prepared appropriately, can be merged with your company's or company-owned customer data and then streamed into your analytics, visualization, and interaction automation systems.

Recent innovations in technology are making it possible for hospitality companies to move beyond the limitations of traditional web analytics (i.e., aggregated data and historical performance analysis as opposed to predictive modeling). Marketing departments can now integrate digital data with offline guest profiles, and use that complete picture of the guest in predictive modeling to support personalized content delivery, offers and recommendations digitally as well as when the guest is on property.

INTEGRATED DATA FOR DIGITAL INTELLIGENCE

New technology for collecting and analyzing digital interactions is becoming available that will help move the industry beyond traditional web analytics to a more detailed and flexible view of the consumer. Here is a review of what hotels should be looking out for in the technology sphere as you start down the path to personalization:

- **Single line data collection insert.** Records all online behavior down to the millisecond against the session, visitor, and most important, the individual guest, while reducing tag management challenges. In addition, the data is liberated to be used in any downstream application. This is in contrast to some digital data providers that only allow aggregated access to historical data.

- **Data normalization.** This is the process of converting raw event data into usable data with business context. This can be extremely challenging to accomplish because of the variety and complexity of digital data. Business rules are typically identified to capture the different permutations of paths to the same goal, resulting in digital data organized into business events that have meaning for your operation. A good digital intelligence solution will facilitate the creation and management of these rules in an operationalized manner.

- **Proprietary data management.** The biggest advantage of a digital intelligence platform over traditional web analytics is that you collect your own data, so you are not dependent on the third-party provider sharing (or not) what they collect. This means you have access to all of your data, you have the flexibility to configure your data model to suit your specific needs, and you can facilitate analysts' access to the data so they can spend more time analyzing and less time manipulating data.

- **Tying digital data to the guest.** Traditional web analytics aggregate data for business intelligence around the performance of the website. Digital intelligence solutions should capture this information for each individual guest, at a level of detail and in a format that is appropriate for data mining, predictive analytics, forecasting, and optimization. We are interested in guest experiences, not just aggregated clicks.

The final crucial component in a digital platform is intelligent visualization. Your analysts should be able to access digital data through a highly flexible visual analytics platform, where they can not only see the trends and patterns, but apply analytics like forecasting or segmentation-centric decision trees to visually predict opportunities (or threats). These visualizations will also help to facilitate conversations between analysts and business owners—making it easier for analysts to effectively communicate results.

REVENUE MANAGEMENT SUPPORTING
THE PERSONALIZATION VISION

All of this guest-facing activity is definitely a marketing challenge and opportunity. Getting it right in front of the guest is crucial, which is where operations will come in. It's also crucial to align the infrastructure and organization to ensure personalization drives revenue, not just engagement. This is where the unique data, analytics, and skill set of revenue management should be involved. The good news is that much of the role that revenue management will play in personalization initiatives is already ongoing in most organizations.

In the constant struggle to balance providing an excellent guest experience with driving revenue and profits, revenue management's role is to ensure that personalization efforts are driving enough of the right kind of revenue to ensure they are profitable and sustainable. This will have to be done in partnership with marketing and operations, of course. As a first step, pricing recommendations will be a key component of the personalized offers and recommendations that go to the guest.

All personalized content, offers, and product selections that include a price require an input from the revenue management system. In many cases it can be just this simple, and it is probably already happening to some extent today, particularly in outbound marketing campaigns, as revenue management and marketing work more closely together. If the company is using a revenue management system, which updates prices in the selling systems, then the content surfaced to consumers during the booking process, in a direct mail or in a conversation with an agent, will be "price optimized," assuming that promotions and offers do not discount below what the revenue management system says the room is worth.

However, this is only the first step to taking full advantage of personalization opportunities to drive revenue and profits. Revenue management holds information about demand patterns, which can be incorporated with the predictions of what content to show a web shopper to ensure that as they are shown the properties they are most likely to be interested in, there is consideration for those properties that "need" that kind of demand. This can be accomplished in the search, but also through the content that is surfaced in the ad space around the search. The guest, of course, will be able to book what they want, but, as much as possible, also encouraged to book where the hotel company needs the demand.

As we established in Chapter 6, "Total Hotel Revenue Management," hotels should be focused on using all of the assets across the enterprise to attract the most profitable mix of business for the hotel as a whole. This discipline can be directly applied to, and supported by, personalization initiatives. Personalized offers should identify which guests belongs to a targeted segment and recommend or offer a package of all revenue-generating assets within the hotel, such as spa and restaurants. However, this needs to be aligned with the forecasted operating conditions at the property. For example, if personalization algorithms recommended spa treatments, the systems in the background ought to have already forecasted demand for spa to ensure that the spa has sufficient capacity during the guest's stay to accommodate the treatments before the offer is made. Revenue management data and analytics can help with packaging decisions as well. They can ensure that the package components drive demand when and where it is needed and that the pricing of that package is profitable according to forecasted demand and optimized price across the enterprise. Again, some of this activity may be happening today, so hotels should simply continue to develop and automate these processes.

In advance of the implementation of personalization initiatives, revenue managers should work with operations in departments across the organization to help instill a revenue discipline. Understanding where opportunities exist, for example, when to offer a discount or special to drive demand, or when to speed up service to increase volume (i.e., maybe the cheapest spa treatments are not available during peak spa periods, or the restaurant offers more expensive specials on weekends), can support the profitable execution of personalized recommendations. Personalization initiatives can be layered over this revenue discipline, so guests are guided to experiences that are aligned with their preferences, but also with the operational conditions and revenue-generating opportunities in the property.

Personalization and Guest-Centric Revenue Management

Personalization initiatives provide a good opportunity to further revenue management's long-term vision of guest-centric revenue management (I discussed this concept in Chapter 6). There are several different ways to execute on guest-centric revenue management. Some would say that guest-centric revenue management is about calculating the lifetime value of a guest, building that into the optimization algorithm, and then either restricting access or delivering a specific price based on that individual customer's lifetime value. In my view, the role of price in personalization does not have to go this far to be successful. There is a spectrum of possibilities, all of which will be effective in both driving revenue and improving the guest experience. In fact, pricing can become more guest-centric even without changing the core revenue management analytic process.

Consider the following scenarios: A guest searches the website for resort properties, and you know that when they have vacationed with you in the past, they've booked suites. When they click check availability, personalization technology kicks in and the suites offers are displayed first, with the offer that is most likely to be accepted as the featured offer. If the price of the suites is the optimal price for that product, based on the revenue management system's recommendations, then revenue management has participated in the personalization process without needing to know anything about the guest, the offer, or the content.

The same goes for the case in which a guest who was browsing a website, but did not book, receives an e-mail offer for the product they were searching for a couple of days later. If the price is based on a revenue management system recommendation, pricing is part of the personalization process without changing the existing revenue management process. The possible exception in both cases is that if you move to selling by room type, a revenue management system that can give optimal price recommendations at a room type level will provide more profitable pricing recommendations. In both cases, if the guest books the offer, the booking becomes part of the data that the revenue management system consumes for future pricing calculations.

As the personalization capabilities become more complex, the challenges facing revenue management increase. Allowing guests control over their experience might include providing a personalized package, where they pick the elements and are given a price based on their selections (which would require accurate estimates of the value of each of the packaged elements, in addition to the value of them together as a package—basically a giant forecasting and optimization problem). Personalized price at the individual level, based on a balance between customer lifetime value and the forecasted value of the product, is also a possibility. In this case, the selling system would have to be set up to deliver a recommendation in real time based on analytics about the specific customer who is booking, as well as the available inventory and expected demand to come. It requires more analytics, technology, and integration, but is certainly achievable should you wish to price and manage demand at this level. Remember that discounting hotel rooms, the core revenue stream, is risky, unless you know for sure the guest's spend across the property and over his or her lifetime will make up for the discount (and also, that the particular guest would not have paid the full price and also spent across the property). This is why I do not necessarily advocate for guest-centric pricing in hotels, but rather, guest-centric marketing, focused on capturing and nurturing value based on the value and preferences of the guest or segment.

The challenge we face as an industry is how to include guest value in decision making without it appearing to the consumer to be price discrimination or price gouging. Encouraging guests to come to you through "private" channels (i.e., logging into the loyalty program) provides you the opportunity to show them pricing or products that are not generally available, getting you around rate parity issues and creating a "fence" that helps the guest understand why their price is different from the publicly available rate. Still, you certainly cannot offer higher prices for the same product when it is so easy for guests to find the generally available price online, so you need to consider how much incentive is required to get your "best" guests to book in these private channels—maybe you do not even need to discount at all.

More important, to maintain the perception of price fairness, guest-centric pricing and personalization should be about displaying products that the guest is most likely to be interested in or creating attractive custom packages, not pricing the same products differently for different guests. There might be some products or offers that are only available to guests who have a certain predicted value to the firm, but evidence has shown that consumers need to feel that "the price is the price," never think that they are being charged more because of who they are or what they do. Remember, consumers accept variable pricing based on demand patterns for the same product because that price is available for everyone who books (Kimes and Noone 2002). They have been shown to react negatively to consumer-specific pricing when it is not framed or fenced fairly. Recall the reaction to Amazon charging different prices to different consumers for the same book, or the negative reaction when Orbitz was presenting different, more expensive, products to Mac users.

Regardless of how revenue management contributes, whether systematic (where the revenue management algorithms are part of the process), or more ad hoc, where revenue management provides analysis and support for personalization initiatives to help analyze their demand or revenue impacts, revenue management needs to have a seat at the table. Personalization will require the involvement of all functions across the organization to be successful.

Price parity agreements with OTAs will reduce the flexibility of personalized pricing, but as long as guests are logged in to their account, they are booking through a "private" channel, and therefore, not subject to rate parity agreements. Otherwise, hotels are going to have to ensure that the parity is respected throughout the guest's interaction with the website. This will continue to require a good deal of effort on the part of revenue management to track and ensure rate parity.

Customer Choice Modeling

An interesting approach to personalized pricing becomes available when selling product through "owned" channels where you control the price presentation. You can use the way that guests shop and ultimately buy to optimize pricing strategies, packaging options, and presentation order. This allows you to not only set the right price based on what elements of the package customers value, but also you can steer guests to the most profitable option for the hotel according to the contents of the package, and the order in which you present the prices.

There is plenty of information on the technical details of customer choice modeling, but at a high level, this process works by tracking and analyzing the choices customers make among all available options, noting what they picked and what they did not pick, and including data from "browsers" who picked nothing. The web is ideal for this type of experiment, because you can change prices frequently and track changes in booking behavior, and a lot of data is generated very quickly, adding to the predictive power of the algorithms. As the patterns of choice are tracked, the algorithms can begin to understand what value consumers place on each attribute of the purchase, as well as test price sensitivity. This methodology is similar in theory to what we used in the studies we talked about in Chapter 4, "Pricing in a Social World," but we conducted those studies in a highly controlled environment. This methodology builds on what we did by using the choice behavior in the real world to estimate the probability of choice for each available product, and then using that information to offer the optimal mix of products to maximize revenue.

Many researchers believe that customer choice modeling is the next big innovation in revenue management modeling. They feel it is the best way to model consumer behavior (because the algorithms are based on actual customer shopping behavior). The challenge will be that although this may be a very accurate methodology to measure sensitivity and preferences, if you are not getting a significant amount of business through a channel that you control (which allows you to collect the data and experiment with the price presentation enough to get valid results), the benefits of choice modeling might not move the needle enough to justify making the changes required to the website, call center agent selling, and revenue management system. Also, it is important to note that the data associated with these problems, and the complexity of the analytics, can get large very quickly, which means that even in a big data world, choice modeling formulations could become too large to be solved in a reasonable amount of time.

CROSSING THE LINE TO "CREEPY": QANTAS AND BRITISH AIRWAYS

In two well-publicized stories, these major airlines struggled with personalization initiatives that ultimately made their most valuable customers feel uncomfortable. Qantas provided tablets with profiles of frequent fliers to the flight attendants, but did not provide adequate training when the program was initially rolled out. Passengers started to feel that attendants were reading from a script instead of genuinely connecting with them, and it made them uncomfortable.[3]

In 2012, British Airways announced a program called Know Me to use facial recognition via Google Image search to identify their most valuable customers while they were moving through the airport. It would then provide information about them from online sources to any agent they may come in contact with, so that VIPs could be recognized, welcomed, and treated as VIPs. Many are highly concerned about invasions of privacy with this initiative (although spokespeople for British Airways maintain that they are in compliance with privacy regulations).[4] This example reinforces the point I made earlier about only using information the guest has provided to you directly.

HOW DO WE GET STARTED?

Personalization in a service context, especially hospitality, is nothing really new. Experienced staff give this level of service to regular guests all the time. The difference is executing that same level of service on a mass scale, and across all interaction points, particularly in the digital environment. Keep this in mind as you design your programs. Your personalization process should replicate the good service instincts of your best staff—that keeps the personal and relevant touch without crossing the line to creepy.

There are many steps you can take now, even if you have yet to implement any technology to support the initiative. Consider any of the following:

- **Leverage your mobile presence.** Consumers are turning to mobile for everything from research, to transactions, to logistics support. Hotels must provide value through their mobile app, or risk losing consumers who prefer the integrated mobile experience they can get from a third party, like an online travel agent. Think creatively with your counterparts about how to set yourself apart with your mobile presence, and how to take advantage of the data generated through those interactions.

- **Evaluate technology offerings and vendor partners.** This step can (and perhaps should) be time-consuming, but you need to make sure that you are making the right choices here such that you can execute your personalization vision, and still leave flexibility to continue to grow, innovate and evolve.

- **Understand how your website is performing.** As competition heats up for the online consumer—between third-party distribution channels and metasearch (and so on and so on), how does your website stack up? Is it easy for consumers to find? To navigate? Does if effectively represent your brand? Does it show up in search? If you are not where your customers are, you'll miss out on the opportunity for them to come directly to you. If they can't find what they are looking for on your website, they'll go to a third party—or to your competitor. My biggest pet peeve with hotel websites is how difficult it can be to find the button that says "book now." Make sure it is very easy for the visitor to navigate to booking—after all, our OTA partners do.

- **Evaluate the cross-channel experience.** Everyone has multiple devices these days, and your guests are no exception. Consumers will look for you through a myriad of devices (mobile, tablet, laptop), and a myriad of channels (website, Facebook). Are you delivering a consistent experience through all of these channels? Is the look and feel the same (adjusting for channel demographics, etc., of course)? Are they recognized through all channels? Can they find the same product or services no matter where they look? Put yourself in your guest's shoes, and be critical of what you are seeing.

- **Simplify the booking process.** As an industry, we need to be sure that we are making it as easy as possible for our guests to do business with us (and holding booking engine providers accountable for ensuring that the booking process if as efficient for the guest as possible!). Looking at it from the guest's perspective, booking a room today can be very confusing and difficult. Booking links are buried on brand.com, so they are nearly impossible to find. Search parameters are confusing, and information has to be entered multiple times. Guests are presented with long lists of room pricing and packages (nearly always starting with the cheapest, whether the guest asks for that or not), many of which they don't qualify for. It is difficult to enter or search for options (room type, special packages). The easier the booking process, the more likely the guest will be to complete their transaction, and use your site next time as well.

- **Rethink your loyalty program.** Think about how the data you collect through your loyalty program, and the rewards you provide in return for that information, support a personalization initiative. There might be more data you should collect in the sign-up process, and better ways to align the rewards with the guests' profile and preferences, reinforcing the value to the guests while growing their value to your organization.

- **Start operations on the path to personalization.** You can start conceptualizing what personalization will look like across the guest experience now, even if you do not yet have the tools to execute it. Start identifying interaction points where personalized recommendations can be offered. Conceptualize a website flow with personalized content. Identify portions of your service process that could be "customized" by a guest. Decide what information you want to access about the guests, and how you want to use it. (Will guests appreciate you printing out a picture from their Facebook page for next to the bed, or will they find that intrusive and "creepy"? Do you want to offer the exact same drink to a guest when they approach the hotel bar, no matter where they are, or just be sure you have their brand behind the bar "just in case"?). As I suggest earlier, figure out how you would get personalized recommendations in the hands of your team members, and how you would like to have them interpret and act on those recommendations. These actions will help to guide your technology, data and analytics strategies, as well as setting a plan for the change management required to execute.

Remember that guests should be at the center of these initiatives, no matter how they reach you.

> First and foremost, we must be easy to do business with. In simple terms, we must offer the consumer a great purchasing experience regardless of the channel *they* choose. We must "sell the way a customer wants to buy" and that will necessitate a diverse and colorful distribution strategy. As much as we try, we can't force usage of brand.com, and so that means being agile enough to participate in distribution strategies across disparate platforms, both in brand and through partnerships, to reach consumers regardless of where they purchase.
>
> —*Scott Pusillo, Vice President, Market Strategy, Viceroy Hotel Group*

You will notice that most of these activities I describe earlier are not under the direct control of revenue management. Some of these will have to be managed through influence with the other departments across the hotel. Personalization is an all-encompassing initiative, however, representing a change to core facets of the operation. Because of this, it is crucial that all departments have a voice in the process, and visibility to the initiatives. After all, if moving in this direction does not generate revenue and profits, what's the point?

EXAMPLES OF STARTING ON THE PATH TO PERSONALIZATION

The complete personalization of the guest journey as I described at the beginning of the chapter is the vision, but how you start on that path will be up to where you as an organization see the low-hanging fruit. It doesn't really matter where you enter the path. I provide some cross-industry examples below to provide inspiration about the "art of the possible."

Webpage Interactions

Lotte.com is the largest online retailer in Korea. Obviously, the website is the company's only channel and therefore, is its source of revenue. It has developed an integrated web traffic analysis system to improve the online consumer experience, increase the returns for its marketing campaigns and drive conversions. The company deployed some advanced customer experience analytics to the website, tracking consumer clicks, and identifying opportunities to improve the experience and drive conversions. It was able to identify popular items, effective promotions, and places where consumers were abandoning carts.

Tracking customer behavior at this level helped the company uncover many "truths," some being "inconvenient truths"—situations where the data and analytics told a different story than the line the business executives had hoped about their product.

Algorithms allow the site to immediately identify highly profitable customers and provide content and incentives to encourage purchases. They can identify and fix the causes of shopping cart abandonment. All of this activity resulted in a first year sales increase of $10 million.[5]

Because Lotte.com is an online retailer, it clearly has a huge opportunity to drive revenue, but any website improvement initiative could be highly valuable to hotels that want to drive traffic to their owned channels. The driving principle behind this initiative was to make it easy for customers to do business with Lotte.com by providing the right recommendations and a smooth booking process. Hotels can definitely learn from this.

Agent Selling Experience

Telenor is the leading tel-co in Norway. They had a desire to ensure a more personalized sales experience with offers that were relevant to the customer but also profitable to Telenor. They developed a sales guidance tool, Automated Sales Tips (AST). Automated analytic models predict the most profitable offer for each customer, driving sales tips that appear on the screen of the agents. However, the program was more than just delivering a recommendation of what the agent should offer the customer. Deployment of this initiative also involved business process change and training programs. The analytics were wrapped in a sales process to ensure that agents knew how to deliver the results in a personalized and respectful matter. Since rolling out the AST program, sales and customer satisfaction have increased.[6]

This example is relevant for both the call center and the front desk of hotels, where direct interactions with guests provide an opportunity for up-sell and cross-sell. To me, the most important part of the AST program that hoteliers should learn from is that the analytics that delivered these next best offers in real time were wrapped in a sales process. The agents were thoroughly trained in how to deliver the recommendations in a personalized and low-pressure manner. Remember that the success of any personalization initiative will depend on how it is operationalized. Training for those who will be in direct contact with the guest will be critical.

During the Service Experience

Vail Resorts operates ski resorts in the western United States. Several years ago, it launched a marketing program called EpicMix, which essentially "gamified" the ski experience. When skiers registered for the EpicMix program, Vail was given permission to tie skiers' personal identities to RFID chips (radio frequency identification) in their badges. The skiers' activity across the slopes was tracked, and they were rewarded with badges and points for achieving certain milestones (skiing a set of difficult slopes, achieving a certain number of vertical feet, skiing on the coldest day of the year). Participants could post activity through their social media channels, and track their achievements against those of their network.

This program proved hugely popular, and dramatically increased engagement and repeat visits. Vail was also able to use this skier behavior matched with skier profiles to create highly specific microsegments for improved targeting for their marketing campaigns. It also used the information in aggregate to improve service offerings, operating hours, and ski slope configurations.[7]

Hotels can look for opportunities to better understand guest behavior during the service experience, whether it's services they use, areas of the hotel they frequent, or activities they engage in. This information is valuable not only to improve your relationship and marketing efforts to individual guests, but operationally, it can identify opportunities to adjust service offerings to better meet the needs of your guests. There are many options becoming available, including iBeacon technology, location tracking through Wi-Fi, or RFID in key cards or bands. Each provides a specific set of data about the user, and can be used with varying degrees of opt-in from the guests. It will be interesting to track how this technology evolves and is used in the coming years.

PROFILING VERSUS TRACKING BEHAVIOR: A CAUTIONARY TALE

I have one final word of caution for any hotel that is embarking on a personalization initiative. In the pressure to develop a complete profile of our guests, it is tempting to gather a complete set of demographic and preference behavior, and then use that information to send offers. Remember that without context, guest profiling can lead to serious mistakes.

Take this example of two men who share quite a bit of demographic and preference details:

Both men were born in 1948, grew up in England, and both have been married twice with two children. These men are wealthy and successful in business. They both spend their winter holidays in the Alps and love dogs.

With this set of information, it would be easy to assume that these men would be interested in and respond to the same marketing offers, and that it would be appropriate to treat them very similarly.

What might you do differently if you found out that one of the men was Prince Charles (British royalty) and the other was Ozzy Osbourne (heavy-metal rock star and reality TV star)?*

This silly example illustrates an important point—applying business rules to a guest profile is limiting. Advanced analytics applied to the intersection of profile and context allows you to build a more complete picture of the guest and provide more relevant recommendations and offers.

FINAL ADVICE FOR REVENUE MANAGERS

The most important role you can take on right now to put your organization on the path to personalization is to start your organization toward the vision of total hotel revenue management as described in Chapter 6. Specifically, you should focus on creating a revenue-oriented culture across the entire hotel or the entire company. This will ensure that as the organization begins to define the guest experience and conceptualize personalization strategies, it is doing so with an eye to opportunities to generate incremental revenue. Revenue management's leadership in defining the most profitable business mix for the hotel, identifying opportunities to leverage existing assets to generate incremental revenue, and keeping the team focused on the critical balance between guest experience and firm profitability will not only ensure the long-term success of the personalization initiatives, but also certainly help the organization develop creative ways to generate incremental revenue across the guest experience.

This chapter brings up yet another expanded responsibility for revenue management, which calls into question what the profile and skill set of a revenue manager, and the revenue management organization, should be moving forward. Having the right resource in place that can navigate relationships with other departments, identify and execute on tactical and strategic opportunities and evangelize for the value of the discipline is and will continue to be key to success moving forward.

---

* This story is attributed to Dr. Peter Gentsh, founder, Business Intelligence Group—B.I.G.

In the final chapter of the book, I address this issue of the right profile of the revenue manager of the future, and the right organizational structure to support continued success.

ADDITIONAL READING

The Future of Guest Experience, ebook by skiff.com. This ebook contains interviews with 28 hospitality CEOs to understand what the industry is thinking in terms of guest experience. Published in early 2015, it will be interesting to see how the industry achieves this vision over time. http://products.skift.com/ebook/the-future-of-guest-experience.

The Path to Personalization Part, 1, www.hospitalityupgrade.com/_magazine/MagazineArticles/The-Path-to-Personalization-The-Vision.asp.

The Path to Personalization, Part 2, www.hospitalityupgrade.com/techTalk/Articles/The-Path-to-Personalization-Part-Two-Digital-Intelligence-for-Hospitality.

Arne Sorenson on the next-gen guest experience, https://www.linkedin.com/pulse/20140325110517–239587237-state-of-hospitality-ask-the-next-gen-traveler.

"Vail Resorts Creates Epic Experiences with Customer Intelligence," SAS white paper, www.sas.com/en_us/whitepapers/vail-resorts-creates-epic-experiences-with-customer-intelligence-105852.html.

REVENUE MANAGEMENT PERSPECTIVES: CONVERGENCE OF DIGITAL MARKETING AND REVENUE MANAGEMENT

There is an ongoing debate in revenue management today about the convergence of digital marketing and revenue management. Over the past few years, revenue management, particularly property level revenue managers, have been called on to manage digital channels, whether they are selling channels (OTAs), marketing channels, or even social channels. As these disciplines converge, the question remains: Are revenue managers also digital marketers? Should they be? I asked a group of revenue management leaders their thoughts on this issue. As you can see, there is no one path at this point, except that revenue management needs to be educated and be prepared to get involved.

> I agree that there is definitely some overlap and convergence between revenue management and digital marketing. I honestly am not sure where digital belongs. I really think, today, it belongs with the person at each property who has the most passion and knowledge of digital marketing. I think that it falls equally between disciplines and the person who is best suited to manage digital should own it, and it should not be driven by the position. I think as time evolves digital will ultimately fall under revenue management and the Director of Sales and Marketing role will transition into just a Director of Sales role. I also think that today a lot of digital marketing is being driven by the brands and management companies and that the people at the hotel level do not have a good understanding of exactly what digital marketing is and how to use it.
>
> —Linda Gulrajani, Vice President, Revenue Strategy and Distribution, Marcus Hotels and Resorts

"Revenue management needs to become educated on digital marketing and perhaps even be an expert in that area, depending on the hotel. These positions need to be cross trained and work very closely. I encourage all of our directors of revenue management to take online courses in digital marketing and become as knowledgeable as possible," says Janelle Cornett, Regional Director of Revenue Management, TPG Hospitality

Time will tell on this issue, but I see two sides of this argument. On one hand, there is a certain danger to spreading revenue management too thin, as crossing into demand generation roles as well as demand control might risk losing the laser focus on the discipline of generating incremental revenue. On the other hand, there are some interesting opportunities happening now as companies are experimenting with consolidating all revenue-generating functions into one group or function, or creating a broader commercial role as opposed to one that is strictly called revenue management or digital marketing. Within this integrated mind-set, there is the opportunity, as I describe in Chapter 5, to put a revenue-minded discipline behind profitable demand generation. If I had to decide today, I would probably lean toward the latter approach, but ensure that all functions on that team had a revenue mind-set, and that I had at least one revenue specialist on the team to look after the system and the deployment of the pricing strategy within the broader revenue generation context.

I encourage you to think through this issue as you read the final chapter in this book. I spoke with revenue leaders from many different types of organizations around the world, who provided their thoughts about this issue specifically and the future of the discipline in general. Their perspectives will help you form your own opinion about the right way to think about revenue management and digital marketing.

NOTES

1. James McCormick, "Digital Intelligence Replaces Web Analytics," Forrester Research, November 11, 2013.
2. The author would like to gratefully acknowledge the expertise provided by Suneel Grover, Principle Solutions Architect, SAS, to this and the following section on emerging opportunities in digital intelligence.
3. https://hbr.org/2013/06/digital-marketings-big-custome.
4. www.businesstraveller.com/news/ba-to-roll-out-a-know-mea-initiative.
5. This story was adapted from www.sas.com/en_us/customers/lotte.html.
6. This story was adapted from www.sas.com/en_us/customers/telenor.html.
7. This story was adapted from "Vail Resorts Creates Epic Experiences with Customer Intelligence," SAS white paper, www.sas.com/en_us/whitepapers/vail-resorts-creates-epic-experiences-with-customer-intelligence-105852.html.

CHAPTER 9

The Future of Revenue Management*

Today's revenue managers need more than just strong analytical skills. They need strong communication skills. They need to be able to work with people with strong personalities and competing priorities and sell their ideas. They need to be comfortable with risk and willing to make decisions with incomplete information. And they need to be confident enough to defend their decisions and actions, even when the results turn out to not be favorable.

—*Lynn Zwibek, Manager, Revenue Management Training Delivery, Americas*

As the discipline of revenue management evolves, as I have described in great detail in this book, the revenue manager and the revenue management organization must evolve as well. The days of simply promoting a front desk agent or a call center manager to the revenue management role are long gone. Today's revenue manager looks very different from the revenue manager of the past, and the revenue manager of the future will be different still. As digital marketing, distribution, and revenue management converge and outlets across the hotel begin to adapt revenue management techniques, revenue managers need to expand their scope of influence and understanding, yet still ensure that proper revenue discipline is maintained in their department, across the hotel and throughout the organization.

Added to this, with the growing visibility and strategic importance of the role, owners, asset managers, and the investment community are starting to pay attention to revenue management. This means that revenue managers will be called on by a wide audience of diverse personas—probably up to the highest executive levels at the hotel and at corporate—to provide performance updates, explain their strategy,

---

and justify decisions. Communication skills and business acumen will therefore be essential for success in the coming years.

The career path for revenue management is also starting to expand. The discipline has only been around for a couple of decades, so career paths are not firmly established. This is a big challenge for revenue management, as it is difficult to attract top talent without a clear and upwardly mobile career path. Still, we are seeing some interesting movement across industries and hotel departments, and up into the executive levels of organizations. Who knows, someday very soon we may have our first CEO of a major hospitality company coming from revenue management.

Different types of hotels are embracing revenue management, so the organizational models of property level revenue managers supported by a regional and corporate structure are changing as well. As revenue management moves into extended stay, economy and limited service hotels, the budget is not there to support a revenue manager at each property— in fact, the lack of complexity at the property level probably means a dedicated on-site revenue manager is not required. However, if there isn't going to be a revenue manager on property, it is even more important that the hotel's management team have bought in to the program (think about Tim from Red Roof's example from Chapter 7). Alternate organization models are evolving, and there has been an ongoing debate about the right organizational model to support an effective revenue management culture both in the traditional full-service environment and now in the evolving limited service models.

Technology has always played a crucial role in revenue management. However, the job of the revenue manager and the job of the revenue management system are not the same. The revenue management system is there to make tactical, day-to-day price recommendations. The revenue manager must interpret those recommendations in light of their pricing strategy, as well as keep an eye on the longer-term market conditions. As technology evolves, companies must keep in mind where the system stops and the revenue manager starts.

In this chapter, I discuss the skills and experience you should look for when hiring or developing revenue management capabilities within your organization. I talk about some alternate organizational models for revenue management departments, and discuss predictions from industry experts about what the job of the revenue manager and the structure of the revenue management organization will look like in the years to come. This chapter is designed to help you think through how to set up the people, organization, and culture to sustain the strength and influence of revenue management within your organization. It is also designed to help you as an individual to strategize about your own career path and the skills you want to develop to achieve it.

PROFILE OF A REVENUE MANAGER

As we have discussed in previous chapters, revenue management is taking on a more strategic role in the hospitality industry, with growing responsibilities and new opportunities to expand the discipline and its influence. In the midst of this evolution, one thing remains constant: the person who fills the revenue management role is the key to a successful revenue management program. This role requires an analytically minded leader, who can successfully work across the organization to drive results.

> A revenue manager today needs to be a revenue manager, a sales professional, and a marketing expert. Gone are the days the director of revenue management can hide in their office behind computer screens.
>
> —*Janelle Cornett, Regional Director of Revenue Management, TPG Hospitality*

Revenue management has traditionally been a detail-oriented, analytical discipline obsessed with data and consumed with spreadsheets. The more analytical, the better. Even as recently as 10 years ago, revenue managers were building their own revenue management systems in Excel and running the pricing of entire large hotels off spreadsheets. As the discipline has matured, the tools and technology have improved and the role has expanded, the requirements to be successful in the job are also evolving.

In the early days of revenue management, before hotels had access to revenue management systems, it was all the revenue managers could do to access data and build a few reports. With this information, they could recognize historical patterns and set up rules to manage demand. This was the *descriptive phase* of revenue management.

Once revenue management systems became widely available for hotels, the forecasting and optimization technology allowed revenue management to move from the descriptive to the *predictive phase*. The forward-looking analytics help revenue managers predict the future and set pricing to achieve the forecasted revenue potential in the market. Systems pick up trends and patterns ahead of time, so the organization can proactively set prices to take advantage of expected demand to come. Most hotel revenue managers are in this predictive phase. They have become adept at understanding and manipulating the output of a revenue management system and deploying prices through the many channels where the hotel is for sale.

The next opportunity for revenue managers is to become *prescriptive*. Instead of just knowing what will happen, revenue managers should be able to develop a plan to manage through it. This is the "so what are we going to do about it?" phase. In many cases, this will require a broader understanding of market forces, and the ability to work with other departments across the hotel, like marketing. If you aren't going to sell out, can demand be sourced through alternate channels? If you are going to sell out, are you being aggressive enough with pricing? Is the operation set up to drive incremental revenue and profits from the guests?

Figure 9.1 depicts this evolution from "what happened?" to "what will happen" to "what are we going to do about it?"

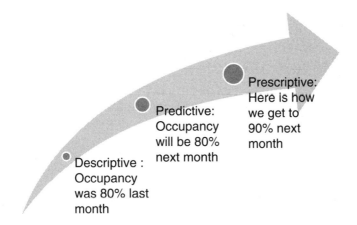

Figure 9.1 The Evolution of a Revenue Manager

For our business model, prescriptive revenue
managers will be essential to moving the business
forward. We need revenue managers with the business
acumen to understand market forces and determine
how to manage through them.

—*Tom Buoy, Senior Vice President, Revenue Management, Extended Stay America*

What the Research Says

Sherri Kimes (2010) conducted a broad survey of revenue management professionals to understand the future of revenue management from the industry's perspective. In her research she identified the direction that the discipline will take and the skill sets that revenue managers of the future will need to be successful. At the time, this was the list of skills that revenue leaders felt would be required to advance the discipline.

- **Analytical.** Revenue management is an analytical discipline, and is becoming even more so as it evolves from inventory optimization to price optimization. Even if you are using an automated revenue management solution, the revenue manager will need to be able to interpret the results, adjust them as necessary, and conduct ad hoc analytical analyses to support special projects. A revenue manager should be very comfortable with analytic techniques like forecasting and predictive modeling. Look for a background that includes some statistics or operations research or, at a minimum, previous experience that included working with numbers.

- **Good communication skills.** Sherri Kimes calls the ideal revenue manager a "geek who can speak." Not everyone in the hotel is, or will be, analytically minded. An ideal revenue manager will be able to clearly and effectively translate complex pricing concepts into understandable actions. In order for revenue managers to be successful in a strategic role within the organization, they must be effective and persuasive communicators.

- **Data-minded.** Successful strategic pricing decisions require gathering and interpreting data from a multitude of sources. The revenue manager must be comfortable with data—where it comes from, how it is collected, how to identify and overcome data quality problems, and how to adjust for missing information. Data is never perfect, so a good revenue manager will be able to identify strengths and weaknesses of data sources that support strategic decision making.

- **Technology-savvy.** Revenue managers have always needed to be comfortable utilizing revenue management software, interacting with databases and performing ad hoc analyses in external analytics packages. Many revenue managers are very familiar with the hotel's PMS (property management systems) as well. The revenue managers of the future will need a basic knowledge of systems integration and should have an interest in staying current with trends in any technology that influences bookings. The rapidly evolving distribution space is putting pressure on revenue managers to also develop expertise in web page design, mobile platforms, and social media channels. They should be able to provide advice and guidance as the hotel considers participating in new channels, launching mobile applications, or making changes to booking engines on the website. Any of these decisions will have an impact on revenue performance. It is imperative that the revenue manager be savvy enough to understand the implications and build a solid strategy around them.

- **Negotiator.** Revenue management is expanding beyond rooms to other revenue-generating outlets within the hotel. Revenue management and marketing are beginning to realize the benefits of synchronizing their activities. As revenue managers begin to work more closely with departments across the organization and influence the decisions that are made by those departments, adept negotiators will be able to navigate tricky political waters to drive results.

- **Education.** Increasing numbers of undergraduate and graduate programs are offering courses in revenue management, and some even offer concentrations. In fact, while revenue management had been the exclusive domain of a few hospitality programs, traditional business programs are incorporating pricing and revenue management into their course offerings. A formal revenue management education is a bonus, but candidates with a general business or economics background would also be valuable, provided they understand supply/demand dynamics and the analytics. In addition to degree programs, there are also many excellent certification programs available. If your revenue manager doesn't come to you with formal revenue management education or previous hotel revenue management experience, you have options for filling in the gaps.

Most of these skills are very relevant today, and many organizations are identifying others that go along with this list. I might argue that given the prevalence of revenue management systems today, while revenue managers should be analytically minded, they don't have to have degrees in math or statistics. Some experience with interpreting analytical results and working with numbers is sufficient for most revenue managers, although larger companies may want to invest in a couple of resources with deep analytic experience to work with the system vendors and perform the more complex ad hoc analyses.

"Revenue management talent should be calculated risk-takers, have strong aptitude and a behavioral economics mind-set," says Sloan Dean, Vice President of Revenue Optimization for Ashford Hospitality Trust.[1] He believes that some of the reluctance the market sees with pushing rates even in good economic conditions comes from having risk-adverse revenue managers.

The challenge is in finding a resource that fits this very unique profile. Organizations need to figure out which of these skills are required, which can be trained, and which are optional. When you have the option to have multiple resources in a revenue management department, you could split the roles such that one person does not have to be everything on the list. For example, you can hire a hard-core analytics expert for the analysis and a business-focused resource for the communication and negotiation responsibilities. One of the biggest challenges

I hear revenue managers talking about these days is the shortage of talent to fill this critical role.

Finding and Retaining Talent

Clearly, the ideal revenue manager must possess quite a unique skill set. Attracting the right talent will require a change in the industry's traditional mind-set. A background in front desk operations or reservations is no longer sufficient, or even required, for a revenue manager. You may have to look beyond the hotel industry to identify someone who has the right business and numbers background (maybe a general business degree), and is willing to learn the industry. Think about what might be easier to teach, business acumen or the inner workings of the hotel industry?

Companies are having to get creative in how they identify and recruit revenue management talent. Sloan Dean says that at Ashford Hospitality Trust, they feel "Ability is just as important as experience," and they use case-study interviews to screen talent as opposed to a behavioral or skills interview.

Neal Fegan from Fairmont Hotels and Resorts thinks it's crucial to educate HR (human resources) on revenue management. "Revenue management isn't very well understood within the hotel culture. It's a fairly young discipline. We have a full program to educate human resources on revenue management." It's much easier for HR to identify the talent if they understand the concept.

Once the talent is hired, organizations need to be able to retain this talent. Ongoing training and development is very important. Calvin Anderson, Director of Revenue for the Hilton Midtown in New York City, requires his team to listen to podcasts and be members of a departmental book club. He feels that constantly exposing his team to new ideas and different business examples challenges them to stay engaged and active in their roles.

One of the unique challenges of property level revenue management is that in many hotels there is just one revenue manager. They do not have a built-in peer group to bounce ideas off of or socialize with. Building a revenue management community in certain markets, or even virtually, is a good way to keep these folks engaged and to continue their career development.

As the skill sets become more specialized and robust, the right talent will get more expensive. The industry must recognize that they need to invest, and continue to invest, in revenue management talent. We will lose talent to higher-paying jobs outside of hospitality, ones that they are increasingly well qualified for, if we don't change the compensation structure for revenue management.

The HSMAI Foundation and ZS Associates conducted a comprehensive survey study of incentive plans and compensation for revenue management roles. The study provides a good perspective into the design and administration of incentive plans, and identifies some perceived issues and opportunities for hotels. Full details of the study can be found at www.zsassociates.com/publications/whitepapers/how-to-upgrade-hotel-sales-and-revenue-management-incentive-practices-and-improve-plan-satisfaction. These findings provide really good guidance about what it will take to attract and retain revenue management talent.

Here is a summary of key findings and opportunities:

Findings

1. The majority of revenue management plans are remarkably similar to each other, particularly for overall plan structure, performance metrics and payout schedules.
   - However, there are differences in performance metrics: while RevPAR Index (revenue per available room) and Room Night Revenue dominate the plans, properties tend to select just one of the two, with RevPAR Index as a slight favorite.

2. Overall, revenue managers have low satisfaction with current incentive compensation practices. In particular, revenue managers feel that effectiveness can be improved by providing:
   - Competitive pay levels.
   - Effective goal setting (most fall short of achieving target payout).

- Differential earning for top performers.
- Valued employee development.
- Recognition programs.

Opportunities

1. Increase pay-for-performance, to reward top performers.
   - Create plan upside and downside risk and set payout levels whereby the true stars consistently earn more than the lower performers.
2. Improve goal-setting effectiveness, to better reflect performance expectations.
3. Ensure opportunities for career growth of high performers within the company, to retain top talent.
4. Improve formal performance reporting, to increase plan motivational impact.
   - In particular, provide more frequent and transparent formal communication to solidify revenue managers' understanding of their plan's expectations, and increase their understanding of how they are performing toward goals.
5. Benchmark pay levels on an ongoing basis, to ensure market-appropriate pay levels.

I would encourage you to review the broader study for more details about this critical component of job satisfaction and employee retention.

REVENUE MANAGEMENT CAREER PATHS

A big challenge for this young discipline is understanding the career path. It is crucial for new revenue management talent to understand that there are great advancement opportunities, whether you would like to stay in revenue management or move into a different area of the hotel industry. Revenue management system vendors are always looking for good talent with experience in hotel revenue management as well.

For a relatively young discipline, a prescribed career path is difficult to identify. As the revenue management discipline has evolved, it has been interesting to watch the many and varied career paths that people who started in revenue management have followed.

Revenue leaders today would argue that the ideal career path for a revenue manager leads to chief revenue officer (CRO). Most hospitality companies have yet to add this role, although many are moving in this direction. Wikipedia defines the CRO as "the corporate officer responsible for all revenue generation processes in an organization, driving better integration and alignment between all revenue-related functions, including marketing, sales, customer support, pricing and revenue management. This role typically reports to the CFO."

I have identified three examples of career paths that are interesting for revenue managers to look to as examples of the possibilities.

Before recently retiring, **Rom Hendler** was Chief Administration Officer for Las Vegas Sands, responsible for Las Vegas Sands' relationship with analysts, investors, board of directors, shareholders, and credit rating agencies. He oversaw and directed the capital expenditure and annual budget process. Rom started his career in revenue management at the Venetian Las Vegas, where he built up the revenue management department and introduced the idea of scientific revenue management in Las Vegas. As director of revenue management at the Venetian, he started working closely with the marketing department to better co-ordinate the company's marketing analysis efforts with the revenue management practice. From there he became vice president of strategic marketing, responsible for both revenue management and marketing for the Venetian. He was then promoted to corporate vice president of strategic marketing, responsible for the marketing and revenue management efforts across the four Las Vegas Sands casinos. The next step for Rom before he became Chief Administration Officer was corporate senior vice president and chief marketing officer for Las Vegas Sands.

Rom's path is interesting, because he was one of the pioneers in integrating marketing and revenue management activities by bringing both departments under the same organizational structure. His success in this area led to rapid advancement through strategic marketing and up to the C suite.

Chris Silcock is Global Head of Sales and Revenue Management for Hilton Worldwide. Chris came up through revenue management at Hilton, eventually becoming global head of revenue management in 2009. Since then, Hilton Worldwide started to consolidate some related disciplines under Chris, first promoting him to senior vice president of commercial services, then adding digital, international marketing, and customer relationship management to his portfolio. Most recently, he took responsibility for sales as well.

As with Rom and his progression, Chris's path, particularly the recent additions to his responsibilities, represents Hilton Worldwide's commitment to synchronizing revenue-generating activities. With marketing, revenue management, and sales analytics working under the same leader, activities can be better organized to support profitable revenue growth, generating demand where it is needed and controlling it where demand exceeds supply.

Leigh Silkunas is relatively early in her career but to me, she represents the cross-functional nature of today's revenue management discipline. Leigh has an undergraduate degree in hotel administration, with a focus in revenue management, from The Pennsylvania State University. After graduation she spent one year as a revenue management trainee with Sheraton Hotels in New York City, and then took a job as area revenue manager for Kimpton Hotels in New York. While in this role, she worked a lot with the Kimpton's online channels in her efforts to generate and manage demand, and became very interested in this space. She became the first area director of online marketing for Kimpton Hotels in Boston, New York, and Philadelphia, and leveraged this position into a role as Western region director of digital marketing, also with Kimpton. Leigh is now Director of E-commerce for Commune Hotels and Resorts.

I find it interesting how easily, and in a relatively short time, Leigh transitioned from revenue management into the digital space. Her revenue discipline combined with exposure to this space when she was a revenue manager made it easy for her to advocate for Kimpton to basically create an online marketing job for her, and that allowed her to rapidly rise through the digital side. With this experience, and in today's market, Leigh could easily move between revenue management and digital marketing roles all the way up to a well-prepared chief revenue officer position.

There are many models these days as the revenue management discipline matures. These are just some examples. The career paths of these three individuals are a good demonstration not only of possible career paths in revenue management, but also of how organizations are adapting to the convergence of revenue management, sales, and digital marketing.

REVENUE MANAGEMENT ORGANIZATIONS

There has been much debate in the hotel industry about the right reporting structure for revenue management, and I don't know that we have solved this issue definitively just yet. The reality is that some of the decisions about where to place revenue management within the organization depend on the business strategy of the company. There does seem to be a consolidation trend happening in many areas of the industry, so it will be interesting to track how this evolves.

> It's crucial that no matter what the organizational structure of the hotel company is from a functional perspective, that there is a chief strategist at the top above the functional areas of sales, marketing and revenue management that is driving the overall strategic revenue direction. It's crucial to have a global strategy in place that aligns with these functional areas, or everyone will just go their own way—and that's not optimal for the company.
>
> —*Timothy Wiersma, Vice President of Revenue Management at Westmont Hospitality and Red Roof Inns*

At the property level, I've seen revenue management reporting through operations, finance, information technology, sales and marketing or even directly to the general manager. I think reporting into IT keeps revenue management too systems-focused. At the property level, finance has a very different mind-set to revenue management, so I am not sure that the demand-generation aspects of revenue management can be fully realized in that reporting structure. Some argue that reporting to a director of sales and marketing is also restrictive to revenue management. They would posit that the demand control aspect of revenue management will be overridden by a role that is so heavily incentivized toward demand generation.

■ ORGANIZATIONAL CHANGE

CASE STUDY

I spoke with Siv Forlie, who is a Vice President of Revenue Management for a mid-sized luxury brand, recently about some of the changes she is making to revenue management's organizational structure at the hotel's properties. Since she joined her company, she has been advocating to move revenue management at the property level out from under sales and marketing to report directly to the general manager. The change was finally approved and was about to roll out when I caught up with her.

"With conflicting goals and incentives that can exist between sales and marketing and revenue management, it has never made sense to me that RM should report into the director of sales and marketing," she told me. "This limits the impact and reach of the revenue management department. RM should be its own department, reporting directly to the GM. Savvy directors of revenue management today know the importance of the right reporting structure. 'Who do I report to?' is the second question out of their mouths in the interview, and when they hear sales and marketing, it makes the job a lot less attractive."

This was a difficult challenge to overcome. Raising the profile of revenue management to this extent had implications on cost structures, incentives, and the culture in general. I asked her how she was able to make this change. She told me it was a long process, but it was the concept of total hotel revenue management and how it should be applied at the property level that finally convinced the organization that this was the right change to make.

"We started using this asset performance report recently that breaks down all revenue-generating departments by key RM metrics, including the

(Continued)

(Continued)

revenue generation per square foot/meter. Once our executives started looking at the entire asset that way—not just rooms—it adjusted our way of thinking about the space and how it is used," she told me. "We are able to slice and dice by region, brand, hotel type, et cetera, which gives us a lot of power to understand and manage the drivers of performance. Our executives across the organization started to see the impact that a holistic revenue mind-set has on the entire operation, and that revenue management has a lot more impact beyond rooms pricing. The value of RM for the asset became obvious, and the team began to understand that in order to foster this kind of thinking, revenue management needed to be its own department. If it weren't for that report, and moving toward total hotel revenue management, I don't think this change would have gone through."

Regardless of the reporting structure, there should be a cross-functional demand management team in place at the property, comprised of sales, marketing, operations, revenue management, and the general manager, that can be responsible for overseeing the overall property strategy, with everyone bringing their unique perspective and data to the table.

The participants in Kimes's 2010 study predict that in the future revenue management will be its own department within the hotel organization, with its own reporting structure through the executive level (presumably to the general manager or CRO, as described earlier). Given the growing strategic importance of revenue management, it makes sense that revenue management have its own seat at the table, with an equal voice in decision making. In order to achieve any sort of overall revenue culture, it is crucial to ensure that goals and incentives across the organization are aligned. The biggest impediment to successful, profitable demand management is misaligned incentives. For example, the sales department is typically incentivized on their ability to generate room nights, meaning that they are only concerned about volume, not revenue. Revenue management typically has an opposite goal, resulting in conflicts between these two groups. As I mentioned earlier, this gets exacerbated when revenue management must report into a director of sales and marketing.

Another trend identified in Kimes's (2010) research is the move toward centralization of the revenue management function. Obviously the unique set of skills described earlier will make it difficult (and expensive) to attract and retain qualified candidates. A centralized revenue management function would require fewer revenue managers to operate, but there are trade-offs. Some pricing decisions do require intimate knowledge of operating conditions at the property. However, automated revenue management systems are making it easier to manage pricing decisions remotely. Many hotels have structured centralized or regional revenue management functions that act as support systems or consultants to the properties. Smaller hotels can be managed as a cluster. You won't have to staff a revenue manager at each hotel, but the cluster revenue manager can still develop an intimate knowledge of the characteristics of the market. The structure you choose will depend on the characteristics of your company and your goals. Just make sure it's a well thought out choice! The next section lays out some recommendations for getting creative with the organizational structure with the support of technology. This is a continuation of the discussion in Chapter 7, where I talked about pricing to support an organization's business strategy. Here the focus is on aligning the pricing organization to a business strategy as opposed to aligning the pricing itself to a business strategy.

Aligning the Pricing Function with Operational Constraints

As revenue management practices become more widely used, both within the hotel industry and outside of it, the number and type of individuals who interact with pricing recommendations are growing. Couple this with a shortage of revenue management talent, and there's more work with fewer people to do it. Companies are beginning to think creatively about how to leverage advanced analytics to apply revenue management discipline broadly. This cannot be accomplished if systems and processes still require revenue managers to manage prices and technology at a detailed level. However, oversimplifying or incorrectly simplifying can negatively affect profitability. Hotels need to first consider how pricing fits within their business strategy, then evaluate any operating constraints (selling systems, people, organizational structure, and culture) that may have implications for pricing processes and practices. Finally, they should seriously consider whether a technology investment could streamline or automate the process further, thereby freeing up key resources.

To get started, it is important to understand the capabilities and skills of the current staff, and evaluate what is reasonable to develop, implement, and sustain with training, time, and new hires. You must understand the current process of setting prices, including what systems need to be updated, how many different products are being managed, how rooms are sold, which channels are utilized and how these channels perform. Understanding this information allows you to get creative about how to operate the revenue management business in a way that drives profits, without adding undue time or cost burdens.

For example, in the full-service environment, it makes sense to have a dedicated revenue manager or revenue management team, depending on the size of the hotel. The budget can support this resource, and the problem is complex enough to keep the resource busy. However, in limited service–type properties, the pricing problem is simpler because there are fewer room types and groups to manage. Margins are also tighter, so it may not make economic sense to have a dedicated revenue manager. Some hotels have gone to area or cluster revenue managers who are responsible for multiple properties for frontline pricing support (full-service hotels are hoping to leverage this strategy as well). Others are wondering if they could rely on an existing person at the property to tactically manage pricing (like a general manager or front desk manager), with the right system and/or regional support. In both of these cases, managing detailed rate and availability controls by slogging through layers of reporting and complex grids of recommendations is simply infeasible. These resources need to focus quickly on pricing or revenue discrepancies and be able to count on automation as much as possible to manage the routine decisions.

This is another example of where organizations can leverage advances in data visualization. Highly visual data displays are crucial to efficient identification and resolution of pricing opportunities, particularly in a limited service or cluster environment. Revenue managers who focus on more than one property must be able to efficiently visualize across their portfolio, first identifying problems and then drilling into the problem areas. I have seen several creative solutions to this issue, many leveraging revenue management technology. The most obvious is to create a revenue management process in the revenue management system that is driven by workflows and alerts, rather than pricing matrices. Users are guided directly to the areas that require attention, and are able to find the right information quickly, enabling more efficient decision making.

I've also seen large companies manage completely centrally, by building a highly analytical pricing function within the headquarters and controlling prices through that function. This is the case at airlines, where prices are set and managed centrally for the entire system. I've also seen examples that are closer to hotels, where pricing is set centrally and the results are communicated out to the disparate sites. In cases like this, a simple, strategy-based communication can be very effective, especially if there is not a lot of sophistication or bandwidth in the resources available at the sites where sales happen. As I discussed in Chapter 7, I worked with one company that decided that instead of translating the demand forecast to an optimal price recommendation, they would translate it into a series of actions that need to be taken to maximize revenue. So, for example, demand condition "A" was a free sell opportunity—set the lowest prices and upgrade freely with no length of usage restrictions, but demand condition "D" was to set the highest prices, not offer upgrades and restrict short durations of use. In this case, detailed and accurate analytics drove highly simplified strategy—that was easy to understand and execute. The innovative element of this process was that "pricing" in this case was not simply raising and lowering rates in a selling system, it was a whole set of activities that took place to drive revenue, both within and outside of the selling system. This is an example of a prescriptive approach, as I described earlier.

Technology is key in deploying a simplified pricing program. However, you must simplify without losing the advantage of the advanced analytics. You cannot afford to put some basic rules in place, and sit back and see what happens (remember the fly story in Chapter 2). Blindly following business rules, or even automatically accepting all price optimization recommendations without intervention might be fine in the short term, but eventually could result in suboptimal revenue generation or in compromising the longer-term business strategy. Revenue management systems perform better when they are managed by a revenue manager.

> Our revenue managers are responsible for a portfolio of hotels. We want them to use the system effectively to support their decision making, but we also don't want them to spend all their time "managing" the system and none of their time making decisions. We are looking at the kind of behaviors that indicate effective use of the RM system so we can better evaluate performance. We're also working closely with our revenue management vendor to ensure the system is designed to facilitate efficient decision making."
>
> —*Tom Buoy, Senior Vice President, Revenue Management, Extended Stay America*

Revenue Leader Predictions

I've talked about the skill sets required for the revenue manager of the future and described possible career paths and organizational structures that can help organizations set themselves up to manage through the challenges presented by the evolving marketplace. I've described how technology can support these organizational changes, but technology will only ever be an enabler. The real value in a revenue management program is in the decisions made by the revenue manager, based on the system recommendations.

With all of the new pressures on the revenue management function that have evolved over the past decade or so, and the associated challenges and opportunities I've presented in this book, I was curious to know how top revenue management leaders "forecasted" the changes to the discipline that will come over the next decade or so. I asked revenue leaders from a wide variety of hotel organizations around the world for their predictions, and here is what they told me:

Evolving roles and responsibilities. "I believe revenue management will evolve into two positions. A lead position that is more strategic and focused not only on revenue management but also on distribution and marketing and a second position that is an analyst who is responsible for data collection, analysis and inventory management. One thing that is evident when you look at current revenue leaders is that they are either very strategic, big thinkers, or very analytical people who can crunch the data. It's rare to find someone with both skill sets. I think revenue management and business intelligence technology will continue to evolve, which will make the data easier to access and analyze than it is today. Revenue managers will need to learn to focus on total hotel revenue and profit and expand their thinking to include other areas of the hotel besides rooms (at least in larger hotels). As bookings and marketing continue to shift to online and mobile channels, I believe that more and more of the marketing decisions and responsibilities will fall to revenue management and the traditional director of sales and marketing in most hotels will focus more on the direct sales efforts," says Linda Gulrajani, Vice President, Revenue Strategy & Distribution, Marcus Hotels and Resorts.

Stay focused on the basics. Rhett Hirko, Executive Director, Revenue Account Management, Preferred Hotels, has the following advice for revenue management leaders:

"As much as we in revenue management focus on either the hot topic (social media and review management), the latest maths (incorporating airline data into hotel forecasting), or the latest technology (true SWOT analysis at your fingertips), the fundamentals still ring true. For every newcomer in revenue management with good business acumen and a keen aptitude for learning disparate tools, you equally have hotel leadership that remains disconnected or uninformed, making organizational decisions that impact a youngun's potential. At times it can be disheartening. I have a few thoughts about the future:

Education

- Education has to be both at the grassroots level and with executive leadership. Money is constantly left on the table if the revenue manager is educated but her ideas are not heard.

- As we know, revenue management is both art and science. Using the latest technology to educate revenue managers on the theoretical and practical application of revenue management is great, but it is best done with an understanding that people learn differently. Dumping all education into online learning is as ineffective as having only classroom teachings. Not everyone will understand it and it will end up costing too much. Using media in all its varied ways keeps engagement, hits people where they learn best, and helps retain talent by making content fun.

- The younger generation has an amazing aptitude for the changing online landscape. We should encourage these new aspiring leaders to educate senior leadership about the power of online distribution, social media, and analytics.

Communication

- Collaborative efforts remain the most effective way of decision optimization—with supportive leadership. Hotel and corporate leaders should encourage creativity and discussion in problem solving, particularly in strategic decisions such as sticky revenue situations. This is especially true of those that recur.

- Everyone is having to do more with less; our revenue managers are multitasking more than ever before. Finding easy ways to communicate standards, updates, news items, and the like that allow a revenue manager to find relevant information they need in the shortest amount of time will create an eager audience for "new stuff" and a more efficient workforce.

- Hubris will be the end of any hotel or organization that thinks they know better. Those who are willing to say they don't know and ask for help to design the best strategy or product will win the game.

"Finally, I think the ever-changing landscape requires revenue management to be open to change and to challenge traditional methods and maths. The discipline can be simple in its application but it is within the analytics that I'm finding some exciting and creative new ideas, and latest technology is enabling its integration more easily than ever before. Integration of airline capacity and bookings into hotel forecasting to sharpen the focus on market demand? Customer ranking sentiment indices to track impact to online booking trends? Scenario based forecasting with dynamic pricing implications? These were dreams not more than a few years ago but are now hitting the marketplace.

"Of course, all of this isn't cheap, and not all of it has a tangible return on investment. How do we know what would work best for my hotel, in my market, for today, this weekend and next month? Time to ask my revenue manager. . . ."

Elevating the discipline. "I think revenue management is ever changing. Increasingly, all revenue channels not just rooms are being revenue managed by the director of revenue management (DORM) of a hotel. Ownership groups are now also hiring this position to help them understand and stay current with trends and strategies. In 5 to 10 years I hope many of today's DORMs will be CEOs of brands, hotel management companies, or professors of revenue management in major universities. I also hope that universities will offer a BS degree in revenue management. This position has become so valuable to our industry the next five years will only help to move this position positively forward. Of course, this value creation will mean our next problem is going to be finding great talent," says Janelle Cornett, Regional Director of Revenue Management, TPG Hospitality.

Demand generation. "Hotel revenue management has historically delivered 'the right product at the right price' through yield and price management. Tomorrow's revenue management will finally shore up the other half of the equation through predictive marketing by answering 'the right time' and the 'the right customer' question. Now, more than ever, technology is able to reveal who that customer is and when is the best time to solicit them. Tomorrow's revenue manager will leave inventory balancing in the hands of advanced algorithms in pursuit of managing the entire commercial process through pricing, marketing, distribution and predictive analytics," says Calvin Anderson, Director of Revenue, New York Hilton Midtown.

Technology, Data, Disruptors, and Global Impacts. Tarandeep Singh, Director of Revenue Management Analytics, Africa, Middle East, and Asia, IHG, provided the following perspective:

- Revenue management will be focused on not just selling the right bed at the right time but more importantly via the right channel. With cost of sales going up to 35 percent, the larger hotel companies will have an immense focus in this area. Not to mention the whole Net RevPAR approach. Expect technology to play an important role here, wherein the revenue management system in business will evolve and start implementing pricing decisions based on the profitability of channel.

- Reputation and rate shopping will be a given in five years time. Which means the pricing decisions will be largely based on these two drivers apart from the regular internal booking data.

- Expect Airbnb will continue to play the disruptor role and therefore *will* pop up in the rate shopping as the more than $10 billion valuation company continues to add rooms across the globe, a figure that has already crossed 1 million. With more than 37 million room nights last year, it's getting ready to be a strong competitor to not just the neighboring stand-alone hotels but also serious players in the business.

- Revenue management organizational model as a function will see some changes. With new hotel growth coming largely in emerging markets, the fight for talent will continue. Expect to see some central/offshore models evolving over a period of time by the big buddies. At the same time outsourcing might be a need rather than a choice for the smaller ones.

- The customer's lifecycle—a lot has been talked about this, but revenue management is yet to cross over completely to leveraging the whole loyalty variable. Technology will again play a crucial role here and how the revenue management system evolves to incorporate this element in the business.

- Expect big clean data to drive the business. From geo-locations to airline promotions to oil prices to GDP data and weather . . . more and more customer-centric data and external data will be combined together and made "Ready to Use" for the revenue manager. The SoLoMo will pay a crucial role here.
- Rate parity will be out. Or rather a trend that has been triggered will now very soon be widespread.

Expanding responsibilities. I also spoke with Melinda Yeoh, Head of Revenue Management and Analytics at the Ascott Limited, based in Singapore, about how she felt revenue management would evolve in the next 5 to 10 years. She provided the following insight:

Within the hospitality industry, the areas of responsibility for revenue management will grow and specializations will emerge within the revenue management team as the demands grow, for example, function space, food and beverage, extended stay and long stay, to name a few. Revenue managers will grow in their understanding and capabilities vis-à-vis the digital marketing arena, where business will be optimized not just at the business unit/channel/market segment level but at the guest/customer level. Customer intelligence will be a core part of the successful execution of revenue management strategies. At the travel industry level, online aggregators/consolidators will evolve to be even more adept at the entire distribution game, with multi-product and city-level/market-wide revenue management capabilities. The hospitality industry—chains in particular—will be challenged to keep up with the technological developments and capabilities of such industry players and may struggle to maintain their value proposition to owners.[2]

Don't just participate, anticipate. Fabian Bartnick, Director of Revenue Generation for Tune Hotels, based in Malaysia, said: "We started as a subgroup of sales. Through the rise of online we moved to equal parts and then ended up, like in my case, on top of sales. I believe marketing will be the next to be incorporated into a revenue-generation role (commercial or whatever you want to call it). Truly being able to control all areas of generating revenue moving toward '1 on 1' revenue management. In traditional hotels, 'operations' always holds accountability and drives the way forward. I believe this will change and revenue generation will take on that role as a true owner of strategy. Companies are already moving toward this with 'VP of revenue strategy' titles.

"So to answer your question about where revenue management will evolve to in 5 to 10 years, revenue management will not exist anymore in its current form but will have evolved into a larger role. Revenue management itself as part of RevGen will become more complex and more personal and more 'life' not just 'now.' In most revenue management systems, we do not take our decisions from the past into consideration when looking into the future, for example, 'the reason my results last year were X is because I decided to do Y, hence this year if I need to decide between A and B, how would have Y impacted my decision today to do A versus B and what would my decision be if I had chosen Z last year?' Of course, all of this would then be across multiple streams of revenue (food and beverage, catering and events, spa, etc.). My point is that we need to start looking at how we can generate lifelong revenue from a guest and their immediate sphere of influence (their friends, their children), not just them in isolation.

"The industry needs to understand that we cannot participate, but we need to start to anticipate. Of course, this comes with risks, but also rewards. We need to stop being risk averse and be more adventurous in our endeavors. The industry, or part of it, is struggling with the millennials—both as guests and as staff—however, we knew they were coming. Yet we did little to prepare. So what will happen when Gen Alpha comes of age?"

Customer segment of one and the road to the CRO. "I see two trends emerging in revenue management. One is the ability to price by consumer, that is, the implementation of the market of one concept. This concept would give revenue managers insight in the lifetime value of each existing (and algorithm-driven future) consumer across a single property and total brand portfolio and allow for personalized marketing and pricing. This would greatly enhance revenue generation, in my opinion.

"The other related trend is the emergence of the chief revenue officer position at more and more hospitality companies. The CRO would lead all commercial functions like sales, marketing, branding, communication, distribution, and revenue management and apply guest-centric analysis to personalize the commercial approach in order to reach, price, and sell to the right consumer in the right market at the right time through the right channel," says Stefan Wolf, Senior Vice President of Revenue and Distribution Strategy, Onyx Hospitality Group.

FINAL THOUGHTS

The common themes that run through the predictions are the convergence of revenue management to a commercial role, the continued pressure on hotels from new distribution channels or disruptive competition, and the importance of meeting the needs of the empowered consumer. As I reflect on the opportunities and challenges in revenue management today, I am both excited and worried. I am excited because, with the attention we are receiving and the new responsibilities we're being given, this is a great time to be in revenue management. A motivated and strategic *prescriptive* revenue manager has the executive attention and the tools at their disposal to make a huge difference in their organization, supporting tactical revenue maximization and a longer-term strategic vision.

I'm worried, however, because the hotel industry has traditionally been very slow to react to market opportunities and very conservative in their approach to analytics, technology, and organizational change. As an industry, we are still dominated to a certain extent by old-school operators who came up through operations and have a very traditional perspective on the business of hospitality. We will need to be willing to be nimble, take risks and rapidly evolve our thinking, as an industry, to be able to overcome the risk of commoditization and shrinking profits associated with the complex digital environment. Revenue management can lead the charge, but it will be a bit like turning the *Titanic*!

Here is a list of five overarching takeaways that will help revenue management position themselves to take advantage of the opportunities to come:

1. **Remember the basics.** With everything that's happening, there's a real temptation to get distracted by shiny objects—data, technology or partners. While the market has dramatically changed, there are many core tenets of revenue management that remain true today. Stay focused on profitable revenue generation, and remember the research that has already been done to form the foundation of how we operate today.

2. **Stay educated.** As I described in the book, technology and practice are evolving rapidly. Make an effort to read articles, talk with peers and attend conferences, particularly those outside of our discipline. As you are able to keep abreast of innovation, you can responsibly bring that innovation back to your organization.

3. **Stay connected to your counterparts.** Organizational and cultural barriers are difficult to break down, and silos will continue to exist. It is crucial for you to work with counterparts, even informally, as your organization evolves to meet the changing needs of the market. You will learn from your peers and they from you, and you may be surprised at what you can accomplish as you anticipate technology investment or organizational structure changes.

4. **Evangelize, clearly.** Despite all that revenue management has accomplished in the past 20 years, there is still a lot of awareness building that needs to happen to continue to justify investment. Be sure that you are able to clearly communicate your value and your accomplishments, and that you take every opportunity to evangelize your success across the organization. Now is not the time to prove you are smart by showing lots of complicated math and rows and columns of data. Articulate your points clearly and compellingly, so that you can inspire action from your peers. In fact, you will look smarter if you are able to explain complex concepts in simple language.

5. **Plan for your future.** I'm specifically talking about *your* future now, my new reader friend. The relative youth of the revenue management discipline is both a challenge and an opportunity. We have not clearly defined a career path, but evidence has shown that a good revenue manager has opportunity to move up through the organization in a variety of different functional areas. Think about what kind of revenue manager you want to be, and find ways to develop the skills you need to get you there. Do you want to understand marketing better? Take on some projects with your marketing colleagues. Is technology of interest? Get involved with your systems implementation and management. Revenue management is in a unique place in most organizations, between operations, sales, marketing, technology, strategy and even finance. You have an opportunity to develop your own skill set to send you on the career path you are most interested in.

In closing, the best advice I can give to revenue managers today to keep us focused on moving forward is a quote from Antoine de Saint Exupéry, in his book, *Citadelle or the Wisdom of the Sands* (1948).

"Your task is not to foresee the future, but to enable it."

ADDITIONAL READING

HSMAI salary report, www.hsmai.org/incentivespracticeresearch.

eCornell courses in RM—Augment your internal training with these courses and certifications from Cornell Hotel School Faculty, www.ecornell.com/certificates/hospitality-and-foodservice-management/hotel-revenue-management.

Eric Savitz, "The CEO's Secret Weapon: The Chief Revenue Officer," *Forbes*, March 13, 2012, www.forbes.com/sites/ciocentral/2012/03/13/ the-ceos-new-secret-weapon-the-chief-revenue-officer.

HSMAI CRME Certification, www.hsmai.org/career/content.cfm?ItemNumber=4863.

REVENUE MANAGEMENT PERSPECTIVES: A CASE STUDY IN ORGANIZATIONAL STRUCTURE

Kathleen Cullen, Senior Vice President of Revenue Management and Distribution for Commune Hotels, recently put forward a proposal for what she believes could be the organizational structure of the future for hotels, both at property (Figure 9.2) and the corporate level (Figure 9.3).

The controversial part of this organizational structure, as we've talked about it with other revenue professionals, is how operations will fit in with this picture. Many hoteliers, rightfully so, argue that the business of hotels is service, and operations needs to stay laser-focused on providing the differentiated service experience that will keep guests

Figure 9.2 Proposed Property Level Structure

Figure 9.3 Proposed Corporate Level Structure

coming back. Having this department report through a director of revenue management or a chief revenue officer could make it too focused on costs and revenue and not enough on guests. At the same time, in order to achieve the vision of total hotel revenue management I outlined in Chapter 6, all of the revenue-generating departments at the hotel need to be aligned with the organization's revenue strategy.

To me (and Kathleen), it's very clear that eventually sales, marketing, digital, ecommerce, distribution, and revenue management will converge organizationally to report into a single organization. It's not as clear how that discipline will be disseminated through the operational functions at the hotel, like restaurants, spa, and function space.

Kathleen's path to her current role, by the way, was via operations. She started at the front desk, and then moved into running the reservation department. The general manager of the hotel was so impressed with her analytical approach to selling rooms that he asked her to try out this "new revenue management" role they were adding, and the rest was history. Goes to show you that there are many paths to the top, and that someone with revenue in their blood will find their way there somehow.

I also spoke to Fabian Bartnick, Director of Revenue Generation, Tune Hotels (based in Malaysia). Fabian had the following to say about his title, which is quite unique. "I have responsibility for revenue management, business analytics (includes feasibility and preopening), voice and channel optimization (central reservations office, customer service, distribution) and traditional offline sales."

I asked him what advantages a revenue-generation role holds over a traditional revenue management title. He told me, "A traditional director of revenue management (DORM) works in the here and now, using pricing, forecasting, et cetera to drive the business. Yet the DORM looks only after one or two portions of the overall picture and therefore relies on other departments to support or drive forward. There is a lot of impacting and influencing required and sometimes other departments have other priorities and you end up 'fighting' for your place. The beauty about my role is that I control the levers themselves. I can decide and steer all of my departments in the same direction with limited influencing required as there is a common goal, not just virtually but also hierarchy wise, it all comes back to one decision maker. Of course, there are always discussions with marketing, operations or other departments, but the benefit is all revenue-generating departments work as one and are seen as one.

"When I started in revenue management," he continued, "we always thought of the job as having four stages: create demand, forecast demand, manage demand and retain demand. Traditional roles have direct impact on two of those. My role allows direct control across all four of those areas. Another key benefit of our role is the aspect of *when* revenue management gets involved. Unlike in traditional revenue management, my role gets involved at the building/conversion stage of hotel development. Revenue management decides on the room breakdown—twins, doubles, et cetera, the size of the meeting space, signs off on revenue projections for the first 10 years, and once the hotel comes into preopening we take over the positioning and then, of course, the managing going forward. So essentially I am part of the active decision making process before the hotel is actually built."

Fabian's new role is representative, I think, of future revenue management organizational structures, although I hope that Tune rolls marketing into his responsibilities soon!

NOTES

1. All quotes from Sloan Dean of Ashford Hospitality Trust were taken from this article: www.hotelnewsnow.com/Article/14399/Take-a-case-study-approach-with-RM-talent.

2. Melinda alludes to an interesting point here that I started to pick up on for the first time during some recent travels in Asia Pacific. Third-party distribution partners have started offering a complete suite of distribution management, property management, and revenue management to independent hotels—effectively managing the entire sales and distribution process, and leaving just the operation of the hotels to the hoteliers. You could see where this might be an attractive offer for some independents, but it does seem like hotels will be giving up a good deal of control to the OTAs in this model—this is one to watch.

Appendix: Practical Tips for Revenue Managers[*]

PRACTICAL TIP 1: TELLING A STORY WITH DATA

Advances in data visualization are providing a huge opportunity for revenue managers to communicate complex information. However, this traditionally very analytical discipline can be more comfortable with rows and columns of data. In this section, I will provide tips for how to move from charts of numbers to telling a story.

Why Are Visualizations So Important?

Seventy percent of all sensory receptors are in the eyes, and the brain devotes 25 percent of its capacity to vision. Visual displays are powerful because sight is one of the foremost ways we learn about the world around us. They support cognition by providing aids to memory, and displays act as a visual cue to trigger thought and analysis responses in our brains.

When data is in a table, we are only able to process the data one value at a time. When the same data is put in a graph, we can benefit from the eye's ability to recognize patterns and relationships, interpret them, and register the values as a whole. At first, producing and interpreting graphs may be uncomfortable for revenue managers who are used to viewing and interpreting spreadsheets. However, as you are called on to present information to other departments, the general manager, asset manager, or owners, graphs will be much easier for them to interpret.

---

[*] Portions of this chapter were taken from: www.hotelexecutive.com/business_review/ 3723/telling-a-story-with-data. HotelExecutive.com retains the copyright to the articles published in the *Hotel Business Review*. Articles cannot be republished without prior written consent by HotelExecutive.com.

The following chart outlines the benefits of using data visualization over spreadsheets:

Spreadsheets	Data Visualization
End-user focus on isolated figures or values	Allows end user to visually register values as a whole
Less emphasis on interrelationships between results	Represents interrelationships in an interactive manner
Higher-level expertise needed for analysis and interpretation	Facilitates collaboration and communication through singular representation of the data
Singular data source	Ability to analyze and incorporate data from multiple sources
Static view	Ability to interact by drill-downs, filtering, and sorting data

As data sets become larger, visualizations offer the ability to interpret thousands or even millions of data points. They facilitate collaboration by allowing everyone to start with the same information (such as a graph of RevPAR for the last month), and interpreting it from there.

VISUALIZATION AND THE REVENUE MANAGEMENT SYSTEM

Keep in mind as well that visualization has always provided key insights into how the revenue management system is performing and into what actions the revenue managers need to take to ensure that the system recommendations are understandable, accurate, and complete. As a window into the analytics, the visualizations also provide a framework for how the users are expected to interact with the system, outlining which actions they need to take in what order. In order for the users to fully trust the system, they need to be able to easily access information that will help them understand why the system is making the recommendation it is making. They also need to be able to input any information that they know that the system might not know.

In my opinion, the development of many technology offerings starts with the feature functions, and thinks about the user experience later. Whether you are designing a report or evaluating an entire revenue management system, you should first think about what you expect a user to do with the inputs and outputs and what you want the user experience to be. The effectiveness of revenue management depends on the interaction of user and system, so defining the revenue managers' experience and understanding whether the system will meet the needs of that experience is a crucial part in making any technology or design decision.

Creating Powerful Visualizations

As opportunities to leverage fancy new technology with slick new visuals increase it is important to maintain a strong discipline around the display of data. Routine reports may be created by business intelligence experts or provided by your revenue management vendor, but revenue managers will always be called on to present either a synthesis of information from various sources or the results of a special analysis. It is important to understand how to create a simple but powerful visualization to support your story.

Here are six tips for creating visualizations:

1. **Determine the purpose of your visualization.** It sounds simple to say, but rather than dumping a bunch of data into a graph, start by defining exactly what point you want the visualization to support. Exploration happens during the analysis, so when you create visuals for a presentation, you need to be more purposeful.

2. **Consider your audience.** How well do they know the subject? What information are they expecting to get out of your presentation? What type of questions will they ask? Do they like to dig into the data or just want the highlights?

3. **Pick the visual that best represents the data.** Flashy is not always better. The visual needs to clearly demonstrate the story in the data, not be masked by fancy graphic effects. I show some examples later of what could work and what definitely doesn't.

4. **Keep your style and formatting consistent.** Viewers can get easily distracted by formatting inconsistencies. They will struggle to process the changes and lose the point of your story.

When you go from graph to graph, stay consistent so they can stay with you.

5. **Don't forget to label.** Seriously. There is nothing more frustrating than looking at a graph and not knowing what it represents. Label everything so you can spend time on the interpretation of the information, not interpretation of the graph.

6. **Show comparisons.** Multiple visualizations, either on the same graph or near each other, are a very powerful way to make a point. Without cluttering the visualization, try to get comparisons on the same visualization. If this is not possible, remember tips 4 and 5, so that when you move from graph to graph, the viewer can easily interpret the comparison.

Think carefully about how the data and visualizations are connected. We default to certain chart formats when we see certain kinds of data, such as percentages. These default formats might not be the best representation of the information. Consider Figures A.1 and A.2.

Figure A.1 is really more of a spreadsheet with a picture next to it. It is not easy to determine how the two pieces of information (numbers and picture) are related. The pie chart (Figure A.1) is so small, it's difficult to relate the percentages to each other. Now look at Figure A.2. It's the same information, but in a stacked bar chart. This is a visualization. The information is connected to the picture, and it is crystal clear what the relationships among the data points are.

Sector Allocation of Holding

■ FINANCIALS	21.45%	■ NONCYCLICAL CONSUMER GOODS	18.09%
■ INFORMATION TECHNOLOGY	13.61%	■ CYCLICAL SERVICES	14.17%
■ RESOURCES	9.61%	■ GENERAL INDUSTRIES	8.99%
■ UTILITIES	3.83%	■ CYCLICAL CONSUMER GOODS	1.87%
■ NONCYCLICAL SERVICES	3.67%	■ BASIC INDUSTRIES	3.70%

Figure A.1 Traditional Pie Chart

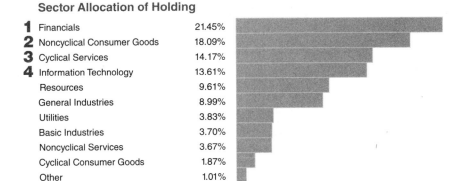

Figure A.2 Stacked Bar Chart

The two pictures that follow are an example of a situation where "flashy" formatting is actually distracting from the main point of the story. In the first picture (Figure A.3), the 3D effect masks the real relationship among the departmental expense categories, and the pointy bars make it much more difficult to see the exact values. In the bottom picture (Figure A.4), a simple bar chart helps to make the relationships clear.

Using Visualizations to Tell a Story with Data

The point of good visualizations is to support the story you want to tell with the data. However, even the best visualizations will fall flat if

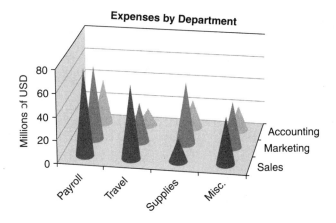

Figure A.3 Flashy Effects

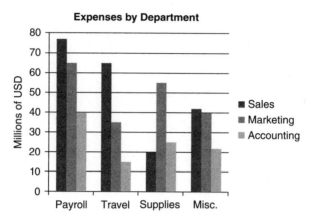

Figure A.4 Simplified Comparison

the context they are presented in is not clear to the viewer. How you organize and present your key points with supporting information is just as important as a clear and compelling visualization. With access to these powerful visualization tools, it is becoming even easier for revenue managers to make their case across the organization, and clearly explain complex information, but you still need to be able to tell that story in a compelling and persuasive fashion.

In fact, this is a good point to stop and remind revenue managers about the importance of strong communication skills. Particularly as revenue management gains visibility and importance within the hospitality organization, it is becoming even more critical that today's revenue manager be a "geek who can speak." Revenue managers have always been challenged with interpreting their data to the "layperson" outside revenue management. This trend will only continue into the future. If this section feels a bit more tactical than the rest of the book, it's meant to. Whenever I ask executives about the most important characteristics of a strong revenue manager, communication skills are always number one. Knowing how to tell the story the right way will increase revenue management's influence within the organization (and make you as an individual look pretty good, too!). Even executives can benefit from being reminded of a few communication best practices.

The format of an effective presentation should look like this:

1. State the action you want the audience to take. "I am here today to explain why we need to increase marketing spend in Q4."
2. Present a couple of key supporting points at a high level. "Our booking pace is slower than last year in Q4. Transient forecast is off by 20 percent. Our competitors are getting aggressive with price."
3. Support each key point with a few visuals and some high-level information.
4. Summarize your action and the key supporting points.

There are three steps to consider when putting together a data-driven presentation:

1. Focus on the audience and the action.
2. Find your story.
3. Support your story.

Focus on the Audience and the Action

Before you start to put together your presentation, make sure you know who the audience participants are and what their expectations from this presentation are. Don't be afraid to follow up with the meeting organizer and some attendees in advance to make sure you are crystal clear on this. Audience expectation will influence everything, from the content to the language you use to the takeaways or actions you propose.

Next, find out about the format that you are presenting in. Will this be in a room or via conference call? How big is the screen? Do you expect questions or discussion? There is nothing worse than watching a presentation with complicated and wordy slides on a teeny-tiny screen from the back of the room (frankly, in my opinion, there is no excuse for giving a presentation that has such complicated visuals; if they have to be that complex, it's not a presentation, it's a report). Being prepared on these basics will make you look much more professional, and help the audience stay focused.

Every presentation must have an action. Whether it's approving a request, getting the go-ahead to move forward, adopting a new business practice or simply gaining an understanding of a current status, every presentation should end with your audience clear on their next steps, and inspired to take the action you recommend.

Revenue managers are frequently called on to present analytically driven material, from performance updates to the results of special projects. The required/expected action for some presentations may be much clearer than others. A status update or hotel performance review, for example, may not seem like a presentation that's supposed to inspire action—but it is. Do you want your attendees to be able to update their stakeholders after they hear your presentation? Do you want them to start or stop selling rooms during a specific time period? Do you want them to simply be better informed about how the hotel is performing? The goals you set for the outcome of the presentation will dictate the script of the story you want to tell and facilitate the structure of the material you are delivering.

Make sure you state the action right up-front in the first few slides, making it specifically directed at the audience. "I want *you* to understand—recommend—approve." The attendees will know the purpose right from the beginning, and will be looking for the information they need to fulfill your request. This will also help you to verify right away whether you properly understood the context and the audience for your presentation.

A subtle tip to heighten audience engagement is to make each participant personally involved in the action. Knowing your audience means that you can tune the content and the action you want to take to something that will benefit the audience personally. Make sure the benefit to the audience is clear in your mind, and right up-front in your presentation. "I'm Kelly, the revenue manager. I'm here today to help you understand the forecast for the next three months, so you can make sure you have hired and trained enough housekeepers." Or, even better, "so you can take credit for our excellent performance in your next departmental meeting."

Find Your Story

Once you have firmly set the action you'd like your audience to take, the next step is to define the key points of the presentation that support and inspire the action you desire. This is the framework for your story. You are intimately familiar with the nuances of your data and analytics, but what does it tell the outsider? What's going to be important for your audience participants to understand to support the action you'd like them to take? What information is just "extra" in case they ask but doesn't need to be included in the main body of the presentation?

Everyone talks about the rules of three in communication, and for good reason. Three key points, following the "tell them what you are going to tell them, tell them again, remind them what you told them" methodology, are easy to communicate, and easy for your audience to remember. This structure will make your presentations very powerful.

So for my forecasting presentation, I might say:

1. Current forecasts indicate we'll be up 10 percent over last year.
2. This is driven by increased bookings in the transient sector.
3. Weekends, in particular, will be very strong.

The action is, since we are going to be busier than expected, Operations, you need to adjust your staffing levels for the weekends; Finance, be prepared to increase the budget.

Supporting Your Story

After you have defined the action and surfaced your key points, find data to support your key points. In the analytical presentations revenue managers must give, presentation of the data is the easiest place to turn off an audience. You will look much smarter/more confident if you can explain a complex analytic result clearly to an outsider than if you use a lot of big words, jargon, and mathematical proof points that no one understands.

This is another place where understanding the audience is crucial. It will help you determine what level of detail (and insider language) they expect. I still recommend keeping data presentation simple and language clear, even if you are confident that your audience is relatively advanced. People can always ask more detailed questions, but they will appreciate that you've made your presentation easier for them to listen to, easier for them to retain, and, importantly, easier for them to communicate to others.

This is where the visualization tips I provided earlier come into play. Supporting data and analytics should be presented as visually as possible. A big hole in the middle of a graph is much more powerful than the viewer having to scan through a row of data to find negative percentage growth. Reports containing rows and charts are more effective when sent via e-mail, or discussed in a one-on-one meeting, as opposed to presented in PowerPoint to a group. Although, I would still argue that even in an e-mail, a visual with description will do a better job of guiding the recipient to the information you want them to consume.

It is very tempting to clutter up a graph with lines and bar charts representing all of the key metrics you track (Figure A.5). This will be extremely distracting for your viewer—particularly in a presentation.

Only include information on the graph that is relevant to the point you are trying to make (Figure A.6). It will not only be easier for the

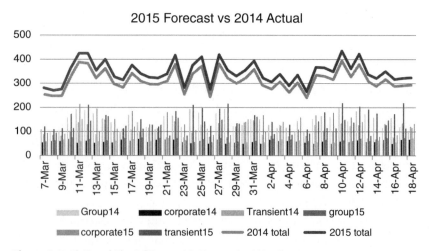

Figure A.5 Cluttered Chart: "Forecast Is Up over Last Year"

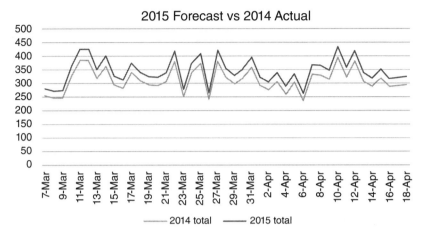

Figure A.6 Simplified Chart "Forecasts Show Us Up 10 Percent over Last Year"

audience to understand, but also for you to explain. You will keep the material focused on what you want to talk about rather than leaving room for tangents. Consider circles, colors, or highlighting to draw attention to the parts of the graph that are most important to your point.

Talk through your visualization in simple but descriptive language. Color coding definitely makes this easier, as do the relative size or position of your lines and bars. I cannot tell you how many times I have given presentations where my interpretation of the graph basically amounted to "Red bar—bad, blue bar—good. Blue bar is higher here, so good! Blue bar is lower here, so bad." This was, of course, followed by an appropriate conclusion like "Transient demand is up on weekends, but down during the week. Marketing needs to increase weekday promotions." I always include a little bit more information on the graph than I speak about (including labeling key data points with numeric values, clear data series labels, indications of statistical significance if appropriate, etc.). Not too much more, but just enough to allow those in the audience who are interested (and comfortable) to draw their own deeper conclusions.

You know the details about how data was collected and analyzed and what the limitations of the analysis were, but don't include too much of this. The audience can ask if they need to know, and again, providing too much information about study design and data collection can take you on tangents that will distract from the main point.

Finally, I will reinforce the point I made above about simplicity. I find that the simpler I make my interpretation, the more the audience trusts me. The audience knows that it's only when you truly understand your material, and are confident in the interpretation, that you can boil it down to the most basic elements that tell the right story. More often than not, they care more about the conclusions you draw and the actions that they should take, than the minute details that justify them.

Ongoing Communication

All of the previous tips are useful in any form of communication, from written reports, to e-mails, to daily or weekly summary reports. Many organizations are moving away from static e-mailed reports with rows and rows of data and metrics toward a more visual and interactive form of data presentation. Rather than forcing users to comb through piles of metrics and do the investigative work themselves, organizations are leveraging dashboards, alerts, and workflows to draw viewers' attention directly to the actions they need to take. Reports can be accessed through mobile devices, so stakeholders can access information no matter where they happen to be.

A major advantage of interactive visualizations over static reports is that viewers can look at trends over time and drill in for more detail if they need it. There are many tools available today that facilitate data access and exploration at this level, and I am seeing more and more hospitality companies investing in this area. My only caution is that the more powerful the visualization tool, the more tempted we are to create unhelpful clutter by cramming more and more information into the interfaces. As with everything we've talked about in this chapter, make an effort to keep things simple, surfacing only the key metrics that facilitate decision making, while allowing users to drill deeper if they need to. Think of this as "detail on demand," and let the viewer decide how much more information they want.

A Word of Caution

Mark Twain popularized the phrase, "There's three kinds of lies: lies, damned lies, and statistics," and there have even been books written on the subject (*How to Lie with Statistics*, by Darrell Huff, being my favorite). Avoid trying to bolster a weak argument with flashy visualizations or misleading statistics. Your credibility is at stake. Even the most anti-numeric of your coworkers will eventually see through weak arguments. Instead, use these techniques to build your reputation as an insightful thinker who can see the forest for the trees and is able to help others to do the same.

Case Study: Visualizing Revenue Data for New Insights

Below, I present a set of data visualizations with revenue management data. These were created in a visualization solution called IDeaS Revenue Performance Insights™, based on a tool called SAS™ Visual Analytics. These examples will show the value of providing a flexible, highly visual interface to help managers discover the answers to both routine and ad hoc questions.

Example 1: Regional Revenue Manager Reviewing the Portfolio

The regional revenue manager is preparing a report on the effectiveness of the revenue management initiative the company implemented last month. This report allows her to segment historical performance by brand, by property, and by property by day (Figure A.7).

The Process

- Limit the report to historical periods with the date slider at the top.
- The pie chart represents the enterprise of hotels that the regional manager is responsible for. The slices of the pie represent the revenue by each level of the hierarchy. Drilling into each slice of the pie changes the other objects on the screen to represent the values within the slice.
- Because the regional manager selected city hotels, the bar chart to the right of the pie chart shows the city level of data and the properties within the cities, color coded by brand. The single axis is Revenue. If you highlight bars on the chart, the table and the bar-line chart below change according to your selection.

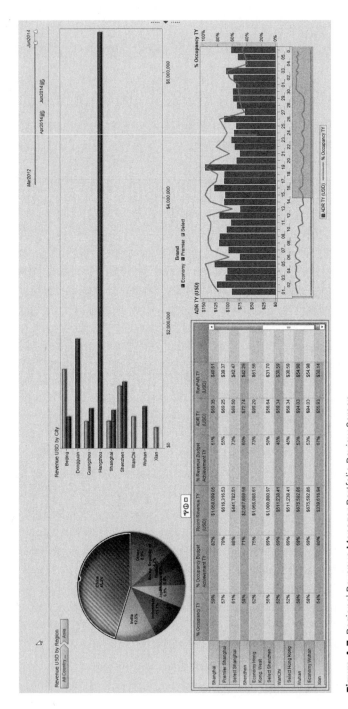

Figure A.7 Regional Revenue Manager Portfolio Review Screen

- The table shows all properties that are in the cities selected, above. The columns show occupancy, budget achievement in rooms and in revenue, ADR and RevPAR.

- The bar-line chart shows the individual dates of interest and an aggregate of all the selected properties. The data shown here is ADR and Occupancy percent. This chart includes an overview access for an easy ability to zoom in upon a set of periods of interest.

Conclusion: The regional manager identifies properties that showed a positive revenue impact from the new program, and those that did not. She can provide additional coaching to the laggard properties and benchmark against those that performed well.

Example 2: Top Executive Reviewing Forecast vs. Budget

A top executive wishes to know what global forecast is and how they are doing vs. budget. He would also like to know how individual properties are performing (Figure A.8).

Solution:

- By using the date slider at the top, the report is forced to look only at future pages. If he needed to, the executive could adjust the chart by brand, hotel type, and country using the drop downs at the top of the chart.

- The map represents the enterprise of hotels and shows estimated ADR (color/shading) and occupancy forecast (bubble size). There is a map control for the executive to slide around the world and zoom as they see fit. As the executive interacts with the map, the gauges to the right and table below change.

- The two dial gauges represent forecast to budget achievement for the period and hotels chosen. The top dial is rooms and the bottom is revenue (normalized to USD). There is a tear drop on each to represent last year's performance on the same metric for the same periods (offset by day of week).

- The table represents specific data elements related to all the properties, but selected ones will highlight. Sparklines are

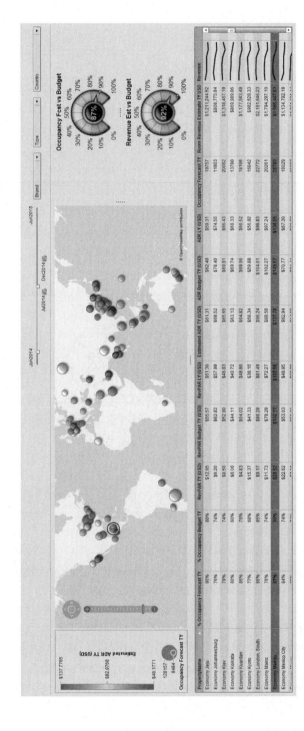

Figure A.8 Executive Dashboard

included for daily revenue estimates for the periods selected at the top.

Conclusion: By swiftly moving around the globe on this report, the executive can easily identify which properties are forecasted to be under budget. He can then reach out to the regionals and find out what they plan to do to address the issue.

Example 3: A Cluster Revenue Manager Evaluates Occupancy

The revenue manager wants to identify which dates are low occupancy for her hotels and see which rates are being sold on those particular dates (Figure A.9).

Solution

- Using the sliders on the top of the report, the cluster revenue manager selects an occupancy percent threshold that she would like to qualify as "low," and selects the months she wants to review.
- Using the check boxes on the upper left, she selects the properties she wants to evaluate.
- The trendline on the graph in the middle shows occupancy percent by date for the periods and property groups of interest. The pink background indicates where the "low" threshold was set.
- As the user selects certain dates (circled), those dates appear in the table. The table shows the date, whether or not that is a weekend or weekday date, the rooms sold and ADR by rate code by property.
- Using the check boxes in the lower-left and the bottom-left slider, the cluster revenue manager selects the rates she is interested in evaluating (BAR or Discount), and uses the slider to highlight "low" ADR performance in the table. She can easily see which dates fall below the ADR criteria.
- The cluster revenue manager subscribes to an alert to let her know when future dates fall below the occupancy and ADR thresholds she set.

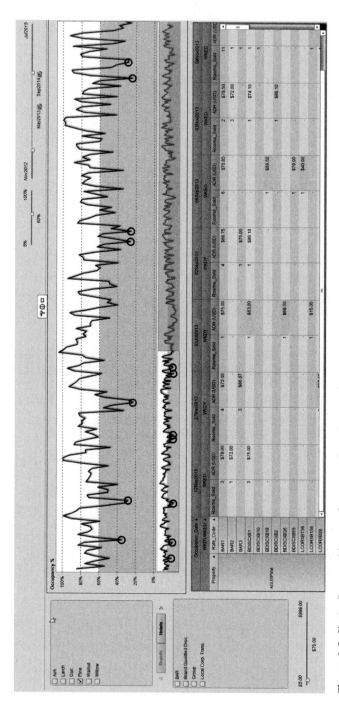

Figure A.9 Cluster Revenue Manager Occupancy Report

Conclusion: The cluster revenue manager can easily see what days she needs to take action on, and will be alerted to similar situations in the future.

ADDITIONAL READING

Darrell Huff, *How to Lie with Statistics* (New York: Penguin, 1954).

"Data Visualization: 7 Considerations for Visualization Deployment," SAS white paper, www.sas.com/en_us/whitepapers/iia-data-visualization-7-considerations-for-deployment-106892.html.

"Visualization Best Practices," All Analytics, www.allanalytics.com/archives.asp?section_id=3365.

Questions

1. Describe the advantages of visualizations over spreadsheets.

2. What are some best practices for building an effective visualization?

3. Using the process outlined here, build a presentation for the hotel general manager where you are giving an update on the forecast for the next three months. Describe what data you might include and how you would represent that data.

4. Review the visualizations that follow. What issues do you identify, and how would you change the visualization to make it more effective?

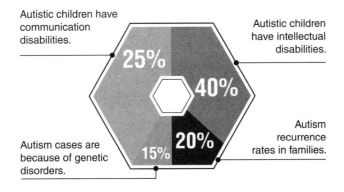

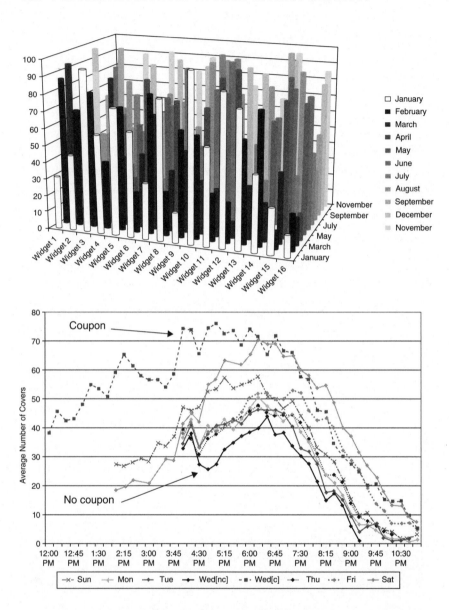

PRACTICAL TIP 2: TAKING ADVANTAGE OF SOCIAL DATA AND CHANNELS

I hope I have convinced you that reputation data will play a critical role in pricing and positioning strategies moving forward. Whether or not your revenue management system is incorporating this kind of data into pricing algorithms, it's a good idea to get used to working with this data, and to keep an eye on the impacts.

Social data and social channels can fit both a strategic and a tactical purpose. With the variety of data available and seemingly unlimited applications, it can be overwhelming to determine where and how to get started with leveraging reputation data in the revenue management decision. To help with this, some colleagues and I developed a framework (Noone et al. 2011) (Figure A.10) that places the direction of social media communication (inbound—or consumer generated; and outbound—or firm generated) against the scope of the decisions that revenue managers must make (short term—tactical; and long term—strategic). Inbound information flow is the data generated in social networks by the consumers, and outbound represents the firm's communications through social media channels. Most revenue managers are used to working with data and with channels, so social media simply adds another data source and another channel.

Here are four examples of how this works in a revenue management context:

1. **Inbound/short term.** Consumer review data could be used to inform short-term promotion and pricing decisions. This information could identify which "add-ons" consumers are willing to pay for, or what types of activities they like to participate in. Revenue managers and marketers could use this insight to create packages that could generate short-term demand or incremental revenue.

		Time Scope	
		SHORT-TERM Tactical	LONG-TERM Strategic
Information Flow	INBOUND Consumer-Generated Content	(1) Inform promotions and pricing decisions	(3) Inform pricing, distribution, and CRM strategy
	OUTBOUND Firm-Generated Content	(2) Drive short-term demand and build brand awareness	(4) Drive customer development and retention

Figure A.10 Evaluating Opportunities to Use Social Data and Channels

2. **Outbound/short-term:** Social channels can be used to push short-term promotions designed to stimulate demand for need periods.

3. **Inbound/long-term:** Consumer feedback can be used to inform pricing, distribution, and customer relationship management strategies. Consumer feedback can provide information about how consumers value your hotel compared to your competition. Reviewing volume and sentiment by distribution channel can contribute to the distribution channel strategy. Enriching consumer profiles with information they provide online can help to enhance customer value calculations.

4. **Outbound/long-term:** Hoteliers can use their outbound channels to engage consumers and cultivate relationships.

What you will realize as you begin to apply this framework, and what I think is key to successful social media analytics, is that the right approach is to start by identifying a business problem you need to solve, and then to determine how social media analysis could be used to improve the solution. Instead of letting social media drive you, think of incorporating it as another data source and channel to augment your existing tool basket. This approach makes it much easier to envision how social media can be leveraged across the organization (and will probably give you more ammunition to justify your organization's investment in social media).

PRACTICAL TIP 3: DRIVING MARKET SHARE—AN AIRLINE EXAMPLE*

The example is from the airline industry. Maarten Oosten, senior manager in the Advanced Analytics and Optimization Services group at SAS, developed the following case study from the airline industry to

---

*Portions of this section were taken from: Maarten Oosten, "Strategic Pricing: The Secret Sauce of Executives," SAS white paper, www.sas.com/content/dam/SAS/en_us/doc/whitepaper1/strategic-pricing-secret-sauce-executives-106561.pdf.

demonstrate how the strategic market share pricing system I described in Chapter 7 might work.

Imagine an airline that serves four airports (A, B, C, and H). All these airports are connected—on any given day, you can get a flight from any airport to the hub (H) in the morning, and then fly out again in the afternoon. That creates 12 itineraries—or 24, if there are two classes. Figure A.11 shows this scenario.

Imagine that H is an airport in North America, A is in India, B is in Australia, and C is in Brazil. The markets to and from North America and Australia are very profitable and have high load factors.

The airline would like to stimulate travel to and from India (B) because it believes that 10 years from now India will be an important market—in other words, it's a growth market. It is not very profitable now; its rates are not competitive with those to and from North America and Australia. So load factors on direct flights between India and the hub may be quite low—perhaps just 50 percent.

The airline's executives will most likely ask the market director why there is not more demand for those flights. The market director may reply that he could probably create enough demand to and from India to fill those flights. But because the fares are lower than for other

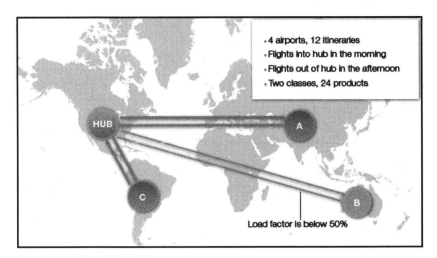

Figure A.11 Airline O/D Map

itineraries, the revenue management system cuts out this demand in favor of the more profitable ones.

In this case, said Maarten, "The revenue management system doesn't seem to understand the airline's long-term goals." That's because the tactical revenue management system is only considering short-term profitability when it restricts bookings to and from India. To compensate, the market director could ask for a larger quota on all the markets to and from India to generate more demand. Then the market director would need to answer the questions "What should this quota be?", "How large should it be?", and "What will it cost?"

Let's say the analysis shows that the market director could fill all the flights—but only at the expense of 5 percent of all revenues. That strategy would have too much of an impact on margins. So the market director would probably try to improve to more than 50 percent without filling all the flights. To do this, analyses could be run to see what would happen if flights were filled to 60, 70, or 80 percent.

Based on the results, the market director might say, "I can get a significant increase in the load factors on my flight—up to 70 percent. That gives me more market share at the expense of only 1 percent of my revenues."

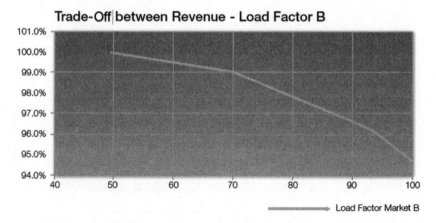

Figure A.12 Trade-Off between Revenue and Load Factor

At this point, how can the market director decide which customers to accept to and from Airport B so that it will take as little revenue as possible? One way is to do a trade-off analysis. Figure A.12 shows an illustration of this type of trade-off.

Obviously you can optimize for profit or you can optimize for revenue—and that will give you two different types of solutions. But you may not like either choice. Because when you optimize, the automated system aims for using your last cent of profit or revenue—and it often recommends extreme measures to achieve that goal. A common solution is to find something that lies between a profit-optimal solution and a revenue-optimal solution.

Still, there are many solutions that are optimal in some way. Using an approach called *Pareto optimal*, you can see that given a certain level of revenue, you can't achieve more than a certain level of profit using a particular solution (and vice versa). And if you increase one of the metrics, it's always at the expense of one of the other metrics. The result of this type of analysis shows how far off your current solution is from something called the *efficient frontier* (a term borrowed from financial services).

Now your trade-off analysis might be acceptable—and you can make a fact-based decision on how to set targets and goals for multiple metrics.

Discussion Questions

CHAPTER 2

1. Define the traditional revenue management optimization problem in terms of objective, decision variables, and constraints.
2. What is price endogeneity and how and why does it impact hotels?
3. What is the difference between yielding and price optimization?
4. What type of pricing methodology—price optimization, or revenue management—would be best for an economy hotel, a limited service, and a full-service? What characteristics of their demand would you use to make this determination?
5. How would the revenue manager interpret a demand forecast if they were using a price optimization methodology? How is this different from a traditional revenue management methodology?

CHAPTER 3

1. How could review and rating data be used in revenue management decision making?
2. For each of the data sources below, apply the list of questions from this chapter, come up with a list of information you would need from the data provider to be certain of the value of that data, and determine how it might be useful in revenue management decision making:
   a. Forward-looking demand data (aggregated reservations on hand in a defined market for the next six months).
   b. Performance benchmarking data like Smith Travel Research reports (your ADR, Occupancy and RevPAR as compared to the average for your comp set).

    c. Web shopping data (click stream data about how many guests browsed the website and whether they purchased anything).

    d. Guest lifetime value.

    e. Projected new hotel openings (number of rooms) in your market by month for the next three years.

    f. Competitor pricing.

3. Why is weather data problematic in a forecast? How would it benefit a forecast?

4. What value would airline lift into a market provide for a revenue manager? What might some of the dependencies be?

5. What are two issues that could arise when you add more variety of data into an analytical model?

CHAPTER 4

1. What are three issues that make reputation data challenging for revenue managers to work with?

2. If you were primarily a business hotel, how might you think about reputation management, versus if you were a resort property with primarily a leisure market?

3. Provide one example for each of the four quadrants from Figure A.10 in the Appendix of how you would use inbound and outbound social media communication for a tactical or strategic business problem.

4. If a hotelier told you they were working on a campaign to improve their TripAdvisor rank, what advice would you give them?

CHAPTER 5

1. What functions would a cross-functional team with the goal of intelligent demand management be comprised of at the property level? How about at corporate?

2. If you were a marketer designing a promotion for the spring, what information would you want from revenue management, and how would you incorporate that into the promotion plan?

3. If you were a revenue manager evaluating demand for the spring, what information would you need from marketing to ensure accurate demand forecasts and how would you incorporate that information?

4. How would you change the revenue manager's incentive structure to incorporate the vision of intelligent demand management? What about the marketer's incentive structure?

5. Design a promotion and describe which elements were produced by each of the functional areas: customer analytics, revenue management, campaign management, marketing optimization.

6. Describe how hotels should think about incorporating customer value into the revenue management decision.

CHAPTER 6

1. What are the necessary conditions for revenue management? List an example of why that condition is important for the application of revenue management.

2. Describe why spas meet all the necessary conditions to apply revenue management.

3. Why is it important to use the metric Revenue per Available Time Based Inventory Unit as a baseline and tracking mechanism?

4. What is the right RevPATI for spa? Which of the three levers (price, time, space) can spa utilize?

5. If you were going to kick off a spa revenue management program, who would you invite to the first meeting? What data would you ask the team to collect to establish the baseline?

6. What are some challenges associated with guest-centric revenue management programs? How would you overcome these challenges?

CHAPTER 7

1. Give an example of a situation where a hotel might be in danger of violating the Principle of Dual Entitlement.

2. Why is the concept of a customer reference price so important for revenue managers to understand?

3. Explain how familiarity and framing impact consumers' perceptions of price fairness.

4. Describe a scenario when you might make a strategic decision to override the revenue management system's price recommendations to offer a lower market price.

5. Explain how you might set up the "red, yellow, green" recommendation system I describe earlier if you were the revenue manager of a chain of 200 small, roadside economy hotels, including the actions you'd expect the hotel managers to take under each condition.

CHAPTER 8

1. In this chapter, I gave the example of Ann Roberts, a business traveler, looking for a weekend getaway. Provide several examples of the importance of understanding the context of an interaction as opposed to just matching the web visitor or guest to their profile.

2. Where and how should revenue management be involved in a personalization initiative? (i.e., what parts of the guest journey does revenue management provide information for, and how is that information consumed by the guest and the operation)?

3. How does personalization relate to customer-centric revenue management? What are some of the dangers associated with personalized pricing?

4. What data and technology challenges will hotels encounter as they start to work toward personalization?

CHAPTER 9

1. Describe how the evolution of the revenue management discipline has impacted the skill set required for a revenue manager.

2. If you had to find revenue management talent outside of the hospitality and travel industry, what type of industries would you target, and what roles within those industries? Why?

3. Recommend a revenue management organizational structure for a 300-property, highly franchised, economy scale chain. What kind of technology solutions would you recommend to support that function?

4. Of the skills mentioned in this chapter, which two do you think are the most critical for the revenue manager of the future? How would you evaluate a candidate to determine whether they possessed this skill set?

5. Create and defend a property level organizational structure for an integrated revenue function as discussed in the chapter and described in the case study in the revenue management perspectives section.

References

Albright, Paul. 2012, March 13. "The CEO's Secret Weapon: The Chief Revenue Officer." *Forbes*. www.forbes.com/sites/ciocentral/2012/03/13/the-ceos-new-secret-weapon-the-chief-revenue-officer.

All Analytics. 2013. "Data Visualization Best Practices." www.allanalytics.com/archives.asp?section_id=3365.

Anderson, C. K. 2009. "The Billboard Effect: Online Travel Agents Impact on Non-OTA Reservation Volume." *Cornell Center for Hospitality Research Reports* 9(16).

Anderson, C. K. 2012. "The Impact of Social Media on Lodging Performance." *Cornell Hospitality Report* 12(15): 4–11.

Anderson, C., and B. Carroll. 2007. "Demand Management: Beyond Revenue Management." *Journal of Revenue and Pricing Management* 6:260–263. doi:10.1057/palgrave.rpm.5160092.

Ariely, Dan. 2008. *Predictably Irrational: Hidden Forces That Shape Our Decisions*. New York: HarperPerennial.

Blal, Ines, and Michael C. Sturman. 2014. "The Differential Effects of Quality and Quantity of Online Reviews on Hotel Room Sales." *Cornell Hospitality Quarterly* 55(4): 365–375.

Burnham, K., and D. Anderson. 2002. *Model Selection and Multimodel Inference: A Practical Information-Theoretic Approach*. 2nd ed. New York: Springer.

Campbell, Margaret C. 1999. "Perceptions of Price Unfairness: Antecedents and Consequences." *Journal of Marketing Research* 36(2): 187–199.

Choi, S., and A. S. Mattila. 2005, November. "Impact of Information on Customer Fairness Perceptions of Hotel Revenue Management." *Cornell Hotel and Restaurant Administration Quarterly* 46(4): 444–451.

Cross, R. G., J. A. Higbie, and D. Q. Cross. 2009. "Revenue Management's Renaissance: A Rebirth of the Art and Science of Profitable Revenue Generation." *Cornell Hospitality Quarterly* 50(1): 56–81.

Dean, Jared. 2014. *Big Data, Data Mining, and Machine Learning: Value Creation for Business Leaders and Practitioners*. Hoboken, NJ: John Wiley

& Sons. www.sas.com/store/books/categories/business-leadership/big-data-data-mining-and-machine-learning-value-creation-for-business-leaders-and-practitioners/prodBK_66081_en.html.

Dietz, Alex. 2013. "Demystifying Price Optimization: A Revenue Manager's Guide." SAS white paper. www.sas.com/en_us/white-papers/demystifying-price-optimization-revenue-managers-guide-106156.html.

Dietz, Alex. 2013. "Can Big Data Help Revenue Management?" *Analytic Hospitality Executive* blog. http://blogs.sas.com/content/hospitality/2014/10/08/can-big-data-help-revenue-management.

Dietz, A., N. Osborn, and T. Sanli. 2012. "Are You Awash in the Sea of Competitive Price Intelligence? Let Analytics Be Your Life Raft." Paper 379–2012, SAS Global Forum 2012 Proceedings. http://support.sas.com/resources/papers/proceedings12/379–2012.pdf.

Dorman, James. 2012. "What Is Personalization." Quora. http://www.quora.com/What-is-the-definition-of-personalization.

Duggan, M., N. B. Ellison, C. Lampe, A. Lenhart, and M. Madden. 2015. "Social Media Update 2014." Pew Research Center.

Dull, Tamara. "Hadoop in a Data Environment: A Non-Geek's Big Data Playbook." SAS white paper. www.sas.com/en_us/offers/15q1/non-geeks-big-data-playbook-106947.html.

Enz, Cathy, and Linda Canina. 2010. "Competitive Pricing in European Hotels." *Advances in Hospitality and Leisure* 6:3–25.

Enz, Cathy, Linda Canina, and Breffni Noone. 2012. "Strategic Revenue Management and the Role of Competitive Price Shifting." *Cornell Hospitality Report* 12(6).

Enz, Cathy, Linda Canina, and Mark Lomanno. 2009. "Competitive Hotel Pricing in Uncertain Times." *Cornell Hospitality Report* 9(10).

Garlick, Rick. 2009, November 9. "What if You Reduced Your Hotel Room Rates and Nobody Noticed?" *Hospitality Net.* www.hospitalitynet.org/news//4044480.html.

Green, Cindy Estis, and Mark Lomanno. 2012. "Distribution Channel Analysis: A Guide for Hotels." HSMAI Foundation.

Hanks, R. B., R. P. Noland, and R. G. Cross. 1992. "Discounting in the Hotel Industry: A New Approach." *Cornell Hotel and Restaurant Administration Quarterly* 33(3): 40–45.

HSMAI CRME Certification: www.hsmai.org/career/content.cfm? ItemNumber=4863.

Hotel Revenue Management (course), eCornell, www.ecornell.com/ certificates/hospitality-and-foodservice-management/hotel-revenue-management.

HSMAI salary report: www.hsmai.org/incentivespracticeresearch.

Huff, Darrell. 1954. *How to Lie with Statistics*. New York: Penguin Mathematics.

IHG Trends Report. 2014. "Creating 'Moments of Trust,' the Key to Building Successful Brand Relationships in the Kinship Economy." http://library.the-group.net/ihg/client_upload/file/2014_moments_ of_trust_report.pdf.

Kahneman, D., J. L. Knetch, and R. H. Thaler. 1986. "Fairness and the Assumption of Economics." *Journal of Business* 59:S285–S300.

Kahneman, Daniel, and Amos Tversky. 1979. "Prospect Theory: An Analysis of Decision under Risk." *Econometrica* 47: 263–291.

Kaplan, A. M., and M. Haenlein. 2010. "Users of the World, Unite! The Challenges and Opportunities of Social Media." *Business Horizons* 53(1): 59–63.

Kimes, S. E. 1989. "Yield Management: A Tool for Capacity-Constrained Service Firms." *Journal of Operations Management* 8(4): 348–363.

Kimes, S. E. 2010. "The Future of Hotel Revenue Management." *Cornell Hospitality Report* 10(14).

Kimes, S. E., and K. A. McGuire. 2001, December. "Function-Space RM: A Case Study from Singapore." *Cornell Hotel and Restaurant Administration Quarterly* 33–46.

Kimes, S. E., and R. B. Chase. 1998. "The Strategic Levers of Yield Management." *Journal of Service Research* 1(2): 156–166.

Kimes, S. E., R. B. Chase, S. Choi, P. Y. Lee, and E. N. Ngonzi. 1998. "Restaurant RM: Applying Yield Management to the Restaurant Industry." *Cornell Hotel and Restaurant Administration Quarterly* 39(3): 32–39.

Kimes, S. E., and B. M. Noone. 2002. "Perceived Fairness of Yield Management." *Cornell Hotel and Restaurant Administration Quarterly* 43(1): 21–31.

Kimes, S. E., and Lee W. Schruben. 2002. "Golf Course RM: A Study of Tee-times." *Journal of Revenue and Pricing Management* 1(2): 111–120.

Kimes, S. E., and S. Singh. 2009. "Spa Revenue Management." [Electronic version]. *Cornell Hospitality Quarterly* 50(1): 82–95.

Kimes, S. E., and G. M. Thompson. 2004. "Restaurant RM at Chevys: Determining the Best Table Mix." *Decision Sciences* 35(3): 371–392.

Koushik, D., J. Higbie, and C. Eister. 2012. "Retail Price Optimization at IHG." *Interfaces* 41(1): 45–57.

Kumar, T. Krishna. 1975. "Multicollinearity in Regression Analysis." *Review of Economics and Statistics* 57(3): 365–366. JSTOR 1923925.

Laney, D. 2001. "3D Data Management: Controlling Data Volume, Velocity, and Variety." META Group. http://blogs.gartner.com/doug-laney/files/2012/01/ad949-3D-Data-Management-Controlling-Data-Volume-Velocity-and-Variety.pdf.

Marn, Michael V., and Robert L. Rosiello. 1992, September. "Managing Price, Gaining Profit." *Harvard Business Review.*

McGuire, Kelly. 2012. "Customer Lifetime Value Analytics—The Holy Grail for Hotels and Casinos." http://blogs.sas.com/content/hospitality/2012/02/29/customer-lifetime-value-analytics-the-holy-grail-for-hotels-and-casinos.

McGuire, Kelly. 2014, June. "The Path to Personalization—The Vision. Part 1." www.hospitalityupgrade.com/_magazine/Magazine Articles/The-Path-to-Personalization-The-Vision.asp.

McGuire, Kelly. 2014, October. "Hotel Pricing in a Social World: The Unmanaged Business Traveler." http://blogs.sas.com/content/hospitality/2014/10/06/chrs_pricingsocial.

McGuire, Kelly, and Suneel Grover. 2014, July. "The Path to Personalization Part 2: Digital Intelligence for Hospitality." www.hospitalityupgrade.com/techTalk/Articles/The-Path-to-Personalization-Part-Two-Digital-Intelligence-for-Hospitality.

Metters, R., C. Queenan, M. Ferguson, L. Harrison, J. Higbie, S. Ward, and A. Duggasani. 2008. "The 'Killer Application' of Revenue Management: Harrah's Cherokee Casino & Hotel." *Interfaces* 38(3): 161–175.

Naipaul, S., and H. G. Parsa. 2001, February. "Menu Price Endings That Communicate Value and Quality." *Cornell Hospitality Quarterly* 42(1): 26–37.

Noone, B., S. Kimes, and L. Renaghan. 2003. "Integrating Customer Relationship Management and Revenue Management: A Hotel Perspective." *Journal of Revenue and Pricing Management* 2(1): 7–21.

Noone, B., and K. McGuire. 2013a. "Effects of Price and User-Generated Content on Consumers' Pre-Purchase Evaluations of Variably Priced Services." *Journal of Hospitality and Tourism Research.* doi:10.1177/1096348012461551.

Noone. B., and K. McGuire. 2013b. "Pricing in a Social World: The Influence of Non-Price Information on Hotel Choice." *Journal of Revenue and Pricing Management* 12:385–401.

Noone, B., and K. McGuire. 2015. "Impact of Attitudinal Loyalty on Road Warriors' Use of Price and Consumer Reviews in Hotel Choice." Working Paper. Submitted to *Journal of Revenue and Pricing Management.*

Noone, Breffni, and Stephani Robson. 2014. "Using Eye Tracking to Obtain a Deeper Understanding of What Drives Online Hotel Choice." *Cornell Center for Hospitality Research Reports* 14(18).

Noone, B., K. McGuire, and K. Rohlfs. 2011. "Social Media Meets Hotel Revenue Management: Opportunities, Issues and Unanswered Questions." *Journal of Revenue and Pricing Management* 10:293–305.

Oosten, Maarten. 2013. "Strategic Pricing: The Secret Sauce of Executives." SAS white paper. www.sas.com/content/dam/SAS/en_us/doc/whitepaper1/strategic-pricing-secret-sauce-executives-106561.pdf.

Ott, R., and M. Longnecker. 2001. *An Introduction to Statistical Methods and Data Analysis*, 5th ed. Duxbury: Wadsworth.

Pan, Y., and J. Q. Zhang. 2011. "Born Unequal: A Study of the Helpfulness of User-Generated Product Reviews." *Journal of Retailing* 87(4): 598–612.

Park, D. H., J. Lee, and I. Han. 2007. "The Effect of On-Line Consumer Reviews on Consumer Purchasing Intention: The Moderating Role of Involvement." *International Journal of Electronic Commerce* 11(4): 125–148.

Phillips, R. 2005. *Pricing and Revenue Optimization.* Stanford: Stanford University Press.

Pinchuk, S. 2007. "A System Profit Optimization." *Journal of Revenue and Pricing Management* 7:106–109.

Polsky, Analise. 2014. "Data Visualization: 7 Considerations for Visualization Deployment." SAS white paper. www.sas.com/en_us/whitepapers/iia-data-visualization-7-considerations-for-deployment-106892.html.

Robson, Stephani, and Breffni Noone. 2014. "Show Me What You See and Tell Me What You Think: Using Eye Tracking for Hospitality Research." *Cornell Center for Hospitality Research Report* 14(17).

Skiff.com. *The Future of Guest Experience.* http://products.skift.com/ebook/the-future-of-guest-experience.

Smith, B. C., J. F. Leimkuhler, and R. M. Darrow. 1992. "Yield Management at American Airlines." *Interfaces* 22:8–31.

Sorenson, Arne. 2014, March. "State of Hospitality: Ask the Next Gen Traveler." Linked-In Pulse. https://www.linkedin.com/pulse/20140325110517-239587237-state-of-hospitality-ask-the-next-gen-traveler?trk=mp-reader-card.

Talluri, Kalyan T., and Garrett J. van Ryzin. 2005. *The Theory and Practice of Revenue Management (International Series in Operations Research & Management Science).* New York: Springer.

Taylor, Wayne J., and Sheryl E. Kimes. 2010. "How Hotel Guests Perceive the Fairness of Differential Room Pricing." *Cornell Hospitality Report* 10 (2).

Tetko, I. V., D. J. Livingstone, and A. I. Luik. 1995. "Neural Network Studies. 1. Comparison of Overfitting and Overtraining." *Journal of Chemical Information and Computer Sciences* 35(5): 826–833. doi:10.1021/ci00027a006.

Thaler, R. H. 1985. "Mental Accounting and Consumer Choice." *Marketing Science* 4(3): 199–214.

Vinod, B. 2004. "Unlocking the Value of Revenue Management in the Hotel Industry." *Journal of Revenue and Pricing Management* 3(2): 178–190.

Weinstein, Jeff. 2014. "HOTELS Interview: Nassetta Reflects on Hilton's IPO, Part 2." *HOTELS Magazine.* http://www.hotelsmag.com/Industry/News/Details/48361.

Worgull, Samantha. 2014, September. "Take a 'Case Study' Approach with RM Talent." Hotel News Now. www.hotelnewsnow.com/Article/14399/Take-a-case-study-approach-with-RM-talent.

Yang, S., S. E. Kimes, and M. M. Sessarego. 2009. "$ or Dollars?: Effects of Menu Price Formats on Customer Price Purchases." *Cornell Hospitality Report* 9(8).

Index